# Managing Mission-Critical Domains and DNS

## Demystifying nameservers, DNS, and domain names

**Mark E. Jeftovic**

**BIRMINGHAM - MUMBAI**

# Managing Mission-Critical Domains and DNS

**Commissioning Editor:** Gebin George
**Acquisition Editor:** Noyonika Das
**Content Development Editor:** Mohammed Yusuf Imaratwale
**Technical Editor:** Shweta Jadhav
**Copy Editor:** Safis Editing
**Project Coordinator:** Hardik Bhinde
**Proofreader:** Safis Editing
**Indexer:** Mariammal Chettiyar
**Graphics:** Jason Monteiro
**Production Coordinator:** Shantanu Zagade

First published: June 2018

Production reference: 1300618

Published by Packt Publishing Ltd.
Livery Place
35 Livery Street
Birmingham
B3 2PB, UK.

ISBN 978-1-78913-507-7

www.packtpub.com

*To my wife Angela, whose resiliency and focus is an inspiration.*
*To my daughter Emily,*
*who never ceases to amaze.*

*– Mark*

`mapt.io`

Mapt is an online digital library that gives you full access to over 5,000 books and videos, as well as industry leading tools to help you plan your personal development and advance your career. For more information, please visit our website.

# Why subscribe?

- Spend less time learning and more time coding with practical eBooks and Videos from over 4,000 industry professionals

- Improve your learning with Skill Plans built especially for you

- Get a free eBook or video every month

- Mapt is fully searchable

- Copy and paste, print, and bookmark content

# PacktPub.com

Did you know that Packt offers eBook versions of every book published, with PDF and ePub files available? You can upgrade to the eBook version at `www.PacktPub.com` and as a print book customer, you are entitled to a discount on the eBook copy. Get in touch with us at `service@packtpub.com` for more details.

At `www.PacktPub.com`, you can also read a collection of free technical articles, sign up for a range of free newsletters, and receive exclusive discounts and offers on Packt books and eBooks.

# Contributors

## About the author

**Mark E. Jeftovic** is the cofounder and CEO of easyDNS Technologies Inc, the managed DNS provider and domain name registrar. He was formerly a director to the Canadian Internet Registration Authority (CIRA) and is currently a director to the Internet Society Canada Chapter.

Mark entered the internet space in the early '90s as a computer programmer and Unix sysadmin, working for the early dial-up ISPs in Toronto before cofounding a web development firm in 1995 that later morphed into easyDNS.

A lifelong guitarist and avid bookworm, Mark lives in Toronto with wife Angela and daughter Emily.

*This book would not have been possible without the generous help from the following people: Tamas Acs, Ranko Rodic, Peter Van Dijk, Matt Pounsett, Patrik Lundin, Cricket Liu, John Demco, George Kirikos, Russ Nelson, Jan-Piet Mens, Jaques Latour, Joe Abley, Bert Hubert, Paul Vixie, Steve Job, Jim Carroll, Rick Broadhead, Richard Lau, Jothan Frakes, Dan Blais, Douglas Patterson, Noyonika Das, Mohammed Imaratwale, and Sandro Pasquale.*

## Packt is searching for authors like you

# Table of Contents

# Preface

Domain names and DNS can be thought of as the basic foundation of the internet. If you want to explain how important DNS is to somebody, you might find the following useful; this has been my "30-second elevator pitch" about DNS for close to 20 years now:

> *"Everytime you send an email; visit a web page; type or receive an instant message, text or SMS; place a VoIP call (or a Skype call), or do anything else involving the internet, it cannot happen until a bunch of computers around the internet have a conversation about it:*

> - *Where does this email need to be delivered?*
> - *What server is holding the file that this web browser is asking for?*
> - *Where is the VoIP gateway that needs to route this call?*

> *These conversations happen very quickly, typically in under 100 milliseconds (less than a quarter of the time it takes you to blink), and typically involve, at a minimum, 3 or 4 disparate servers around the globe. None of those servers have anything to do with the actual email, web page, or application being routed.*

> *These special computers are called* `nameservers`*, and without them, absolutely nothing would happen on the internet.*

What is interesting about DNS, given its importance, is how overlooked it is in the overall scheme of IT. Similarly, domain names (the logical naming entities that anchor DNS lookups) are often the most profoundly misunderstood facets of IT as well, even by otherwise advanced technical personnel.

For some reason, DNS and domain names seem to be a blind spot in many organizations' infrastructure. As we have fondly quipped since our early days as a managed DNS provider, *"DNS is something nobody cares about ...until it stops working"*.

It never fails to amaze me that a company can spend thousands, hundreds of thousands, even millions of dollars on redundancy, high availability, firewalls, disaster recovery plans, and even cyberthreat insurance, and yet the entire technical infrastructure of the organization is held up by a couple of unpatched, forgotten nameservers gathering mold in a closet somewhere. Often, this can be the case without a given company being aware of it, because they simply allow their (pick one) web host, registrar, ISP, data center, or some other vendor to handle the DNS for them, perhaps as part of a bundled offering, and they have absolutely no knowledge of the state of the DNS infrastructure deployed by that vendor.

Following on from that theme, perhaps the DNS infrastructure may be beyond solid: anycast deployments, DDoS mitigation, hot spares, uptime monitoring, and 24x7 NOC support; but the portfolio of domain registrations are managed haphazardly or on an ad hoc basis. The smooth running underpinning of the organization is ripe for disruption by an unintentional domain expiry or a domain registration getting "slammed".

Truth be told, I am *not* a DNS *expert* per se, unless you use Neils Bohr's definition of an expert as "somebody who has made all possible mistakes within a very narrow field".

What I am is somebody who came up the DevOps side and then wound up running a business in the DNS and domain space for nearly 20 years. In that time, I've been dealing with all manner of use cases and customer profiles, and I've seen almost every DNS and domain-related failure condition imaginable.

# Who this book is for

Your time will be well spent in reading this book if the following is true:

- You are responsible for at least one mission-critical domain that must be online 24x7x365, or you are part of a team that manages large groups of domains, in the hundreds, thousands, or above, on behalf of your company or on behalf of your downstream users.

- Your responsibilities include maintaining your organization's core DNS or DNS for its downstream users or clients, even if you accomplish these tasks by outsourcing DNS management to external providers. (This can include sysadmins, webmasters, IT consultants, and developers.)

- You work for a technology company, or you are in tech, your core competency is something other than domains and DNS, but you or your company relies on functioning domains to carry on your business (which is almost everybody these days).

**Here's a basic acid test**: If your company's or perhaps one of your client's key domain names went offline for any reason, would *you* be one of the people who will be paged after hours, woken up in the middle of the night, grilled, yelled at, or possibly fired afterward? If the answer is "yes" or "maybe", this book is for you.

# What this book covers

Chapter 1, *The Domain Name Ecosystem*, describes what parts of the naming system affect specific functions of your domains.

Chapter 2, *Registries, Registrars and Whois*, outlines the relationship between registrants and registries, and the database that houses your registrant data.

Chapter 3, *Intellectual Property Issues*, examines issues like which domains your organization should register and how IP-based domain disputes work.

Chapter 4, *Communication Breakdowns*, lists the various ways in which a key domain can go offline because of procedural and organizational mishaps, and also details common scams to be aware of.

Chapter 5, *A Tale of Two Nameservers*, looks at the difference between resolvers and authoritative nameservers and how they work together to answer DNS queries.

Chapter 6, *DNS Queries in Action*, looks at the anatomy of a DNS query and how queries actually get from a resolver to an authoritative nameserver and back to the client.

Chapter 7, *Types and Uses of Common Resource Records*, takes you through each DNS Resource Record (RR) type on an individual basis.

Chapter 8, *Quasi-Record Types*, goes through record types that don't actually exist within the DNS protocol but are frequently managed from within the DNS infrastructure.

Chapter 9, *Common Nameserver Software*, looks past the near ubiquitous BIND server and examines alternatives, such as PowerDNS, NSD, tinydns, and Knot DNS, with an eye toward nameserver diversity.

`Chapter 10`, *Debugging Without Tears – DNS Diagnostic Tools*, digs into debugging tools for DNS, both command-line and web-based.

`Chapter 11`, *DNS Operations and Use Cases*, delves into DNS use cases; we will cover all the things people often want their nameservers to do (even if it breaks protocol.)

`Chapter 12`, *Nameserver Considerations*, explains that as your portfolio of names under management grows, it becomes more difficult to change some of the deployment decisions made early on. With this in mind, we want to try to create a sensible approach from the outset.

`Chapter 13`, *Securing Your Domains and DNS*, covers securing your naming infrastructure, including DNSSEC.

`Chapter 14`, *DNS and DDoS Attacks*, looks at DDoS mitigation considerations.

`Chapter 15`, *IPv6 Considerations*, is a short but sweet chapter where we look at IPv6 considerations and how they relate to DNS.

# To get the most out of this book

This book is *not* about how to learn the basics of operating nameservers. It is assumed that the reader already has working knowledge of at least one nameserver daemon or knows how to use an external vendor or system to manage zone data.

The book sets out to build on previous works in the field and is meant to fill what I perceived to be a vacuum that starts somewhere after "everything you need to know about running a nameserver" and runs up to "the byzantine and arcane labyrinths of domain policy".

In the former case, when in the case of BIND servers, there are standard must-reads, such as Paul Albitz and Cricket Liu's DNS and Bind (O'Reilly Media) and Ron Aitchison's Pro DNS & Bind 10 (Apress), or the exhaustive look at bind alternatives found in Jan-Piet Mens Alternative DNS Servers (UIT Cambridge).

On the domain policy side, there hasn't really been anything since Rony and Rony's *The Domain Name Handbook* (2000, Publishers Group West), exhaustive in its day but never updated, and nothing has really appeared to build on it. Milton Mueller's *Ruling the Root* (MIT Press) should be mentioned as it also endeavors to bridge a gap, in that case between an understanding of the technology and the economic and political drivers that shape the landscape within which the DNS is deployed.

It is also assumed that you are familiar with at least the technical basics of the DNS naming system. Worth mentioning here is that the Wikipedia pages about DNS are typically up to date, accurate, and accessible to the non-specialist.

# Download the color images

We also provide a PDF file that has color images of the screenshots/diagrams used in this book. You can download it here: `http://www.packtpub.com/sites/default/files/downloads/ManagingMissionCriticalDomainsandDNS_ColorImages.pdf`.

# Conventions used

There are a number of text conventions used throughout this book.

`CodeInText`: Indicates code words in text, database table names, folder names, filenames, file extensions, pathnames, dummy URLs, user input, and Twitter handles. Here is an example: "Mount the downloaded `WebStorm-10*.dmg` disk image file as another disk in your system."

A block of code is set as follows:

```
<OWNER-NAME> <TTL> <CLASS> <TYPE> <DATA>
```

When we wish to draw your attention to a particular part of a code block, the relevant lines or items are set in bold:

```
# Example of a very simple Knot DNS configuration.

server:
    listen: 0.0.0.0@53
    listen: ::@53

zone:
  - domain: example.com
    storage: /var/lib/knot/zones/
    file: example.com.zone

log:
  - target: syslog
    any: info
```

Any command-line input or output is written as follows:

```
$ dig -t mx easydns.com @dns1.easydns.com
```

**Bold**: Indicates a new term, an important word, or words that you see onscreen. For example, words in menus or dialog boxes appear in the text like this. Here is an example: "Select **System info** from the **Administration** panel."

 Warnings or important notes appear like this.

 Tips and tricks appear like this.

# Get in touch

Feedback from our readers is always welcome.

**General feedback**: Email feedback@packtpub.com and mention the book title in the subject of your message. If you have questions about any aspect of this book, please email us at questions@packtpub.com.

**Errata**: Although we have taken every care to ensure the accuracy of our content, mistakes do happen. If you have found a mistake in this book, we would be grateful if you would report this to us. Please visit www.packtpub.com/submit-errata, selecting your book, clicking on the Errata Submission Form link, and entering the details.

**Piracy**: If you come across any illegal copies of our works in any form on the Internet, we would be grateful if you would provide us with the location address or website name. Please contact us at copyright@packtpub.com with a link to the material.

**If you are interested in becoming an author**: If there is a topic that you have expertise in and you are interested in either writing or contributing to a book, please visit authors.packtpub.com.

# Reviews

Please leave a review. Once you have read and used this book, why not leave a review on the site that you purchased it from? Potential readers can then see and use your unbiased opinion to make purchase decisions, we at Packt can understand what you think about our products, and our authors can see your feedback on their book. Thank you!

For more information about Packt, please visit `packtpub.com`.

# The Domain Name Ecosystem

1

A long time ago, on my first day of college at the Music Industry Arts school at Fanshawe College in London, Ontario, our recording engineering teacher-to-be told us:

> *"Today we're going to teach you how to unplug a microphone cable and then roll it up. Yes, you are all sitting there thinking, I already know how to do that. We also used to think you arrived here already knowing that. Then, one day a few years back, I asked a first-year student to do it and he walked over to the wall over there... and proceeded to yank the guts right out of a brand new Neumann U87 microphone..."*

As it turned out, there was a trick to rolling microphone cables that I did not know, which was why until then all my cables always gnarled into twisted, random barbs of spaghetti in my gig bag. But after I learned "the trick," all my cables henceforth fell into ordered, neat, clean loops, and remained that way, even after transport. It was worth the price of admission to college.

This chapter is the "learning to unplug and then roll a microphone cable" of naming. We're going to get an overview of important aspects of naming beyond your own network and outside your own domain's nameservers. We're going to do this because it is necessary to have this knowledge in hand and have processes within your own organization to manage these functions of the names you are responsible for. If you don't, then you can do everything else in this book, from setting up your nameservers, to cluefully selecting an outsourced vendor, to defending against **denial-of-service (DoS)** attacks absolutely correctly, and with flawless execution, yet still find yourself experiencing a catastrophic outage because of something from outside your operations that affected a key domain name.

We'll start by taking a high-level overview of a domain name itself and breaking it into logical components that have different meanings and, with that, different implications.

By the end of this chapter, you should have a greater understanding of the overall workings and life cycles of your domain names, from inception (registration), through resolution (nameservers), to death (expiry), than many IT professionals have

In this chapter, we will cover the following topics:

- Why domains are important
- Domain names 101
- Anatomy of a domain name
- Understanding the domain name expiry cycle

# Why domains are important

Without the DNS or "hostnames" or domain names, we would be left having to reference all endpoints of our internet connections by their raw IP addresses.

While some people (mostly cranks) occasionally argue that this wouldn't be a bad thing, the fact remains that this name-to-number (and vice versa) translation is necessary because it adds a level of abstraction that allows seamless changes in our internet endpoints and destinations. Take a look at this:

Without hostname and domain name labels, and a universal mechanism to map between the two, all applications would have to somehow acquire end-to-end knowledge of all their peers, servers, or clients.

There is also another aspect of the DNS, which has emerged relatively recently, that takes it beyond a protocol simply for mapping names to IP addresses and back. The DNS is now, and will increasingly be, used to publish metadata.

Because of its ubiquity and relatively light footprint, especially combined with DNSSEC to authenticate responses, the DNS lends itself well for publishing other data that applications and clients will be searching for. I am speaking specifically now of authentication, reputation, and encryption processes such as X.509 certificates, PGP/GPG keys, DNS-based **Real-Time Blackhole Lists** (**RBLs**), and **response policy zones** (**RPZs**). The relatively widespread adaptation of SPF and DKIM signal the early beginnings of these types of DNS applications.

In the future, I see more activity occurring in these fields. As organizations and individuals come to grips with "surveillance-as-a-fact-of-life" and other shenanigans (such as third-party **Certificate Authority** (**CA**) debacles), an inexorable move toward taking control over your own data integrity and privacy is taking place. Thus, we see DANE as a response to having to rely on (possibly compromised, or corrupt) third-party CAs. We see increasing adaption of encryption and privacy enhancement, utilizing more uptake of DNSSEC and more authentication credentials being deployed over the DNS.

 The terms "hostname" and "subdomain" are often used interchangeably. Whether a particular label is a domain, hostname, subdomain, or superdomain depends on your reference point and its relation to a zone cut, which we'll explain later.

# Domain names 101

You probably already know that a domain name is simply an alphanumeric string that is mapped—via the **Domain Name System** (**DNS**) to other data—like an **Internet Protocol** (**IP**) address.

So, asking, *What is a domain?* may seem self-explanatory. `example.com` is a domain.

However, when you get into the specifics of the DNS protocol and the documents that describe it, we start to run into some odd nuances in terms of what the formal specification of a *domain* is, versus what you can actually register online at some domain registrar as "your domain name."

For example, underscores are permitted in domain names. This is why certain types of records and practices use them. Later in this book, when we're examining SRV records, we'll see underscores. Take a look at this:

```
_xmpp-client._tcp.example.com.
```

However, you cannot go to a registrar website and successfully register something like `example_domain.com`. The underscore would not be allowed. A hyphen would be permitted, as long as the domain does not begin or end with one.

Now, how about a "hostname"? Those are easy too, right? `www.example.com` is a hostname. But, now, you can't use an underscore in your hostname, ever. But you can still use hyphens, just as long as they're not at the beginning or the end of a label.

(The labels are the alphanumeric strings between each dot. `www`, `example`, and `com` are the labels that comprise the hostname `www.example.com`.)

What we are seeing here is an example of the difference between what I call "the domain name ecosystem," which entails the world of registrars, registries, and oversight bodies, and "the DNS," which is what happens on your domains' nameservers or on the operations side of your organization. Take a look at this diagram:

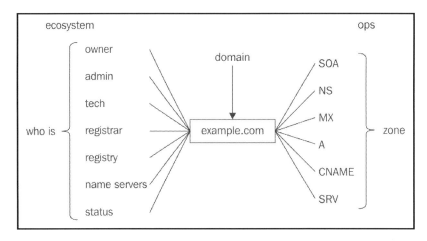

Figure 1: The two logical realms of a domain name

As another example, we will very shortly look at the *Anatomy of a domain name*, where we will look at the various data components that go into a domain name registration. One of those components is called "the registrant," which is effectively the domain owner. It is the entity that owns the domain name. This is pretty straightforward, but it is not to be confused with the owner name as part of a DNS **resource record** (**RR**), which is all the individual records that your nameservers hold and serve up to make your domain—or, more specifically, your zone—visible across the internet.

In *Figure 1*, those myriad resource records are on the right side of our diagram, under the **ops** realm, collectively forming a zone, and each record in there will have an owner name, which carries a completely different meaning than the **owner** of the domain name, shown on the left side, under the domain ecosystem realm

The various components of "the ecosystem realm" are best depicted by the registration details that must be provided at the time a domain is registered, which are held in a database called "WHOIS."

The reason we've gone to such lengths to define these two, seemingly disparate, realms of factors that go into a domain name is this: In my 20+ years of experience in this field, as a sysop, as a CTO, and then CEO of a managed DNS provider, and as a former director for a registry operator, I have observed that a significant portion of domain-related outages occur because of a disconnect between these two realms. Organizations operate with an artificial divide between the overall domain name ecosystem and the nuts-and-bolts operations of their domains, and that can cause problems.

# Anatomy of a domain name

In this section, we'll break out the functional components of a "domain name" from the perspective of the overall ecosystem on the left side of the diagram in *Figure 1.1*.

The "domain name" in this context is a naming entity such as `example.com` or any other domain we register via a domain registrar.

Registration details for domain names are kept in publicly accessible databases called WHOIS servers. The record for a given domain name is typically called a WHOIS record.

We'll look at a WHOIS record for a domain name and break out the logical components of the registration details. Each section has a distinct meaning and function within the overall ecosystem.

If you run the following example `whois` command on your own system, you may see a different output depending on what kind of WHOIS client you are using. For our examples, we are just using a command line `whois` command, which you typically find on most Linux or Unix systems.

A note on examples and `example.com`.

example.com is an example of a domain name. It (and several others) are specifically reserved by IANA to serve the purpose of providing examples without requiring prior permission from anybody. RFC 2606 describes "Reserved Top-Level DNS Names" and their functions. Throughout the book, I use example.com wherever possible. In cases where I need to show some specific element not present within example.com, I'll use different domain names as required. I sometimes employ the nonexistent **top-level domain** (**TLD**) .dom in examples (even though the reserved TLD .example exists and has been reserved for this purpose, it is, like so many of these "new TLDs," long and cumbersome).

WHOIS output for https://www.packtpub.com/—the publisher of this book is shows as follows:

```
$ whois packtpub.com
Domain Name: PACKTPUB.COM
Domain ID: 97706392_DOMAIN_COM-VRSN
Registrar WHOIS Server: whois.easydns.com
Registrar URL: http://www.easydns.com
Updated Date: 2015-09-15T21:46:16Z
Creation Date: 2003-05-09T14:34:02Z
Registrar Registration Expiration Date: 2024-05-09T14:34:02Z
Registrar: easyDNS Technologies, Inc.
Registrar IANA ID: 469
Domain Status: clientTransferProhibited
https://icann.org/epp#clientTransferProhibited
Domain Status: clientUpdateProhibited
https://icann.org/epp#clientUpdateProhibited
Registry Registrant ID:
Registrant Name: Domain Manager
Registrant Organization: Packt Publishing
Registrant Street: 2nd Floor Livery Place, 35 Livery Street
Registrant City: Birmingham
Registrant State/Province: West Midlands
Registrant Postal Code: B3 2PB
Registrant Country: GB
Registrant Phone: +44.1212656484
Registrant Phone Ext:
Registrant Fax:
Registrant Email: packtsupport@packtpub.com
Registry Admin ID:
Admin Name: Domain Manager
Admin Organization: Packt Publishing
Admin Street: 2nd Floor Livery Place, 35 Livery Street
Admin City: Birmingham
Admin State/Province: West Midlands
Admin Postal Code: B3 2PB
Admin Country: GB
```

```
Admin Phone: +44.1212656484
Admin Phone Ext:
Admin Fax:
Admin Fax Ext:
Admin Email: packtsupport@packtpub.com
Registry Tech ID:
Tech Name: Domain Manager
Tech Organization: Packt Publishing
Tech Street: 2nd Floor Livery Place, 35 Livery Street
Tech City: Birmingham
Tech State/Province: West Midlands
Tech Postal Code: B3 2PB
Tech Country: GB
Tech Phone: +44.1212656484
Tech Fax:
Tech Fax Ext:
Tech Email: packtsupport@packtpub.com
Name Server: DNS3.EASYDNS.ORG
Name Server: DNS1.EASYDNS.COM
Name Server: DNS2.EASYDNS.NET
Name Server: DNS4.EASYDNS.INFO
DNSSEC: unsigned
Registrar Abuse Contact Email: abuse@easydns.com
Registrar Abuse Contact Phone: +1.4165358672
```

WHOIS record formats differ between TLDs—and we'll discuss some of the key differences in these when we take a closer look at WHOIS—but they all share similar characteristics that can help us dissect the various "moving parts" of a domain; they are the following:

- Registry details
- Domain registrant
- Administrative contact
- Technical contact
- Domain status
- DNS details

# Registry details

This tells us who the registrar is and key dates such as these:

- When the domain was registered
- When the associated record was last modified
- The registrar's name, URL, and abuse contact

The registry details also contain the following elements that require a more in-depth explanation.

## Registrar WHOIS server

This is a server that can be queried directly for a specific WHOIS record for a domain using the -h switch from the command line:

```
whois -h whois.easydns.com packtpub.com
```

There are a few reasons you may need to do this. Some WHOIS clients do a reasonably good job of figuring out which WHOIS server to query. Sometimes, for factors outside of their control, such as a change in WHOIS output format, this doesn't happen.

Furthermore, with the flood of new top-level domains ("new TLDs") now coming out, there are sometimes cases where a new TLD's WHOIS server has not yet been added to various WHOIS lookup tools. Each new TLD must operate a WHOIS server accessible on port 43, using the hostname whois.nic.<tld>.

From a command line WHOIS lookup, you would then use the -h switch. For example, if the hot new TLD everybody wants a piece of is .blargh, you would use this:

```
$ whois -h whois.nic.blargh example.blargh
```

## Expiry date

At first glance, the field that contains a domain's expiry date may seem pretty self-explanatory. It's the date after which the domain expires at the registry, right? Mostly. Sort of.

The reality is that when a domain expires at the registry, it goes into a cycle called "the expiry cycle", which takes several weeks, or even months, to play out, and it is absolutely critical that you are familiar with this cycle and what is permitted and not permitted at each stage within it. For this reason, the next section steps through the entire expiry cycle.

The other thing to know about the listed expiry date in the WHOIS record is that the date shown might not actually be the expiry date. It may show the expiry as roughly one year from now, but the domain is actually already past expiry. WHOIS snippet of an expired domain displaying expiry date next year is shown as follows:

```
Domain Name: EXAMPLE.NET
Registry Domain ID: 1853290837_DOMAIN_NET-VRSN
Registrar WHOIS Server: whois.easydns.com
Registrar URL: http://www.easydns.com
Updated Date: 2018-04-04T07:47:36Z
Creation Date: 2014-04-03T21:32:39Z
Registry Expiry Date: 2019-04-03T21:32:39Z
Registrar: easyDNS Technologies, Inc.
Registrar IANA ID: 469
```

The reason for this is most registries use a mechanism called "auto-renew" at the registrar level: When the domain expires, the registry will automatically charge the registrar for another year renewal on the domain, which causes the expiry date in the WHOIS output to display an additional year.

However, if the registrar's customer hasn't renewed the domain, then the nameservers for the domain will be removed from the TLDs zone, causing the domain and anything that depends on it to stop working.

If you are looking at a domain that expires on or just before the current day, and the expiry date is one year in the future, but the domain does not resolve across the internet, then this is a likely cause. We cover what happens next in more detail in the next section.

# The registrant contact set

It cannot be overemphasized how important it is that your organization gets this part right, especially given how many times over the years I've seen companies get this part wrong, sometimes with catastrophic results. Any other mistake we can make when it comes to the administration of the registration details of our domain portfolio is fixable. Sometimes this one isn't. When that happens, it can result in a permanent "lock out" condition.

The listed registrant for a domain must be the legal name of your business, organization, or the ultimate user of the domain.

Too often, it is one of the following:

- An employee of the organization (using the employee's own name)
- An outside consultant
- "Fake" data of a nonexistent entity (in an effort to avoid spam or shield underlying data)
- The party who facilitated the domain registration (such as a web host or ISP) – "free domain included" offers are notorious for this
- The entity the domain was purchased from on the aftermarket whose contact details were never modified after control was transferred, which happens frequently

It's not completely clear whether domain names themselves are actual "property" or whether they simply convey rights. There have been arguments and legal decisions going both ways in differing jurisdictions. Suffice it to say for our purposes, the owner or rightsholder, whomever or whatever is listed as a domain's "registrant," is the *ultimate authority* over what happens to that domain.

This means that if you find yourself in a domain "lock-out" situation, the only entity that will be able to regain access and control over the domain is the one listed as the domain's registrant. If that is somebody else other than you, your company, or your organization, then you are at their mercy. If that somebody else doesn't exist, then you are probably screwed.

# The administrative contact set

This contact set looks a lot like the registrant contact set, and in many cases they are the same or contain the same data. In the early days (when Network Solutions had the monopoly on `.com`/`.net`/`.org` domain registrations), there were only two contact sets: administrative ("admin") and technical.

Historically, it's the admin contact that exerts control over the domain name; even today now that the registrant contact set exists, if you have to do a password reset, or your registrar sends out some kind of notice, it'll often go to the admin contact email.

For this reason, it's very important that this email address be chosen with some care; I always recommend the following best practices.

## Use a domain you control

Make sure your email address is under a domain name you directly control, not some third party.

## Use a different domain than the name in the record

Don't use `hostmaster@example.com` in `example.com`, use `hostmaster@example.net` instead. Even if all your other domains use `@example.com` addresses, it is then especially important that you never lose control over the admin access to `example.com`. It is worth provisioning a separate domain just for this purpose.

## Use an exploder

Have that email address explode out to multiple personnel within the organization, ideally also feeding into some process-tracking system, such as a ticketing queue.

## Use a unique address

Specify a role account address that is specific to your domain names, such as `hostmaster@`—it gives you the option to filter on it.

## Alternatively, use canaries

If your organization has a large portfolio of domains to manage directly, you could register a domain specifically for use as your point-of-contact info and then use email canaries for each domain or department or team: `example.net@packtpub-hostmaster.com`, `example.com@packtpub-hostmaster.com`—you can then filter and track each domain individually.

# The tech contact set

This contact set typically exerts no operational or administrative control over the domain. It is primarily a point of contact that network operators can use to establish communications in order to work through various network issues that may arise.

This usually included net abuse issues until the advent of the abuse contact set.

# The billing contact set

Historically, this set was created to provide a separate point of contact for billing issues related to a domain name, and was a boon for domain slammers (see Chapter 2, *Registries, Registrars, and Whois*). Again, this contact provides no operational control over the domain and is frequently the admin contact set duplicated.

# DNS details

Here, finally, we get to the actual "guts" of what makes a domain name actually "light up" on the internet: the DNS details, such as the nameserver delegation and its DNSSEC status.

The nameserver delegation is the set of authoritative nameservers for the domain. The nameservers listed here are the ones that will receive and respond to all DNS queries for the subject domain name. Most of this book is concerned with operating these types of nameservers while minimizing mental anguish; that is, sysadmin angst or "blood in the streets"-style DNS outages.

# Status

While many country ccTLDs use the same or similar status codes to the **generic TLDs (gTLDs)** we are about to describe, some do not. The following codes are the ones used under gTLDs.

One or more status fields will be present to indicate what operations can be carried out on the domain name and what state it is in. These statuses are set by either the registry of the parent TLD, or by the registrar of the domain name.

# Status flags set by the registry

The status flags set by the registry are as follows:

## Ok

No prohibitions or restrictions are in place against this domain. It is somewhat counter-intuitive to see this because it means there are no transfer locks enabled, making the domain susceptible to unauthorized hijackings or domain slamming. (In other words, when I see a domain with this status, it's something of a "red flag": something that needs to be rectified.)

## inactive

The domain has no nameserver delegation associated with it and thus does not resolve across the internet.

## autoRenewPeriod

The domain has expired and is in a grace period. The domain does not resolve across the internet—or it may be delegated to interim nameservers set by your registrar that intercepts your DNS and outputs a landing page ("The domain you are trying to reach has expired"). In most cases, the domain may still be renewed in the normal fashion and doing so will restore normal operations and DNS resolution almost immediately. (Also, see the *Understanding the domain name expiry cycle* section.)

## pendingTransfer

The domain is currently being transferred from the current registrar (aka the "losing registrar") to a new one (the "gaining registrar").

## redemptionPeriod

The domain has expired, the expiry grace period has also ended, and the domain's registrar has gone ahead and issued the "delete" command to the registry. `redemptionPeriod` is a 30-day grace period, during which it can still be renewed ("redeemed") by your registrar. (See the *Understanding the domain name expiry cycle* section.)

## pendingDelete

The `redemptionPeriod` has ended and the domain will be completely deleted from the registry within a few days (usually five). Once that happens, the domain comes available for reregistration by interested parties. (If the domain has any marginal value, it will be reregistered within milliseconds.)

# Status Flags set by the Registrar

## clientHold

The domain has had its nameserver delegation revoked, and it will not resolve across the internet. This can be the result of an unfulfilled WHOIS Accuracy Program verification or some other legal or billing dispute against the domain.

## clientDeleteProhibited

Automatically reject any requests to delete this domain while this flag is present.

## clientTransferProhibited

Automatically reject any transfer requests while this flag is present. This is usually desirable and protects your domain from unauthorized hijackings and will help thwart inadvertent slamming attempts.

## clientUpdateProhibited

Automatically reject any modifications or updates to the domain. Again, it is prudent to have this flag set. Many registrars set this and `clientTransferProhibited` as the normal state for domains. When you need to make changes to your domains, the systems temporarily clear these locks, make the updates, and re-instate them, provided the request is coming from an authorized party.

## clientRenewProhibited

The domain cannot be renewed in its current state. Contact your registrar to find out why.

# Understanding the domain name expiry cycle

Registration terms typically run in one-year cycles. If you register a domain today for one year, it will expire one year from today. The expiration date will be listed in the domain's WHOIS record. (See the previous section, *Anatomy of a domain name*, and recall that the expiry date listed in the WHOIS record may not be the actual, for-real, expiry date.)

On that day, if you have not renewed your domain via your registrar, the registrar will remove your nameserver delegation out of the TLD and your domain stops resolving.

This is the point at which many people erroneously assume that somebody else can now come in and reregister this expired domain. But this is not the case. Let's plod through this cycle.

The expiry cycle varies between TLDs. Not all TLDs allow or facilitate "parking" as we shortly describe it; some have different "drop" procedures in place. This cycle describes it as it functions for the largest TLDs (`.com`/`.net`/`.org`, for instance) and most of the new gTLDs.

## Domain expires (day 0)

Domain expires. The registrant's rights have lapsed. The domain stops working. (The expiry date in the WHOIS record may display next year's date if the registry uses "auto-renew with registrar.")

## Domain gets parked (days 3 to 5-ish)

Somewhere after a few days, many registrars will "park" the domain by inserting new "domain parking" nameservers into the TLD zone for your domain.

You may recognize this when you see it; you may arrive at a web landing page that says something to the effect of, "This domain has expired." It may be peppered with pay-per-click ads, or there may be an offer to backorder the domain.

You may also notice when you look at the WHOIS record that the nameservers are no longer the "usual" nameservers for the domain, but have other names such as `ns1.expireddomain.dom` or `ns2.expireddomain.dom`.

Doing this ostensibly serves to alert end users and, hopefully, word will get back to somebody who is in a position to do something about it to renew the domain.

What is also happening is that the registrar is doing one or more of the following:

- Monetizing clicks
- Measuring traffic
- Running free ads for their own stuff
- Soliciting interest ahead of an auction of the domain

This is a critical window in the domain life cycle because it is at this point where the registrant's (yours) and the registrar's interests may have diverged. This is because if your domain is a good one (defined as being one or more of the following: old, generic, dictionary, popular, high-traffic, or heavily backlinked), then it may be worth more to your registrar if you neglect to renew this domain rather than if you renew it.

If you renew your domain, it's worth a few bucks to your registrar. If you forget to renew it and they can auction it for $10,000 or $100,000, well then, that's another matter entirely....

# RGP – Registrant Grace Period (up to 45 days)

For the next 35 or 40 days, or maybe 45 (yes, it's that inexact, the registrar can do this next step at any time), the domain is in a state called the registrant grace period (RGP).

During this period the domain can be renewed "normally." For example, if this is a non-production domain, nobody had noticed it had expired, then after a couple weeks you find your renewal notice and renew the domain, then the domain gets renewed like any other renewal. It just starts working again and everything reverts back to normal.

But at any time during the RGP, the registrar may also "direct transfer" your domain to another party. They can do this because your rights terminated back on "day 0," the day the domain expired. This is a grace period, and toward the end of the grace period, the registrar will reserve the right to move this domain off to auction, or to sell it directly to another end user.

Domains in this state can still be transferred by the registrant to another registrar (thus triggering a renewal in the process)—however, not all registrars allow it.

# Redemption period (day 45-ish)

We have previously talked about the expiry date and how many registries operate under something called "auto-renewal" (this is a different context from end-user auto-renewal; we'll cover that shortly).

It means when the domain hits the expiry date, the registry automatically renews it and bills the registrar. The registrar has paid for, and is out-of-pocket on this domain name until they issue a "delete" command to the registry.

If the domain is nearing the end of the registrant grace period (up to 45 days), and if the domain looks of marginal value, meaning that nobody has expressed an interest in buying or bidding on it, and the domain isn't earning enough in pay-per-click to cover its renewal fees, then the registrar will issue that "delete" via an **Extended Provisioning Process** (EPP) call to the registry, and then they get their money back from the earlier auto-renewal.

The domain then enters the next phase of the expiry cycle: the redemption period. This lasts for an additional 45 days.

During this period, the domain can still be "redeemed," but only by the original registrant from before the domain expired. The registrar must not direct transfer it to another party, and they must not change the owner or registrant details aside from those which were in place before expiry. The ship has sailed on the registrar's ability to "direct transfer" it to another party.

The registry charges the registrar a "redemption fee" typically much larger than the normal renewal cost. If a domain has a wholesale cost for renewal by the registrar of $9, a redemption can cost the registrar $80 or over $100. Of course, that elevated cost will be passed back to the registrant and then some.

You can recognize the redemption period on a domain from the `DomainStatus` field of the WHOIS record. Take a look at this code:

```
Domain Name: EXAMPLEEXPIRY.COM Registrar: EASYDNS TECHNOLOGIES INC.
Sponsoring Registrar IANA ID: 469 Whois Server: whois.easydns.com Referral
URL: http://www.easydns.com Name Server: DNS1.EASYDNS.COM
Name Server: DNS2.EASYDNS.NET
Name Server: DNS3.EASYDNS.CA
Status: redemptionPeriod https://icann.org/epp#redemptionPeriod Updated
Date: 25-apr-2017
Creation Date: 15-mar-2011 Expiration Date: 15-mar-2017
```

This period is the "last-ditch" chance to renew a lapsed domain. It would be extraordinary for a busy production domain to get to this stage. Too much infrastructure and too many dependencies would be broken for too long (we're up at about 90 days of total nonfunctional DNS by this point). I have seen it happen, but more typically this affects domains that people have but aren't actively using. That doesn't prevent some pretty monster names from going the way of the expiry cycle, however.

## PendingDelete – day 90 (5 days)

Finally, after 45 days in the redemption period, the registry sends the domain into its final state before it's eventual deletion: `PendingDelete`. As usual, this status will be visible in the `DomainStatus` field of WHOIS. Take a look at this:

```
Domain Name: EXAMPLEEXPIRY.COM
Registrar: EASYDNS TECHNOLOGIES INC.
Sponsoring Registrar IANA ID: 469 Whois Server: whois.easydns.com Referral
URL: http://www.easydns.com Name Server: DNS1.EASYDNS.COM
Name Server: DNS2.EASYDNS.NET
Name Server: DNS3.EASYDNS.CA
Status: pendingDelete https://icann.org/epp#pendingDelete Updated Date: 25-
apr-2017
Creation Date: 15-mar-2011 Expiration Date: 15-mar-2017
```

A domain in `PendingDelete` status cannot be renewed or redeemed; it's too late for any of that.

After five days in `PendingDelete`, the domain will finally be deleted and available for reregistration by anybody. If the domain has any marginal value (but somehow got through the registrar's expiry-stream mining), then the "drop-catchers" will now converge and the domain will be reregistered within a few milliseconds.

## Never do this

It's important to understand that you should never intentionally allow a domain name you care about to expire with the plan of reregistering it elsewhere after. If the domain has any marginal value whatsoever, in terms of backlinks, percieved "type-in" value, and so on, it most likely will be backordered and scooped by a name sniper.

# What to do if you lose a key domain

Sometimes it happens: that key domain or one belonging to your downstream customer or user slips through the cracks and before anybody notices it, it's in `PendingDelete` status, and you have no way to retrieve it.

You still have one avenue left to try to obtain it before it becomes reregistered to another party: you can utilize the services of a "drop-catcher." These are companies who have developed systems specifically optimized to grab expiring domain names within seconds of them being finally dropped at the registry.

Some drop-catchers include the following:

- `http://www.namejet.com`
- `http://www.snapnames.com`
- `http://www.pool.com`

If we're dealing with a `.CA` domain:

- `https://www.egatedomains.ca/content/tbr.php`
- `https://www.sibername.com/tbr/`

And there are specialized services appearing such as these:

- `http://park.io`, which specializes in `.me`, `.to`, `.io`, and `.ly` drop catching

# Summary

While the simplest explanation for a domain name may be "a unique name that identifies an internet resource such as a website," to convey the full spectrum of interlocking issues that govern and maintain them, it is useful to examine the data entities, DNS hierarchy, and objects that comprise the typical WHOIS records that describe them.

The basic, prerequisite knowledge of the overall domain name ecosystem includes individual domains and the data elements that describe them, their corresponding registries, which manage each domain's parent TLD, and the registrars, which provide the interface between our names and their registries.

# References

The following points give further insight into the topics we have covered in this chapter, including internet addresses where you can find out more about domain names and related topics:

1. One example that springs to mind was a Canadian bitcoin exchange where the CEO used a purely fictitious name in the WHOIS record because both the exchange and himself personally were constantly under various forms of attack. The problem manifested through a unique combination of unfortunate events (don't they always?). The company lost access to their registrar account at roughly the same time that a hostile third party was attempting to hijack the same account, causing the then-registrar to put the account into "lockdown." The exchange had no means to prove its legitimate claim to a domain name that was, at the time, handling millions of dollars in bitcoin exchange volumes and was registered to a nonexistent person. They operated for over a year in a state of limbo, having no access to the account controlling their prime domain name and in constant dread that some third party would successfully hijack it at any moment.

2. ICANN maintains a complete list of EPP status codes and meanings at `https://www.icann.org/epp`.

3. Some sections of this book were hard to write because I feared veering off into "infomercial" territory. There is a service that exists solely to monitor various aspects of your domain names, including expiry dates and those windows when your registrar's interests are opposed to yours. It's called `https://domainsure.com`. But here's the thing - we created it. Sorry if that's self-promotion, but it's the only service of its kind that exists at the time of writing.

4. This applies mainly to gTLD and new TLD domains. Many ccTLD registries tightly control the expiry process and this is not possible. For example, CIRA runs the "To Be Released" (TBR) process and `.CA` registrars cannot "direct transfer" `.CA` domains or otherwise auction expiring names.

5. Even my company operates `web.to` as a pseudo-TLD for "Toronto," but it's really the ccTLD for the Kingdom of Tonga.

6. `.aero`, `.biz`, `.coop`, `.info`, `.museum`, `.name`, and `.pro` in 2000 and then `.asia`, `.cat`, `.jobs`, `.mobi`, `.post`, `.tel`, and `.xxx` in 2004.

7. See Victor Mayer's *Danger + Opportunity != Crisis* (`http://pinyin.info/chinese/crisis.html`).

8. I added this section after a high-school friend from my hometown contacted me asking for advice on getting his business's domain name back up and running. It turned out he had paid for his domain renewal to his Canada-based reseller, who had gone bankrupt years earlier. The defunct reseller still had a server online somewhere which was on autopilot, sending out renewal invoices which would never be actioned when somebody actually paid them. The registrar was in India and took 24 hours or more to respond to email support requests, to which they initially replied, "Please speak to your reseller." They never did rectify the situation and we ended up transferring his domain over to our system, which took another seven days under that TLD. All told, his business website was down for over two weeks.

9. NameCheap was sued by a Dutch company for alleged "cybersquatting" because their offending domains were using their WhoisGuard service - see `http://www.domainnamenews.com/featured/namecheap-sued-domain-whois-privacy-service/5198`.

10. For a long period of time easyDNS refused to offer WHOIS privacy for these reasons, but people really seemed to want it, so we did an "`official flip-flop`" and started offering it.

11. We submitted public comments recommending against changing the current policy until WHOIS could be redesigned from the ground up.

12. Via Wikipedia (`http://en.wikipedia.org/wiki/Domain_name`).

# 2
# Registries, Registrars, and Whois

In this chapter, we will look at Registries and Registrars, the differences between them, and why it matters to you. Then, we will look at "The Whois," a global database that contains data about domain name registrants, which leads us into intellectual property issues, such as trademarks and domain name disputes.

In this chapter, we will cover the following:

- Registries and Registrars
- Types of Top-Level Domains (TLDs)
- Registrars and Resellers
- Whois
- Whois Privacy
- Where Whois is going

## Registries and Registrars

So far, you've seen references to registries and registrars. It's important to understand the difference between them, and how you interact with these entities that exercise direct control over your domain names.

Your domain names are subject to, and impacted by, external and internal factors. Internal factors are the operation of the DNS and the management principles you apply to your portfolio. External factors come from registries under which your domains are registered and the oversight bodies that administer them. Those factors manifest on your portfolio via the conduit of the registrars for each given domain.

To effectively manage your portfolio, you must both be cognizant of, and understand, the influence of these external entities.

A domain registry operates a **Top-Level Domain** (TLD) for a given namespace .COM is a TLD. Your country has its own County Code TLD (a ccTLD), mine is .CA, for Canada. (Each country takes its two-character country code from the ISO 3166 `https://en.wikipedia.org/wiki/ISO_3166` list.)

Different TLDs have different registry operators. Some registry operators run more than one TLD.

A registry can operate under a "fat" model, in which the registry operator provides most or even all of the functionality at both the registry level and the end user Registrant level. In other words, a registry may operate as its own registrar; those who would like to register domains in it would deal directly with the registry itself.

More often, a TLD is operated under what I call a Triple-R model: the registry accredits registrars who then facilitate domain-name-registration services to the end users (The Registrants). Take a look at this diagram:

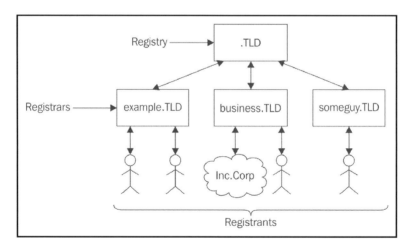

Figure 2.1: Registrars provide services to registrants by acting as a conduit to the registries.

(Some ccTLDs are hybrid models, operating a direct-to-registrant model from the registry while also allowing third-party Registrars to provide registration services , `.TO` and `.IO` come to mind.)

Know your Registries.

There is an official IANA taxonomy (`https://en.wikipedia.org/wiki/Top-level_domain#Types`) for the various types of TLDs. For our purposes, we are going to limit our scope to a few of the myriad TLDs/Registries:

- Generic TLDs (gTLDs)
- Country Code TLDs (ccTLDs)
- The "new" TLDs
- Internationalized (IDN) TLDs
- Infrastructure TLDs

# Generic TLDs

While .COM, .NET, and .ORG originally had charters (.COM was for commercial entities, .NET for network infrastructure, and .ORG for non-profit entities), those distinctions are largely blurred today and certainly not enforced in any meaningful way.

Today, these three are the big, incumbent gTLDs because domains under these namespaces are unrestricted and can be registered by any entity in any location for any reason.

There have been other TLDs over the years attempting to position themselves as gTLDs, prior to the advent of the New TLDs. These have been Country Code TLDs (ccTLDs) attempting to position themselves as gTLDs.

For example, .CO markets itself as ".CO means Company," but the reality is .CO TLD exists as the Country Code TLD for Colombia. .TV isn't really a TLD about television. It's the country code for the small island nation of Tuvalu. WS touts itself as .WS = Website, but it's actually the ccTLD of Western Samoa. The list goes on.

# Country Code TLDs (ccTLDs)

Every country or territory in the world that has its own ISO31664 designation as the two-character version of that designation available as its ccTLD. Not all two-character country codes are actually delegated to an operating registry.

The ccTLDs have their nameserver delegations maintained via ICANN (see the *Oversight Bodies* section) but each one sets its own policies governing the registration of domains within their respective ccTLDs.

Some, such as Canada's .CA, China's .CN, and the USA's .US, have local presence requirements. This means that only citizens and entities native to those countries are permitted to register domains within the TLD.

Others, as we've seen, are wide open and may actively position their ccTLD as something other than their geographical context.

# New Top-Level Domains

As of 2013, things officially "got real" as the ICANN's new TLD process kicked into motion and released the wave of the new top-level domains into the naming ecosystem. While New gTLDs are defined as any TLDs entered into the Root after January 1 2013, the TLD expansion began in earnest during 2014.

The 2013 expansion is distinct from earlier new TLD expansions in that, for the first time, it became possible for practically any entity to apply for a new TLD. The previous two rounds of expansion, 2000 and 2004, were much more limited in scope and produced only seven and eight new TLDs, respectively. The 2014 round opened the floodgates, and so far over 1,000 new TLDs have been delegated into the root.

This means that the number of generic TLDs has expanded over 20-fold in a few short years.

Examples of the new TLDs include `.website`, `.press`, `.rocks`, `.support`, `.email`, `.pics`, `.lgbt`, `.red`, `.blue`, and my personal favorite, `.wtf`.

The complete list of all TLDs currently awarded can be found at `https://newgtlds.icann.org/en/program-status/delegated-strings`.

# IDN TLDs

Internationalized Domain Names contain characters that are outside the usual alpha-numeric character set. They contain characters with accents or non-English entities.

Because labels within the DNS are encoded in ASCII, these types of entities must be converted to an ASCII representation before they can be used within the DNS system. This is facilitated by converting them to punycode.

Punycode uses a function called to ASCII to strip out the characters that need encoding and appends them to the remaining string separated by a hyphen. (The entire encoding process is described in *RFC 3492*.) Take a look at this:

Motorhead:                      Motörhead

Hong Kong's TLD:          .危危

Screen shot

$ host -t ns .危危

host: '.危危' is not a legal name (empty label)

In other words: Motörhead would become motorhead-p4a, then we also need a mechanism to signal that this label or domain was not originally an ASCII label to begin with, so the prefix `xn--` was selected.

Thus, `Motorhead.com` becomes `xn-motrhead-p4a.com` (alas, that domain is already taken).

# Online tools for converting punycode

Verisign's IDN Conversion Tool: `http://mct.verisign-grs.com/convert Servlet?input=Mot%C3%B6rhead`

All About Charsets: `http://www.charset.org/punycode.php`

Prior to the 2014 expansion of the TLD space, IDNs existed within many of the legacy TLDs. In other words, the label to the left of the dot could support IDN strings while the domain suffix, the TLDs themselves, were all ASCII.

With the advent of the new TLDs, IDNs are now supported to the right of the dot, such as Hong Kong's 危危 Again, at the level of DNS lookups, you can't simply dig this suffix's internationalized label:

```
$ host -t ns . 危危
host: '. 危危' is not a legal name (empty label)
```

Rather, the label is converted to punycode (`xn--j6w193g`):

```
$ host -t ns xn--j6w193g
xn--j6w193g name server C.HKIRC.NET.HK.
xn--j6w193g name server Y.HKIRC.NET.HK.
xn--j6w193g name server V.HKIRC.NET.HK.
xn--j6w193g name server U.HKIRC.NET.HK.
xn--j6w193g name server B.HKIRC.NET.HK.
xn--j6w193g name server W.HKIRC.NET.HK.
xn--j6w193g name server Z.HKIRC.NET.HK.
xn--j6w193g name server D.HKIRC.NET.HK.
xn--j6w193g name server X.HKIRC.NET.HK.
```

# Infrastructure TLDs

The aforementioned special case `.arpa` TLD is "the" internet infrastructure TLD ("Address and Routing Parameter Area"). In fact, it was the very first TLD and it was intended to be a temporary measure to facilitate the migration from the original Arpanet to the domain name system we have today.

As with many temporary measures, it stuck around and is used as the TLD to anchor various internet infrastructure functions:

- `.in-addr.arpa`: The "reverse mapping" or reverse lookup for IP addresses (specifically IPv4 addresses, which we will look at in `Chapter 11`, *DNS Operations and Use Cases*)
- `.e164.arpa`: Used for creating telephone number mapping (see the section on NAPTR RR's in `Chapter 11`, *DNS Operations and Use Cases*)
- `.ip6.arpa`: The reverse-mapping domain for IPv6 addresses (`Chapter 11`, *DNS Operations and Use Cases*)

# Registrars and Resellers

Registrars are organizations that facilitate the registration and maintenance of domain names in specific TLDs. Sitting between the Registrant and the TLD's registry, as depicted in *Figure 2.1*, they act as a conduit to the various name spaces their end users have domains under. They may specialize in this or do so in conjunction with some other service they provide (such as web hosting providers or managed DNS services). Most Registrars provide registration services to multiple TLDs.

The basic responsibilities of Registrars include providing the ability to do the following:

- Register and renew domain names
- Modify/update contact data associated with domain names ("Whois" records)
- Control security parameters of a domain (lock states)
- Update and maintain the nameserver delegations of domain names
- Enter DS records into the parent TLD zone for DNSSEC-enabled domains (where available)

There are thousands of Registrars worldwide that are directly accredited by ICANN—the organization who oversee the naming and numbering of the internet, to register domains.

While domain registrations are today considered largely commoditized, not all Registrars are created equal. I've provided a concise checklist of what to look for in a Registrar to which you entrust your domains.

# An effective Registrar should...

- **Offer live support**: You should be able to call them and get a human on the phone in a timely manner.
- **Have a robust DNS infrastructure**: Both for serving any customer domains that elect to use the Registrars' nameservers, but also for their own platform. You need to be able to log in and manage your domains when needed. It won't do if your Registrar is offline at the time you need to make a change. To that end, they should have their own DNS deployed via anycast (which we'll look at in Chapter 11, *DNS Operations and Use Cases*) and have adequate protection from **Denial-of-Service (DoS)** attacks. Registrars and nameserver operators are a favorite target for these types of attacks (we cover DoS mitigation strategies in Chapter 13, *Securing Your Domains and DNS*).
- **Be secure**: This is an open-ended topic, but the minimum we want is that Registrars offer some form of multi-stage authentication for accessing your account, that they're using sensible password storage, management, and recovery procedures, and that they are resistant to social engineering attacks. Always remember that your Registrars have arbitrary and total control over your domains. Even if they will not act against your best interests, it doesn't help if a hostile party can use their platform to do so.

- **Support DNS Security Extensions (DNSSEC)**: We will look at this in `Chapter 12`, *Nameserver Considerations*. Even if you are running DNS yourself or using a third-party vendor, such as a managed DNS provider, if you have a requirement to deploy DNSSEC-signed zones, then it will be your Registrar that has to facilitate creation of a chain of trust with your parent TLD.
- **Have a clueful abuse desk**: You may think that since you are not a spammer or some other kind of malevolent actor, you don't need to worry about dealing with abuse desks. Sadly, abuse desks are themselves routinely abused. People file complaints with abuse desks for the most spurious of reasons, and the poorer quality Registrars take down your domains first and ask questions later.

Your domain may also be registered via a Registrar reseller, which means there is a further level of abstraction between your names and the Registries they are under. A reseller is not directly accredited under your domains' parent Registries. They have wholesale agreements with Registrars, and they operate under their Registrars' accreditation agreements.

Problems can occur if there is any kind of problem with the reseller, such as a dispute, or worse, business failure. When that happens, you and your domains can be in limbo because the Registrar may initially deflect all inquiries back toward their Reseller. While under most Registrar Accreditation Agreements, all obligations to the end user Registrants are incumbent upon the Registrar, even if they use resellers, it doesn't help you in that moment when your critical domains are down because if a reseller failure.

There are, of course, many stable resellers. Many times, web-hosting companies will be a reseller because of the high volume of domains they deal with. If the company is competent at their core business, they will be competent in their role as reseller.

But it brings us to a key rule of navigating the domain name ecosystem, which is this: Know who each domain is registered through, and what their relationship is to each domain's registry.

# What is Whois?

As we outlined in the *Anatomy of a domain name* section, the domain name can be split into logical sections, such as Registrant, Admin Contact, Tech Contacts, and Nameservers. All of these sections are described and enumerated in records called Whois records and Whois servers serve those records. While in the early days, Whois records were merely informational repositories of points-of-contact for domain names, as the internet became more integral to everyday living and business, these records became of the utmost importance. They have legal bearing now; they are used to decide ownership disputes and liability issues. There exist forensic Whois record auditors who trace domain ownership using these records to assess whether a given domain may be stolen.

The Whois servers are internet hosts that listen for Whois requests (typically on port 43), and they respond to queries about given domain names with the associated Whois records for them. While traditionally there have been best practices for the format of Whois records, every registry and registrar has their own output format.

## Thin versus thick Whois

Most Registries today are operating under the thick Whois model. That means the Whois servers are operated by the registries themselves and the Whois records returned by the registry are the full and complete records. Take a look at this:

```
$ whois easydns.org
Domain Name:EASYDNS.ORG Domain ID: D19300541-LROR
Creation Date: 2000-02-07T16:36:30Z Updated Date: 2014-02-05T19:35:20Z
Registry Expiry Date: 2015-02-07T16:36:30Z
Sponsoring Registrar:easyDNS Technologies Inc. (R1247-LROR) Sponsoring
Registrar IANA ID: 469
WHOIS Server:
Referral URL:
Domain Status: ok
Registrant ID:tuFR6qyd4IzCW0LK Registrant Name:Hostmaster Role Account
Registrant Organization:easyDNS Technologies Registrant Street: 304A – 219
Dufferin St. Registrant City:Toronto
Registrant State/Province:ON Registrant Postal Code:M6K3J1 Registrant
Country:CA Registrant Phone:+1.6474788439 Registrant Phone Ext: Registrant
Fax: +1.6474386227 Registrant Fax Ext:
Registrant Email:easydns@myprivacy.ca Admin ID:tukBnUT7S6DIXC3g
Admin Name:Hostmaster Role Account Admin Organization:easyDNS Technologies
Admin Street: 304A – 219 Dufferin St. Admin City:Toronto
Admin State/Province:ON Admin Postal Code:M6K3J1 Admin Country:CA
Admin Phone:+1.4165358672 Admin Phone Ext:
```

```
Admin Fax: +1.4165350237
Admin Fax Ext:
Admin Email:easydns@myprivacy.ca Tech ID:tu4jwsWgdFxARStq
Tech Name:Hostmaster Role Account
Tech Organization:easyDNS Technologies Tech Street: 304A - 219 Dufferin St.
Tech City:Toronto
Tech State/Province:ON Tech Postal Code:M6K3J1 Tech Country:CA
Tech Phone:+1.4165358672 Tech Phone Ext:
Tech Fax: +1.4165350237
Tech Fax Ext:
Tech Email:easydns@myprivacy.ca Name Server:DNS1.EASYDNS.COM Name
Server:DNS3.EASYDNS.ORG
Name Server:DNS2.EASYDNS.NET Name Server:DNS4.EASYDNS.INFO
DNSSEC:Unsigned
```

This is in contrast with a thin Whois model. Under this model, the full record is returned by a Whois server operated by the Registrar, not the registry, which is largely the exception (only .COM, .NET, and .JOBS still use it) and officially on the way out. ICANN adopted the GNSO's Thick Whois Consensus Policy in 2014, and thus will move any remaining thin Whois services toward a thick model.

# Whois privacy

A major issue with registering a domain name is that your contact details (or those of your customer) are supposed to be true and valid contact details in order to fulfill the requirements of your registry's Registration Agreement, and those details must be published in the Whois database which is, as you now know, publicly accessible.

### What on earth is a Whois?

My estimation is that the majority of internet users, even the majority of *domain name registrants* have no idea that the Whois database exists, let alone publishes their contact data for all to see. Sure, *you* may know that but the thing is, a lot of your customers may not.

The problem is that spammers, advertisers, and marketers mine the Whois database and extract data from it, so before you know it you are getting various emails, marketing pitches, and junk faxes all because of the information you had to supply when you registered the domain name.

To mitigate this, Registrars invented Whois privacy. Whois privacy hides your Registrant contact details from public view. Since it is against the rules of nearly any registry to supply false data in a domain name registration, Registrars responded by creating actual corporate entities that would act as the Registrant for your domain in your place. When somebody looks up the Whois record for a domain name, they would see the contact details for some privacy-providing entity or other suitable proxy, as shown here:

```
$ whois antiguru.com
Domain Name: ANTIGURU.COM
Registry Domain ID: 1549312202_DOMAIN_COM-VRSN
Registrar WHOIS Server: whois.easydns.com
Registrar URL: http://www.easydns.com
Updated Date: 2014-03-24 10:00:05
Creation Date: 2009-03-25 19:05:18
Registrar Registration Expiration Date: 2015-03-25 19:05:18
Registrar: easyDNS Technologies, Inc.
Registrar IANA ID: 469
Registrar Abuse Contact Email: abuse@easydns.com
Registrar Abuse Contact Phone: +1.4165358672 Domain
Status: clientTransferProhibited
Domain Status: clientUpdateProhibited
Registry Registrant ID:
Registrant Name: Contact Privacy
Registrant Organization: MyPrivacy.net Ltd.
Registrant Street: 300A-219 Dufferin St.
Registrant City: Toronto
Registrant State/Province: ON Registrant Postal Code: M6K 3J1
Registrant Country: CA Registrant Phone: +1.6474785997
Registrant Phone Ext: Registrant Fax:
Registrant Fax Ext:
Registrant Email: antiguru.com@myprivacy.net
Registry Admin ID:
Admin Name: Contact Privacy
Admin Organization: MyPrivacy.net Ltd.
Admin Street: 300A-219 Dufferin St.
Admin City: Toronto
Admin State/Province: ON
Admin Postal Code: M6K 3J1
Admin Country: CA
Admin Phone: +1.6474785997
```

This accomplishes what it set out to do, and it masks your Whois data and your private contact details from marketers and spammers. But... it comes with associated risks that you need to be aware of.

Most importantly, when you use Whois privacy, the actual owner or rights holder for your domain name is the privacy entity that is listed in the Whois record for your domain.

In practical terms, there is usually a secondary agreement between you and that privacy entity that presumably upholds your rights to the domain name. But in the event of a dispute or lost contact details or a lockout situation, it is the privacy entity that owns or holds all the rights to your domain names, not you.

ICANN-accredited Registrars are contractually obligated to escrow their Whois data with an escrow provider to safeguard against business failure on the part of the Registrar. If Whois privacy is enabled, then they are required to escrow the underlying Registrant details. Whether that actually happens in every case is something you would only find out after the fact, in the event of a catastrophic failure on the part of a Registrar.

# RegisterFly – The Lehman Brothers' moment of the domain industry

The RegisterFly debacle is what many might point at when they assert that Registrars need to be better regulated or to make some other point about how crappy the overall domain registration ecosystem is.

With over two million domains under management when it all fell apart, this chapter in naming history has it all: a love affair gone bad between estranged business partners, widespread allegations of fraud, criss-crossing lawsuits and counter-suits, appeals, and overturned decisions. A bizarre schism in which RegisterFly split out into two separate but outwardly identical websites: one operating on `RegisterFly.com` (which briefly sucked my company directly into the crossfire when one of the partners moved that domain to easyDNS in an effort to place it beyond the reach of the other partner) and the other on `RegisterFly.net` (being run by the other partner who was locked out of `RegisterFly.com`).

ICANN made an arguably rare stand on the myriad compliance issues and eventually stripped RegisterFly of their ICANN accreditation...and that's when things became even more unglued.

RegisterFly had not been properly escrowing their Registant data (as is required by all Registrars) and were ordered to turn customer data over, which they failed to do.

Out of all this, many Registrants simply lost their domain names, as they expired during this process, without any means to renew them.

In the aftermath of this, ICANN became far more vigilant in making sure Registrars are properly escrowing their data. Since RegisterFly, numerous Registrars have failed, exited the business, or in some cases, been de—accredited and their Registrants have all been successfully and seamlessly transitioned to new Registrars.

# How to tell whether Whois privacy is enabled

If you do a look on a "Whois" record, a lot of times there is no set field inside the record that says "privacy is enabled," but after you look at enough of these you start to get a feel for it. The following table lists common privacy providers (cutouts) and the domain registrars they are associated with. Take a look at this table:

| Privacy Entity | Registrar |
|---|---|
| Domains By Proxy | Godaddy |
| WhoisGuard | Namecheap |
| MyPrivacy.net Ltd. | easyDNS |
| Contacy Privacy Ltd. | Tucows/OpenSRS |
| WhoisGuard Inc | eNom |
| Oneandone Private Registration | 1&1 Internet Inc |
| Whois Privacy Services Pty Ltd | Fabulous Pty. |
| Protection Service INC d/b/a PrivacyProtect.org | Public Domain Registry |

All these privacy providers are entities that are usually created by the Registrar specifically or solely to facilitate Whois privacy. One of the key reasons is to compartmentalize potential liability from domain names, where the Privacy Entity is listed as the "Registrant".

# Why you should always use Whois privacy

There are a few reasons you would want to use Whois privacy:

- You don't want your personal contact details harvested by spammers.
- You may be in "stealth mode," registering domain names about new products, services, or financial events (such as a merger) and you may want to shield yourself from the scrutiny of your competitors
- You're doing something controversial, such as whistleblowing

# Why you should never use Whois privacy

You should never use Whois privacy if you consider the risk of not directly owning and controlling your domain names unacceptable. The other thing about Whois privacy, especially for e-commerce websites and companies doing business on the Internet, is that it tends to look "scammy." If you are taking people's credit card data or other **Personally Identifiable Information** (**PII**), you should be as transparent as possible and make it easy for users to look up exactly who they are doing business with. Few would disagree that in this context, anonymized Whois records may be off-putting to potential customers.

The problem is when the signup process for many domain registrations is so convoluted and oversaturated with "upsells" and "addons," in many cases Whois privacy may be enabled for your domains without the domain Registrants actually being aware of it.

Another caveat to using Whois privacy is that it can also be used (intentionally? Who knows?) to create lock-in situations. For people not immersed in this industry, transferring domains between Registrars can be a daunting task. It gets even harder when the domains have Whois privacy enabled.

When signing up a domain with a given registrar, adding Whois privacy is trivially easy (perhaps, too easy). It's just a checkbox! For your convenience, it may have already been checked.

Then when the time comes to transfer it out and turn it off, it's another story. Once you're at a point where you decide to transfer your domain to another Registrar (perhaps because of the stellar service?), you have to disable Whois privacy before you can transfer the domain out.

Usually, the Registrar creates a separate Privacy Entity. If they are nice about it, you have the ability to disable Whois Privacy from within the same control panel where you manage everything else. If they're not so nice about it, they may force you to contact the Privacy Entity separately to disable it, and that Privacy Entity may erect more hurdles, such as providing written authorization or photo ID.

# Where is Whois going?

Within the industry, it is widely agreed that the current port-43-based Whois was never intended to function at the scale the internet has achieved today, that it is fundamentally flawed and that, in light of various stakeholders, which include law enforcement, intellectual property owners, network operations, and end users, there needs to be a comprehensive revision, if not a complete rebuild.

The effort to reform or redesign Whois has played out in fits and starts for years, if not decades (I have a faint recollection of serving on a task force that was trying to address this back in 2003 or so).

As I write this, the most appropriate description of the Whois reform process is "stalled." There was a public comment period in 2015 about the possibility of eliminating Whois Privacy, which elicited a strong backlash.

That said, there is a successor protocol, RDAP, designated by ICANN, that was supposed to come into effect in 2017, but, at the time of writing (mid-2018), we're not there yet.

# Europe's GDPR and its effect on Whois

However, one significant even that did occur as this book was undergoing final edits was that Europe's General Data Protection Rules (GDPR) came into effect. The current practices for collecting and disseminating Registrants' contact details contravene GDPR. This is a problem for domain registrars who are contractually obligated, under their ICANN accreditation agreements, to maintain the Whois database and provide registrant data through them.

ICANN asked the EU for an exemption under GDPR and was denied. The registrars asked ICANN for a moratorium on compliance and were also denied. The result was The Day The Whois Died, May 25, 2018, when across the world, many domain registrars simply stopped displaying Whois data for all domains, while others did so only for registrants in the affected EU countries.

The reality is, right now the entire Whois landscape is gripped with uncertainty and inconsistency. There will likely be some kind of gated-access Whois operating under RDAP in the near future, perhaps by the time you read this.

# Registration Data Access Protocol (RDAP)

While reform and updates of the current Whois process is largely stalled, the aforementioned "do over" is proceeding in the form of the **Registration Data Access Protocol (RDAP)**.

The key differences RDAP will bring include these:

- **Accessed over the web**: It will function via a RESTful API, not port 43.
- **Standardized output**: Records will be JSON-encoded. Currently Whois output varies between Registries and even Registrars.
- **Authenticated**: Right now, pretty well anybody and anything can query Whois records. That leads to widespread scraping, data mining, and associated headaches, but is balanced against the transparency of anybody being able to query domain registration information. RDAP will be authenticated access, there will be some kind of framework around who can access the records and under what circumstances, as I write this, that framework is largely unknown. Various concerns enter here. As is human nature, everybody will want privacy for themselves and accountability for everyone else. Queue the policy battle-bots.

The timing of the RDAP implementation is subject to revision, but after a transition period where RDAP and Whois co-exist, as one of the technical reviewers put it "RDAP will have completely supplanted WHOIS long before there's a chance to do a second edition of this book." We'll see.

# Further reading

ICANN publishes a comprehensive "Whois Primer" that details the requirements and implementations of the current Whois system.

We look at the **Whois Data Reminder Program** (**WDRP**) and the Whois Accuracy Program (WAP) in Chapter 2, *Registries, Registrars, and Whois,* and we do so because if you are not aware of these two programs, the difference between them, and how to adhere to them, your domains can stop functioning.

# Summary

In this chapter, we further explored the various components of the domain name ecosystem. We looked at how the TLDs are operated by various registries, and how we interact with those registries when we register, move, or modify domains, via registrars.

We introduced the Whois database, which tracks registrant details for all of these myriad domains across the multitude of registries, and touched on the state of flux that the Whois landscape is undergoing because of the recently-introduced European data privacy laws, the GDPR.

# Intellectual Property Issues

# 3

This chapter will hopefully reduce the mental paralysis that may result once the full spectrum of possible Top-Level Domains available is fully grasped.

As renowned venture capitalist/blogger Rick Segal was fond of telling me, *Choice = Confusion = Inaction*. However, after reading this material, you will know how to create a defined scope for your organization's domain name portfolio.

You will also have an understanding of the rules that govern disputes, how to proceed against parties infringing on your IP rights, and what to expect, including how to respond if a third-party makes a move against a domain owned by you or one of your customers.

You'll be familiar with the domain aftermarkets and domain backordering platforms that you'll need in the case of emergency claw-backs, or even for those times when you have your eye on the perfect name that is coming up for expiry.

Finally, you'll have a general framework for constructing an **Acceptable Use Policy** (**AUP**) that can guide you through takedown requests, data-sharing requests, and other interactions with the general public, rights holders, and **Law Enforcement Agencies** (**LEA**).

In this chapter, we will cover the following:

- Which domains should your organization register?
- Asserting your trademarks within a new TLD
- The rollout phases of new TLDs
- Trademark Clearing Houses
- Dispute mechanisms
- What do to if somebody tries to take your domains
- What happens in a UDRP
- The Transfer Dispute Resolution Procedure

# Which domains should your organization register?

Under which TLD suffixes should your organization register? In the old days (before 2014), a lot of registrars would try to goad their customers into registering their organization or brand names in every TLD that was available.

"Get your name before somebody else does!" was the well-worn mantra that was constantly broadcast at registrants every time a new generic TLD came out or some country code decided to brand themselves as some sort of pseudo-TLD.

In a lot of cases it worked, because managers, IP departments, or lawyers would think that there is an obligation to defend the organization's intellectual property in any way they can. What that meant was that a lot of organizations would make it a habit to register their name in every TLD that they possibly could.

Now that the new TLDs are here, there are over 1,000 TLDs. It is effectively impossible to defend every one of your marks in every single one of these TLDs. Some organizations have a large portfolio of trademarks, products, call-to-action URLs, or other meaningful names, protecting them all under every TLD would make for an exponentially large number of names.

For example, one of our clients at easyDNS is a pharmaceutical conglomerate that has the domain name of every single product they own plus a few other "call-to-action" domain names in their portfolio. On its own, it is about 6,000 to 10,000 names. The level of complexity involved in taking that IP portfolio and then registering them in as many TLDs as practical before the 2014 rollout of the new TLDs was daunting enough. Now that the new TLDs are out of the bottle, I think it is categorically impossible.

Which brings us back to the question, "What domain suffix should organizations register in?"

There is a rule of thumb espoused by a legendry domainer by the name of Frank Schilling, who always advocated registering the .COM, .NET, .ORG of your name, plus the ccTLD of your primary country of business and any other countries you are doing business in.

So, if you're The Example Corporation, you would register (if you can) `example.com`, `example.net`, `example.org`, and if you're here in Canada, you would get example.ca. That's a pretty good rule of thumb. Your mileage may vary, sometimes you can't get the .COM (conventional wisdom holds that ".COM is king," but it can be open to debate). It certainly is the most popular TLD in existence, as this table shows:

| Top Level Domain | Domain count |
|---|---|
| .COM | 130,393,052 |
| .CN | 20,868,593 |
| .DE | 16,314,502 |
| .NET | 14,250,545 |
| .UK | 12,095,794 |
| .ORG | 10,303,123 |
| .INFO | 6,401,406 |
| .NL | 5,797,041 |
| .RU | 5,370,035 |
| .BR | 3,894,363 |
| .EU | 3,815,055 |
| .FR | 3,158,523 |
| .AU | 3,119,485 |
| .IT | 3,094,083 |

Table 3.1: Top Domain Counts by TLD. Source Matthew Zook/Zooknic.com as at Dec 2017

Sometimes you can't get the .COM and make a calculated decision to launch without it. This was already becoming more prevalent in the "Web 2.0" phase of the internet, with companies launching on alternative TLDs, such as .IO and .LY.

What this rule of thumb suggests is that you're going to make a rational decision around a small set of core TLDs. I would modify this rule as follows:

- Try to get the big generics: `.COM`, `.NET`, `.ORG`.
- Get the country code(s) that you're doing significant business in.
- Register in any of the new TLDs that make direct relevant business sense to your organization and its products or services.

You may want to cover off obvious compliments to your business such as .support or .email, if only to block off the most obvious candidates for any phishing campaigns that may directed against your customers. If I had to compose a shortlist that would be these:

- .support
- .website
- .email.company

You have to choose your own balance, a set of criteria that will whittle all the potential TLDs down to a strategic group of them that you want to defend your marks in, and then you just leave the rest behind. Then you deal with any issues of outright infringement or abuse (such as phishing) on a case-by-case basis. We'll look at this next.

### Should we register mycompany.sux?

Worth a short discussion on its own is whether companies should make a special case to "protect their name" in this new TLD landscape under disparaging TLDs such as `.sucks`.

The short answer: no. You should treat these TLDs as any others peripheral to your business or activities: Deal with them if some infringing activity originates from them.

Any hopes that registering the .sucks versions of your names can head off any negative chatter about your company or your brand are misplaced. It falls prey to what I call The Domainer Fallacy, that is, of confusing the map with the territory.

Owning the .sucks versions of your brands *does not* control the narrative about your brand. The way you conduct yourself does that. Even if you successfully grab "mycompany.sucks" before somebody else does, if your customers are disgruntled enough to *want* to register that name and set up a website on it, you have other problems. They'll just do it under some other name anyway.

See `http://blog.easydns.org/2015/04/10/why-we-will-not-be-regist ering-easydns-sucks/`
as well as an interview I did with CBC's Nora Young on this topic.

# Asserting Your trademarks within the new TLD landscape

As we've covered, there are so many new gTLDs rolling out we will be well into the thousands within a few years (all of these new TLDs originate in the first great TLD expansion round of 2013. The next TLD expansion round is estimated to commence in 2020).

You will want to register some or all of your marks in some (but not all) of the new TLDs. You may also want to make use of the Trademark Clearing House for those marks you do want to defend, but not by registering every possible domain. We'll cover both aspects here.

The bad news is when you add up the various fees (Trademark Clearing House, Sunrise Applications, not to mention all the extra domains themselves), it starts to get expensive.

# Rollout phases of a new TLD

Once a new TLD delegation is added to the root, it goes through a ramp-up phase before it is widely available on a first-come, first-served basis.

# Sunrise

In the Sunrise phase, Intellectual Property owners may register for domains that match their trademarks. Usually the trademarks must be registered (in any jurisdiction) to qualify, and trademarks may not "span the dot." In other words, when .bar enters Sunrise (yes, that's a real new TLD) and your organization holds a registered trademark on "`foobar[tm]`", you cannot enter a Sunrise application for `foo.bar`. You can only enter a claim on a matching label for your trademark, in this example: foobar.bar.

If multiple trademark claimants enter Sunrise applications for the same label, it will usually go into an auction process.

Sunrise claims typically cost significantly more than a normal "Landrush" registration (in the $300 to $500 USD range each), yet another barrier making it unfeasible in many cases to defend all of one's registered marks under all possible gTLDs.

For the "new GTLDs" that recently started rolling out, you have to have your trademarks registered with the Trademark Clearing House to qualify for a sunrise round.

# Landrush

Landrush is the "free-for-all" phase where, presumably, everything left after Sunrise becomes available on a first-come, first-served basis. That said, the common practice among most new TLD operators now is to reserve a list of domains designated as "premium," which cannot be registered via Landrush.

Many Registrars pre-sell Landrush by building up waiting lists beforehand. Similar to the Registries "premium lists," they will take preorders on upcoming domains and if they encounter contention (multiple orders for the same name), they will endeavor to "snag" the domain upon commencement of Landrush and, if successful, they will then auction it.

# Premium auction

The Registry will often reserve most of the highly desirable names under a specific new TLD, as well as all of the one-, two-, and perhaps some of the three-character labels and designate them as premium names. They will then either auction them off, or broker them to interested parties on a case-by-case basis for vastly inflated fees.

# The Trademark Clearing House

For a good number of new TLDs under which you won't or can't directly register your names, you can gain some defence of your marks by making use of the Trademark Clearing House.

This provides a mechanism where you register your marks, allow other parties to register labels matching those marks, provided they go through an additional step where they are made aware of the contending marks and affirm that their use of the domain does not infringe on the mark.

When registering an affected domain, you may see an additional step, as in the following screen, which occurred upon registering our `planb.works` domain and ran into the trademark asserted by the Plan B contraceptive (one reason why we never ended up using that name after all). Take a look at this screenshot:

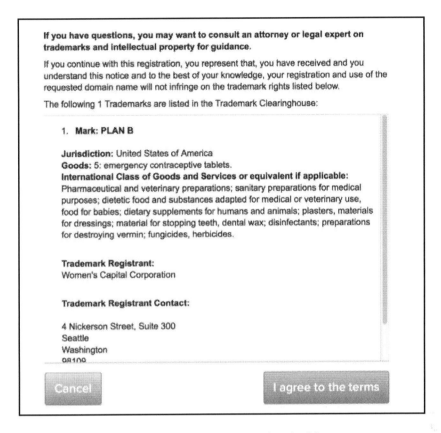

If you have questions, you may want to consult an attorney or legal expert on trademarks and intellectual property for guidance.

If you continue with this registration, you represent that, you have received and you understand this notice and to the best of your knowledge, your registration and use of the requested domain name will not infringe on the trademark rights listed below.

The following 1 Trademarks are listed in the Trademark Clearinghouse:

1. **Mark: PLAN B**

**Jurisdiction:** United States of America
**Goods:** 5: emergency contraceptive tablets.
**International Class of Goods and Services or equivalent if applicable:** Pharmaceutical and veterinary preparations; sanitary preparations for medical purposes; dietetic food and substances adapted for medical or veterinary use, food for babies; dietary supplements for humans and animals; plasters, materials for dressings; material for stopping teeth, dental wax; disinfectants; preparations for destroying vermin; fungicides, herbicides.

**Trademark Registrant:**
Women's Capital Corporation

**Trademark Registrant Contact:**

4 Nickerson Street, Suite 300
Seattle
Washington
98109

Cancel          I agree to the terms

Figure 3.2: Confirmation to acknowledge a non-competing trademark for a name

The problem in my mind with the Trademark Clearing House is that you need have your marks in it before you can apply for Sunrise applications for any of the new TLDs, but the terms only last 90 days to a year. Which means yet another service you're committed to subscribing to and renewing in order to "defend your marks."

# Typo domains

Another decision that you will have to incorporate into your strategy is what to do about obvious typos of your domains. Defensively securing misspellings and typos of your portfolio will, again, boost the complexity of the portfolio itself an order of magnitude. (Think about trying to defend your mark in all TLDs with all possible typo variations, it becomes impractical very quickly).

Here are some examples of obvious typos: We're easyDNS, so we have easydsn.com; it is a common typo to make. We do this because it brings in traffic from our own user base that may commonly make this typo. It makes sense because it contributes directly to usability.

Contrast with a typo that will rarely if ever be made: easydsn.biz. Who cares? We don't and the reason we don't is because nobody has ever typed that trying to get to our website.

There is a reason why it is safe to ignore entire swaths of typos under most TLDs. If somebody else actually grabs a derivation of one of your marks, whether it is a typo or a cyber squat under any other TLD, in other words, any use that can be deemed "confusingly similar" to yours, there are mechanisms available for you to have those domain names shut down and seized if they are in fact trading on your intellectual property (we will explain them in the next section).

# What is "CyberSquatting"?

There is a lot of confusion around the term "cybersquatting." It is frequently misconstrued as any time somebody registers a domain and doesn't actively use it for something. But that is not cybersquatting. A lot of people feel there should be some manner of use-it-or-lose-it rules around domain names and they view those who don't use their own domains as cybersquatters.

It's a fallacious argument, since "use" is entirely subjective. Use versus non-use is an opinion. Even if a domain is intentionally not delegated in its TLD, it may be that way for a reason and thus constitute "use." More often, the cybersquatting charge is leveled against "domainers," defined as people and companies who register large numbers of domain names and then either offer them for sale in the aftermarket, monetize them via ads or lead generation, or both.

There is a perception that doing so is not a "legitimate" use of the domain; however, that is a purely subjective opinion (not to mention a sanctimoniously Marxist one).

My stance on this has been borne out in repeated findings by UDRP panels that "domain parking" is a legitimate use of a domain name, and further, that asking for an "inflated sum" of money in the aftermarket is again, subjective, and not evidence of a bad faith registration." ("Bad Faith" being a key requirement in a domain dispute proceeding)

**So, what is "CyberSquatting" then?**

It is when some party deliberately and intentionally registers misspellings or alternate TLD versions of your domains and does the following:

- Uses it in a way that is "confusingly similar" to your own (passing off)
- Benefits from your trademarks, that is, running ads for your products or those of a competitor
- Intends to profit from the domain through these methods or from an eventual sale of the domain to you or otherwise

A textbook example of cybersquatting would be the registration of yourtrademark.co (capturing typo traffic from people missing or neglecting to type the final "m" in yourtrademark.com) and then redirecting that traffic to an affiliate program selling your own products, or that of a competitor.

# Dispute mechanisms

Processes exist to handle disputes between contending claims on a given domain name. The Terms of Service your Registrar will have you agree to at the time you register a domain will include the provision to abide by these processes. Disputes are not handled or arbitrated by ICANN but rather by Dispute Resolution Providers, who are sanctioned by ICANN to render decisions according to the defined policy.

## Uniform Domain Name Dispute Resolution Policy (UDRP)

The **Uniform Domain Name Dispute Resolution Policy** (**UDRP**) is the primary mechanism by which **Intellectual Property** (**IP**) rights are asserted over domain names. If the complainant is successful in bringing a UDRP procedure against an offending domain, it can be canceled or ordered transferred to the complainant. The remedy in successful cases is effectively always a transfer. If the domain is simply canceled, some other Registrant may grab it and you are back to square one

In order to successfully bring a UDRP against a domain name, all three of the following elements must be present:

"(i) your domain name is identical or confusingly similar to a trademark or service mark in which the complainant has rights; and:

- you have no rights or legitimate interests in respect of the domain name; and
- your domain name has been registered and is being used in bad faith."

In a UDRP, the party bringing the action is the Complainant, while the current domain holder defending against the action is the Respondent.

To bring a complaint against a domain, the Complainant selects an authorized Dispute Resolution Provider, such as the **National Arbitration Forum** (**NAF**) or the **World Intellectual Property Rights Organization** (**WIPO**), files the complaint, and pays the administrative fees.

# How the UDRP works

Here we'll take you through the basic flow and "things to know" of the UDRP procedure. It is highly recommended that you retain a lawyer that specializes in these matters (See the Domain name lawyers sidebar). It is still recommended that you be familiar with the procedure even if you retain counsel. Finally, I strongly caution against representing yourself on either side of a UDRP unless you are a full time professional domainer or otherwise immersed in the industry and are familiar with the governing rules and precedents, which are as follows:

- The Complainant selects a Dispute Resolution Provider, prepares background material, submits complaint, and remits fees.
- The Dispute Resolution Provider notifies the current Registrar for the domain and requests that the Registrar verify various aspects of the Registration.
- The Registrar then sets the `clientTransferProhibited` and `clientUpdateProhibited` flags on the domain status. This prevents the domain from changing its `Whois` record or from transferring away, but the domain will continue to be resolved over the internet.
- The Resolution Provider will then forward a copy of the complaint to the Respondant.

- Unless the Respondent elects to use a three-member panel to hear the case, the procedure will be heard by a one-member panel. If the respondent opts for a three-member panel, additional fees apply and the total fees will be split between the Complainant and Respondent.
- The Respondent will have until the stated deadline to file its rebuttal. If the Respondent fails to file a response, the Panel will decide the case without input from the Respondent. There have been rare cases where a Panel has decided in favor of an unresponsive Respondent.
- The panel then renders its decision and forwards a copy to both sides. If the complainant prevails, their Registrar will commence a domain transfer and the Respondent's Registrar will allow it. If the Respondent prevails, their Registrar will simply remove any restrictions on the domain and life continues unabated.

# Uniform Rapid Suspension System (URSS)

The **Uniform Rapid Suspension System** (**URSS**) is a newer policy designed to make a faster and more affordable dispute resolution mechanism available to rights holders. A URS action can only be initiated against domains under the new TLDs. (A UDRP may also be filed against a domain under a new TLD, but not the inverse.)

The URS contains similar elements to the UDRP:

- The Complainant files their complaint via a sanctioned URS provider
- The Complainant must pay fees within 24 hours of filing or it is summarily denied
- The Complainant must provide details of the complaint as outlined in the URS procedure

As with the UDRP, three key elements must be asserted and all must be present:

- The domain is identical or confusingly similar to an existing mark
- The Registrant has no legitimate interest in or use for the name
- The name was registered in Bad Faith

There are two big differences in a URS decision, which are different from an UDRP:

- If it is in favor of the Complainant, the domain is not transferred to them, but rather put on hold and into an unusable state. The complainant does have an option to extend the registration period of the frozen domain at market rates.
- There is an appeal process. The UDRP doesn't have one.

### What is "Bad Faith" ?

Other than a decent name for a rock band, "bad faith" is a required element of any successful UDRP or URS proceeding. The URS cites a non-exclusive set of "bad faith" conditions, including these:

### Illegitimate gain

This means the Registrant has obtained the domain primarily for the purpose of profiting from the domain (via sale, rent, or otherwise transferring it) *to the Complainant* or *to a competitor of the Complainant*. This is important. Offering a domain name for sale does **not** in itself amount to bad faith. There has to be a specific impetus to somehow gain from the Complainant's own marks. Offering a domain for sale that happens to coincide with a Complainant's mark, but either predates it (was registered before the trademark) or also has other legitimate uses or connotations is not bad faith.

### Blocking/Denial of Service

The registration of a domain to specifically deny a rights holder from obtaining it. Grabbing "google.somenewtld" would qualify here, especially if it were done by say, Bing. But, that said, if somebody registered macdonalds.blargh and their name, or the business really was MacDonalds, then it would not.

# What if somebody tries to take your domains?

Provided that you have a legitimate interest in the domain and you are not cybersquatting (leveraging other people's Intellectual Property), you should be able to prevail in a UDRP or URS challenge.

Here are some things that will help you win:

- A matching registered trademark (domain: example.com with a trademark, "example")
- If you registered the domain prior to the Complainant's trademark or commencement of business activities
- Unambiguous legitimate use, such as your own active business, blog, or hobby page

It is becoming a more frequent occurrence that various entities are attempting to use the existing domain dispute proceedings to strip domains away from their registrants; however, in many cases, those current registrants are not cybersquatting. The term for this is Reverse Hijacking.

Fortunately, dispute panels are recognizing this, and when they see it and they often penalize the aggressor for it. We've covered the three "must-have" conditions that need to exist for a dispute resolution process to strip a domain and order it transferred. In lieu of any of those three, and especially in the absence of all of them, you would have a case for a finding of reverse hijacking.

# What happens when somebody initiates a UDRP against your domain?

This plays out as the flipside of the dispute protocol outlined earlier. Instead of being the Complainant, you are now the Respondent.

Your Registrar will send notice via email to your admin contact email address (and possibly others) that they have received a UDRP complaint from either WIPO, the National Arbitration Forum, or one of the other accredited Dispute Resolution Providers. They will ask you to confirm or correct the data in the domain `Whois` record. They will also put the domain on "registry-lock" status: This lets the domain continue to resolve over the internet but it cannot be transferred or otherwise modified until after the UDRP proceeding concludes.

As the Respondent, you have 20 days to file your reply. One of the decisions is whether to go with a one-person or a three-person panel. If both you and the Complainant seek a single panelist, then one will be appointed by the governing body (WIPO or NAF). If the Complainant specifies a one-person but the Respondent wants three, the additional costs in doing do will be split between the Complainant and Respondent.

### Domain name lawyers

Yes, there are lawyers who specialize in domain name matters and the closely related area of IP law. Here are a few of them:

**Canada**:
Zak Muscovitch: http://dnattorney.com
**United States**:
John Berryhill: http://johnberryhill.com
Derek Newman: http://newmanlaw.com
Mark Randazza: http://randazza.com
Ari Goldberger Esq: http://esqwire.com
Stevan Lieberman: http://APLegal.com

From experience, I can tell you, if you are embroiled in a legal issue you are served best by retaining a lawyer that specializes in the field. Leave your uncle (the family lawyer) to file your incorporation documents and draw up your will. If you get a UDRP against your prized domain, don't mess around, and call in a specialist.

# Transfer Dispute Resolution Procedure (TDRP)

There are rare occasions when either you want to transfer a domain and your Registrar, for some reason, will not let you, or somebody else has managed to transfer away one of your domains and you want to reverse it.

The TDRP procedure is not invoked by end user Registrants, but rather by the Registrars themselves when faced with a situation in the Losing Registrar will not relinquish control over a given domain and allow it to transfer-out to the Gaining Registrar.

Under the ICANN Inter-Registrars Transfer Policy, there are very clear reasons why a Losing Registrar may deny a transfer-out to another Registrar, those reasons are the following:

- Evidence of fraud. In this context, it includes things such as the domain was paid with a stolen credit card. It specifically does not mean that the domain is allegedly engaged in fraud.
- An in-progress UDRP.
- A court order by a court of competent jurisdiction.
- Dispute over identity of the Registrant of Admin Contact (this is why you never use bogus information in these fields).
- Lack of payment for the previous registration period, including credit card charge-backs or NSF checks.
- The current Registrant objects to the transfer (unauthorized transfer).
- The domain itself is less than 60 days old.

These are the only valid reasons for a Losing Registrar to deny a transfer-out. Unfortunately, at the time of writing, there is no mechanism available to end user Registrants who feel their domains are being held captive in contravention of these conditions to directly initiate a dispute. It has to be initiated by the Registrar, thus a Registrant with captured domains must engage a Gaining Registrar with the will to initiate and pursue this process.

The first step in doing so is for a Registrar to file a **Request For Enforcement** (**RFE**) with the Registry of the domains in question. The Registry will solicit the Losing Registrar for a response and render one of three possible decisions:

- In favor of Gaining Registrar
- In favor of Losing Registrar
- No decision

If the Gaining (or Losing) Registrar disagrees with the decision and still wants to pursue the manner, they must now do so via an appeal, which is facilitated via a Transfer Dispute Resolution Provider in a manner similar to the UDRP. Whichever Registrar initiates the appeal must pay the panelist fees associated with the arbitration (starting at roughly $1,100 USD for one domain in a one-member panel and $2,500 USD for a three-member panel). The arbitration loser ultimately pays these fees. If the initiator wins, the loser must then remit the fees and the initiator receives a refund.

TDRPs rarely get to the second stage. My company successfully filed one in 2014 where we prevailed but were surprised to learn it was only the second time a second- level TDRP appeal had ever been filed. I have not heard of one being filed since.

# Summary

In this chapter, we examined the Intellectual Property issues around your naming portfolio.

Given the overwhelming choice afforded by the reality of the new TLDs, we covered how to narrow down the naming options and how to assert your organization's trademarks within this space.

We also covered the steps in rolling out a new TLD and the role the Trademark Clearing Houses play within them.

This brought us to the inevitable disputes that will arise occasionally, both from the perspective of somebody attacking our names through them, and how to assert your rights against somebody else's infringing domains.

We have also definitely answered the age-old question: What is cybersquatting? It is one of the most misunderstood terms around naming.

# References

1. A "call-to-action" URL or domain is one used to bridge the gap between mediums. For example, a billboard offering services with an URL on it saying "`http://calltoda`y.ca"—that's a "call-to-action" URL. It may be easier to remember the call-to-action than the actual product or service name and thus can increase response rates. It can also make it easier to measure effectiveness.

2. `https://www.icann.org/resources/pages/policy-2012-02-25-en`

3. **Examples:** `Insight Energy Ventures LLC v. Alois Muehlberger, L.M.Berger Co.Ltd.` re: Powerly.com; `Igor Vaksv. WebmasterCast.com` re: socialedge.com.

4. `http://newgtlds.icann.org/en/applicants/urs`

5. When a domain is transferred between Registrars, the two parties are commonly referred to as the "Gaining Registrar" and the "Losing Registrar" for obvious reasons.

6. `https://www.icann.org/resources/pages/registrars/transfers-en`

7. See the NAF ruling in the case of easyDNS v Public Interest Registry: `http://blog.easydns.org/2014/01/09/ domains-locked-in-london-police-takedown-ordered-to-be-transferred/`

8. `http://domains.adrforum.com/main.aspx?itemID=643hideBar=FalsenavID=270news=26`

9. `https://www.easydns.com/blog/2014/01/09/domains-locked-in-london-police-takedown-ordered-to-be- transferred/`

# 4
# Communication Breakdowns

This chapter looks at common foibles that can derail your domains, as well as certain external policies that any organizations that register domain names for themselves or on behalf of others must be aware of and understand how to navigate.

The policies covered are those operated by ICANN, the body that oversees naming and numbering for the internet. It is important to understand that ICANN is not an *enforcement* body. They are not the internet police. They enact policies that the registrars must adhere to and enforce.

The foibles covered may seem trivial; there were large sections of this chapter that I frequently considered cutting out altogether. These sections seemed so "obvious" that I thought it wasteful to devote space to them.

Then, without fail and seemingly on cue, I'd get an email from a customer, friend, or acquaintance asking me about the exact section I was thinking of cutting. People who are *smart*, people who grok technology, people with big companies who know what they're doing, were forwarding me a copy of "the foreign infringer" scam emails, or the Whois Accuracy Program emails and asking me: "Is this real?" or "Do we have to do anything?"

By simply registering a domain name, you will begin to receive communications related to them.

You can take a look at the **Internet Corporation for Assigned Names and Numbers (ICANN)**—see `https://icann.org`. For an outtake of this book that covers a brief history of oversight bodies see `https://domainhelp.com/tag/ICANN`

Of the deluge of messaging you'll receive, there are a small number of buckets they can fall into. Some are real and can be ignored. Some are real and *cannot* be ignored. Many are scams and *should* be ignored.

By the end of this chapter, you will know exactly what you can ignore and what you must action.

In this chapter, we will cover the following:

- Domain policies you must be aware of
- The Whois Accuracy Program
- Bad Whois reports
- Domain slamming, phishing
- Unintentional domain expiries
- Domain scams
- DNS Failures

# Domain policies you must be aware of

ICANN-accredited Registrars are contractually obligated to send you certain emails to comply with various policies under the terms of their contracts with ICANN. Some of these emails you can safely ignore, while others you can't. However, all of them are, from time-to-time, spoofed-in phishing attempts by nefarious third parties to attack you, and we'll examine *that* in the *Common pitfalls* section.

It used to be relatively rare that ICANN *policies* could cause domain names to be suspended by their Registrar or even deregistered (such as an **Invalid Whois Data** complaint).

Then, alas, a new policy came out, and now it's not so rare at all. This relatively new ICANN policy causes many domains to be suspended at inopportune times for flimsy reasons, and it causes a lot of damage and mayhem.

This book has taken me so long to write. I was always hoping that by the time I got to the point where I'd be submitting the manuscript, the lunacy of this policy and the carnage it's caused would result in it being rescinded or fixed. Unfortunately, this has not happened. It's still in full effect and causing live, production domains to suddenly go dark and disappear off the internet every single day.

I am of course referring to the following...

# The Whois Accuracy Program (WAP)

The stated goal of the **Whois Accuracy Program** (**WAP**) is to ensure the accuracy and validity of contact data supplied by Registrants in the Whois records for their domains.

However, it does not accomplish this. All that is required is that the end user assert, via some out-of-band mechanism, that the contact data they supplied previously is accurate. If this assertion is not received within 15 days of the event that triggered the process, the Registrar is bound under the terms of their ICANN **Registrar Accreditation Agreement** (**RAA**) to suspend the domain.

The WAP process is set into motion every time you do one of the following:

- Register a new domain
- Transfer an existing domain between Registrants
- Update the name, address, or email of the Registrant contact set of an existing domain Whois record

...and the condition exists that the contact set used in the registration record has not already been verified.

Once this is triggered, the Registrar is required to send an out-of-band verification request to the *new* (and previously unverified) contact set. While the RAA allows for several methodologies, the near-ubiquitous preference is to send an email request to the new contact set requesting that you "Verify your new contact info."

Of course, most security-minded people train themselves, their clients, customers, and downstream users never to fall for the old "verify your contact info" trick because (up until this came along) they were almost certainly spear-phishing attempts to compromise your various accounts.

It is hardly surprising, then, that many of these requests get discarded or ignored until after the 15-day deadline and the Registrar is obligated to suspend the domain.

The tragedy of this policy is compounded by the following, as shown in this screenshot:

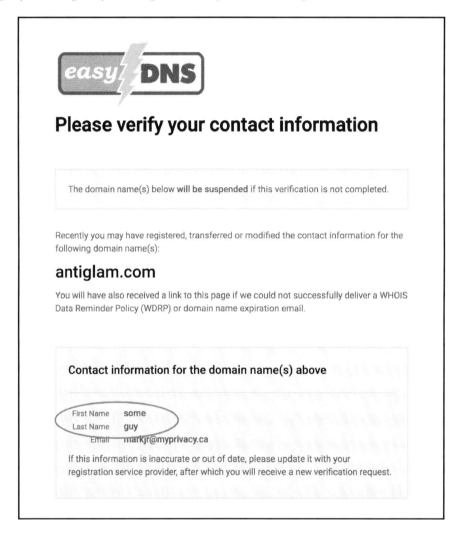

Figure 4.1 Some guy verifying his contact info

Since there is no actual "verification" occurring of the details entered, people are still totally free to enter any kind of bogus contact data they want, so long as they then "verify" said data along the lines prescribed by the Registrar, and...

There is *another* mandatory ICANN program, called the **Whois Data Reminder Policy (WDRP)**, which forces Registrars to email you current copies of your Whois records at least once per year, per domain ("WDRP Notices"). The intent of which is that the end user Registrant review and, if necessary, correct the data in these records:

```
Subject: WHOIS Data Confirmation for easydns.info
From: "easyDNS Technologies Inc." <hostmaster@easydns.com>
To: markjr@easydns.com
Message from easyDNS Technologies Inc.

Dear Valued Member,

This message is a reminder to help you keep the WHOIS (registration) data
associated with your domain up-to-date.

ICANN, the organization responsible for the stability of the Internet,
requires that each domain name registrant be given the opportunity to
correct any inaccurate contact data (WHOIS data) associated with a domain
name registration.

Our records for your domain are as follows:

DOMAIN: easydns.info

    Domain Name: EASYDNS.INFO
    Domain ID: D2273946-LRMS
    Updated Date: 2018-01-30T20:04:05Z
    Creation Date: 2002-07-13T19:47:11Z
    Registrar Registration Expiration Date: 2024-07-13T19:47:11Z
    Registry Registrant ID: C9504720-LRMS
    Registrant Name: Mark Jeftovic
    Registrant Organization: easyDNS Technololgies Inc.
    Registrant Street: 219 Dufferin St. Suite 304A
    Registrant City: Toronto
    Registrant State/Province: ON
    Registrant Postal Code: M6K3J1
    Registrant Country: CA
    Registrant Phone: +1.4165358672
    Registrant Phone Ext: 225
    Registrant Fax:=20
    Registrant Fax Ext:=20
    Registrant Email: markjr@easydns.com
    Registry Admin ID: C9504720-LRMS
Listing 2.2: WDRP notice for a domain. Safe to ignore.
```

This has a pernicious compounding effect because of the following:

*WDRP notices can safely be ignored, while WAP notices cannot.* The difference is likely only readily apparent to people such as me, not to people such as you. I've seen people who know DNS inside-out. People who've written RFCs, puzzle over why some given domain has disappeared from its TLD-zone when the answer was that it had been zapped by a WAP suspension.

Further, *acting on a WDRP may trigger a WAP.* If you actually *heed* an inaccuracy reflected in a WDRP notice and act to rectify it, *that may trigger a WAP* process, and if you are unfamiliar what it means to have one's domain in need of a WAP verification, it can result in a very nasty surprise 15 days later. The time lag doesn't help anybody figure out what happened or why some key domain is suddenly absent from the internet.

Both WDRP and WAP notices provide fertile ground for spear-phishing attacks. Registrars can help mitigate this by PGP-signing their WAP and WDRP notices.

Until the policy is fixed or rescinded, this is just part of the new landscape–if by reading this book, you manage to avoid getting blindsided by it, that alone should be worth the price of admission.

# Incorrect or bad Whois reports

End-user Registrant agreements contain a provision that the contact details supplied be true and accurate. Supplying bogus information in a Whois record, even when motivated by a legitimate need for privacy, will put you in violation of your Registrant agreement and leave you open to having your domains suspended.

Even the Registrar will sometimes summarily terminate an account. If some other unrelated matter attracts their attention to an account and they see it's all obviously fake data, they may surmise it's a fraudulent-spammy-troublemaker and nuke everything. I know we do that, and we're not alone.

Anybody in the world who suspects that a domain contains fake or bogus Whois contact data can report the domain directly to ICANN via their *Whois InaccuracyComplaint Form*.

Doing so triggers a **Whois Inaccuracy Process** via the domain's Registrar, who must action the report with their end user/Registrant, make any corrections to the record, and report back to ICANN Compliance the outcome of their investigation.

If the Registrant is unresponsive to the Registrar or otherwise uncooperative (such as they cannot provide proof the contact details are accurate and refuse to update them), the Registrar *must* suspend the domain.

The risks associated with providing bogus contact data in an effort to acquire privacy can and should be avoided by using Whois Privacy (see the *Whois* section in `Chapter 2`, *Registries, Registrars, and Whois*).

Now let's start looking at the scams and the stuff you should ignore.

# Domain slamming

The term "slamming" owes its ancestry to the practice of "telephone slamming," where a subscriber's phone service would unwittingly be transferred to another telecom provider. In our context, it means having your domain name transferred to another domain registrar without the registrant explicitly intending to do so, or understanding that it has occurred.

This is particularly pernicious in the context of domain slamming, because it is fairly common that the DNS service for a victim domain can stop operating in the course of the transfer (see the *Domain transfers* section in `Chapter 11`, *DNS Operations and Use Cases*) and thus takes the domain offline.

Domain slamming works by mining Whois data for domain contact information and then sending "notices", or what appear to be invoices, to those contacts. Billing departments unwittingly complete these forms and remit payment, and in the process trigger the initiation of a domain transfer.

One characteristic of domain slamming is that they often tend to come via postal mail, not just email. Care is taken that they look like "invoices," as the entire ruse depends on them being blindly forwarded to the accounts payable department and treated as such.

The damage from a successful slam can range from a minor irritant to catastrophic system outage.

If your Registrar transfer-lock is always enabled (and it should be, see `Chapter 13`, *Securing Your Domains and DNS*), then even if you remit payment on it, the transfer will automatically fail. Hopefully, at that point, somebody inside the organization realizes something is amiss and can halt the entire process.

However, if your Registrar transfer-lock is *not* engaged and the transfer winds all the way through and completes, and if your old Registrar also provides your DNS, then they will likely *drop* your DNS after the transfer-away from them completes.

The following image is an example of a postal mail solicitation billing itself as a Domain Name Expiration Notice. Take a look at this screenshot:

Figure 2.2 Sample domain-slamming postal email

# Phishing

Phishing is the practice of setting up a blatantly fake website (or sending a forged email) purporting to be somebody else in the hopes of tricking end users into logging into the fake website, thus capturing their authentication credentials.

This is a multi-faceted attack with many vectors because there are multiple objectives for attackers and there may be some overlap when it comes to the following:

- Capturing authentication credentials to access the information and resources of the target.
- Gaining a base of operations from which to launch further attacks.
- Facilitating identity theft.
- Purchasing services to be used in ongoing operations of the attackers.
- Ordering goods to be fenced offline.

In the case of financial phishing (banks, online brokerages), they may use access to brokerage accounts to purchase stocks in which the attackers have already taken a position (pump-and-dump).

Writing an end-to-end defense guide against phishing, such as how end users can avoid falling prey to it is outside the scope of this book. What we will hone in on here is how to handle it, as it relates to domains under your management.

## Email phishing (spearphishing)

Publish **Sender Policy Framework (SPF)** data and/or **Domain Keys Identified Mail (DKIM)** keys on your mail domains. These mechanisms signal to the world which hosts are allowed to originate or relay email for your domains and helps authenticate messages against spoofing.

However, they only preempt forgeries and spoofs against your legitimate mail domains.

If you run `example.com` and publish SPF and DKIM records on it, it doesn't stop anybody from emailing example.com's customers from `example.email` or `example.support`, or even `example-support.com`. The possibilities are endless.

For SPF to be fully effective, it should be published with `-all` (hard fail), which is a major leap of faith in production domains. Most opt to use the more forgiving `~all`, which means email violating the policy will be accepted anyway, but spam filters can use this to tag the email, which end users can subsequently filter.

DKIM is used to validate the contents of the email, it requires the presence of **Domain Message Authenticating Reporting and Conformance** (**DMARC**) data to assert which hosts can originate email from a given domain (it can also be used to this end with SPF).

We cover each of these mechanisms in `Chapter 11`, *DNS Operations and Use Cases*. In the meantime, this article does a good job of explaining the interrelationship between the three.

Ideally, you would be GPG-signing your communications to your customers. (We've only just started a pilot program doing this at easyDNS, but we want to go all the way with it.) That way, if a customer receives an email from `example-login.com`—even one that may ostensibly be validated by SPF and DKIM data *for its own fake domain*, any end users with GPG integration in their mail clients would be warned that they have no matching public keys in their keychain. This assumes the end user is actively using GPG encryption, something we always advise everybody to start doing. If it's a company they are doing business with already, a missing or unknown GPG key signing an email ostensibly from that company would be conspicuous in its absence.

## Web phishing

Similar to authenticating your email communications, you can secure your web channels by forcing all connections through `https` and having your server validated via **Transport Layer Security** (**TLS**) certificates. Attackers can still set up fake domains impersonating yours and "authenticate" them with TLS certificates validating the fake names.

Often, if your business attracts this type of attack (and pretty near any online enterprise does at some point), you are on to the remediation phase.

As you become aware of attacks, you can send takedown requests to the abuse desks of the key vendors who will inevitably be involved, which are as follows:

- Web hosts or VPS providers
- Managed DNS providers (providing DNS for domains)
- Registrars through whom the offending domains are registered

In extreme instances, the rare case where you have an unresponsive web host, an unresponsive DNS provider, and even an unresponsive Registrar, you can resort to The Nuclear Option and file a UDRP or URS proceeding against the offending name. However, these take time, cost money, and do not immediately cause the domain to cease functioning (we looked at how to file, and respond to, UDRP/URS dispute resolution mechanisms in the *Intellectual property and legal issues* section).

# Unintentional expiry

The most common form of domain name and DNS unplanned outage is the unintentional domain expiry.

I'll say that again: *the most common cause of a domain name and DNS unplanned outage is the unintentional domain expiry.*

### Key domain expires, hilarity ensues

- Christmas weekend, 1999: Microsoft let passport.com lapse, bringing down the entire Hotmail email system. A good samaritan paid the $35 renewal fee out of their own pocket to re-enable services over the long holiday weekend.
- July, 2014: SonyOnline.net expires, bringing down Everquest, Planetquest 2, and all Sony online games.
- November, 2014: Some guy who's writing a book for Packt Publishing, outlining best practices for managing your key domain assets lets a domain upon which his company is operating a managed blogging platform expire, bringing down thousands of customer websites (DNS Company Allows Key Domain To Expire.).

It's happened to Microsoft (including Hotmail, Passport), it's happened to Sony, it's happened to Foursquare, and, yes, it's happened to me. Also on a production domain, also on one that was holding up a large volume of production customer websites.

Thankfully, most of the time, these types of outages are short. When a production domain suddenly goes dark, taking down everything that has dependencies to it, it tends to get noticed quickly and then the domain is renewed within minutes.

Most TLDs now update in real time. Gone are the days when, if this happened to you, you were stuck waiting *24 hours* for the next TLD-server update to bring your domain back online. Now when a domain expires, everything that relies on it breaks, somebody renews the domain, and then everything comes back up within 30 to 60 seconds of that happening. Edge cases of clients referencing a resolver that has NXDOMAIN in the negative cache will have after-effects in the range of 5 to 15 minutes.

Alas, not all TLDs update in real time. When it happened to us, we were in a TLD that didn't. Our base domain name, upon which rested CNAMEs and aliases for every single customer installation, was within a TLD that only updates once per hour, and it takes 40 minutes to fully deploy across all of their top-level nameservers. That made for an agonizing 1 hour and 40 minutes, one that drove a lesson home.

We covered the *Domain Expiration Cycle* in `Chapter 1`, *The Domain Name Ecosystem*. Don't let it get that far.

We will also look at TLD selection for your infrastructure domains in `Chapter 12`, *Nameserver Considerations*.

# Search engine/trademark registrations

You categorically do not need to pay for a search engine submission or listing. Similar to the domain slammers, these are outfits that troll the Whois database and email everybody an "urgent renewal reminder" to remit an outlandish fee to "make sure you're listed in Google."

Unless you've done something to explicitly deny search-engine spiders, or you've been removed for some policy violation, you're listed in Google.

You don't need to pay anybody to put you in there (yes, there is a submit URL tool for Google and most other search engines), the reality is those search-engine spiders will find your domain within minutes of it being activated in the DNS and start spidering it. Take a look at this screenshot:

Figure 4.3 You don't need to do this

Closely related to this I may as well mention Trademark Listings, which have nothing to do with DNS but the mechanism is the same: a boiler-room outfit trolls the Trademarks databases for new registrations, sends the rights holder official looking notices to "list your trademark." The timing works in their favor, since you are expecting to hear back from the trademark office anyway; it's possible this just gets shunted over to accounts payable... and paid.

# Domain scams

Anywhere you can find readily available data that is for the most part wide open to harvesting and mining, scams are not far behind.

Because domain names are listed in Whois databases, that information is frequently used against you in nefarious attempts, ranging from socially engineering toward gaining unauthorized access somewhere, to tricking targets into paying for vaporware or outright fraud attempts.

We'll outline the various domain-related vectors, we still see these passed on to us by our customers every day.

# The Foreign Infringer scam

This is simply an attempt to entice registrants under one TLD to register ("defend their marks") in some other TLD that they would otherwise have minimal interest in. The approach is to make the solicitation sound less like an advertisement and more like a grave intellectual property affront.

Here's an email I received recently:

> *Dear Manager,*
> *(If you are not the person who is in charge of this, please forward this to your CEO, Thanks)*
>
> *This email is from China domain name registration center, which mainly deal with the domain name registrations.*

*We received an application from Huaxing Ltd on August 11, 2014. They want to register " example " as their Internet Keyword and " example .cn ", " example .com.cn ", " example .net.cn ", " example .org.cn " domain names etc.., they are in China domain names. But after checking it, we find "example " conflicts with your company. In order to deal with this matter better, so we send you email and confirm whether this company is your distributor or business partner in China or not?*


*Jim*
*General Manager*
*Shanghai Office (Head Office)*
*3002, Nanhai Building, No. 854 Nandan Road, Xuhui District, Shanghai 200070, China*
*Web:* `www.yg-registry.cn`

This could more accurately be summed up as follows:

Dear Sir, we datamined your contact details from the Whois database and saw that you own example.com. We would like to offer you a chance to register `example.cn`, `example.org.cn`, and `example.net.cn`, which you will never use, and they will never be a meaningful source of traffic to you.

This is just a sales pitch. It's not an urgent matter of your intellectual property in a far off land.

I mention it here because I get about one of these a week forwarded to me by customers who are in a state of inner turmoil about it. Refer back to the *Which TLDs should my organization register our domains under* section. So, just bear this in mind: Ignore these type of emails

# Aftermarket scams

There are times when your organization may want to buy or sell a domain in the aftermarket. Sometimes a client domain has expired and been reregistered and you want to buy it back, or perhaps it's time to sell off a domain that is strong and valuable, but no longer part of the strategy.

The aftermarkets can be perilous to the inexperienced, when possible, it is always advisable to utilize the services of a professional domain brokerage, such as `nameninja.com` or `sedo.com`, to handle the negotiations and an escrow service, such as `escrow.domains` or `escrow.com` (two different companies), to facilitate the handover.

## Buy-side scam

You may receive an email offering to purchase one of your domain names, often one of debatable value (for example, `lolcats.ws`). Piqued at the prospect of unloading an otherwise marginal-value name, the domain holder enters into negotiations and talks converge on an attractive price.

"Just one thing," the buyer reports. Their partner (they have a partner? This is the first they've mentioned that...) needs us to obtain a proper domain appraisal of the name first. "Purely a formality,"; they then send you some links to "domain appraisal services," controlled by... them. You end up paying for a "domain appraisal," after which they lose interest in the deal. Yes, it happens.

My personal opinion is that domain appraisals in themselves are sketchy since domain aftermarket values are highly subjective. A domain is worth whatever a buyer is willing to pay, not what some self-anointed appraisal methodology says it's worth. If you are ever in an aftermarket negotiation and the other party brings up "appraisal," just head over to `estibot.com`—if that isn't good enough, be wary that you may be in the midst of this particular grift.

# Sell-side scams

The Sell side of aftermarket scams are all variations of the same theme: pocketing your money and screwing you on the domain.

The most brazen is selling an outright stolen domain, which does occasionally happen (usually unsuccessful). Despite what I said earlier about domain appraisals being ephemeral and taken with a grain of salt, domain names can be valuable, and there are certain rules of thumb around value that hold up more often than not.

So if you own "Sam and Sues" and somebody offers to sell you `SS.DOM` for $20,000, you want to be *very careful* that you properly vet the ownership and lineage of `SS.DOM` before you put up that kind of money for it. Two-letter .COMs have a basic "floor" underneath them that put their aftermarket values in the six- to seven-digit range, so having an opportunity to purchase one at low five-digit price looks attractive and would be a great pay day for somebody when the domain wasn't actually theirs to sell.

# DNS failures

The final group of Communications breakdowns your domain is exposed to is that of the DNS failure. This is defined as when, in one form or another, all of your nameservers stop responding for your domain. This either occurs because they are not answering queries, they are providing wrong or inconsistent answers, or perhaps originating from the wrong nameservers altogether.

This is a broad topic, so broad in fact, that this takes us into the remainder of the book, which is all about **DNS operations.**

# Summary

In this chapter, we looked at the myriad ways your domain can be impacted by external actors. We looked at policies enacted via ICANN, which much be enforced via your domain registrar, and we made a distinction between which of these can be safely ignored and which ones cannot.

From there, we took a look at various scams and fly-by-night outfits that inundate domain registrants with communications made to appear as if they have some official capacity. We briefly touched on common sales ploys that also attempt to look official but are not, and common scams that are often plied against unsuspecting registrants.

We mention all of these here because they can all lead to outages, which lead to downtime.

# References

1. See `http://blog.easydns.org/2015/05/20/unfortunately-we-have-renewed-our-icann-accreditation/`
2. The technical reviewers were (rightly) all over my case for habitually writing "SSL" throughout this manuscript when referring to securing Internet traffic. SSL (Secure Sockets Layer) has been obsoleted by TLS. The PCI Standards council dropped SSL (and TLS v1.0) from their Data Security Standard (DSS), ruling they can no longer be used past June 30, 2016. That said, you still find SSL used in common parlance all over the internet. A quick note: When we say TLS, it is referring to what you may know as SSL.

# 5
# A Tale of Two Nameservers

As distinct from various nameserver daemons, software, or appliances (which we'll look at later in `Chapter 8`, *Quasi-Record Types*), nameservers can be typed into two broad categories defined by what kind of function they are fulfilling.

Most of the issues we examine in this book are concerned with running DNS operations for a portfolio of domain names and making sure that anybody and anything that queries our domain names always, reliably, obtains a valid response. Doing that involves both main types of nameservers.

The two main functional variations are as follows:

- Resolvers or recursors
- Authoritative nameservers

**Resolvers** or **recursors** make DNS queries on behalf of their clients and relay the responses back to those clients.

**Authoritative nameservers** hold zone data for their client domains or zones and reply to queries coming in for those zones.

If you're reading this book because you are concerned with operating your own domains, you are likely running the latter type: authoritative nameservers, or outsourcing to a vendor who is doing that for you. Authoritative nameservers answer queries for specific domains.

In this chapter, we will cover:

- Introducing resolvers
    - Differences between stub resolvers, caching resolvers, and full resolvers
    - Negative caches: How resolvers handle nonanswers.

- Authoritative nameservers
    - The master or primary nameserver
    - Replication via secondary nameservers

# Introducing resolvers

The two main variants of nameservers represent both sides of a DNS lookup process: a query (resolver) and a response (authoritative nameserver).

Remember my original "elevator pitch" about how DNS works:

*"Every time you send an email, visit a web page, type or receive an instant message, text, or SMS, place a VoIP call (or Skype), or anything else involving the internet, it cannot happen until a bunch of computers around the internet have a conversation about it: Where does this email need to be delivered to? What server is holding the file that this web browser is asking for? Where is the VoIP gateway that needs to route this call?"*

The computers, or applications or daemons that are actually asking these questions are the resolvers.

Your clients are more often applications such as web browsers or email clients, than they are people. Those clients are querying their local resolvers who are asking your authoritative nameservers for answers. Then they will send those responses back to their clients.

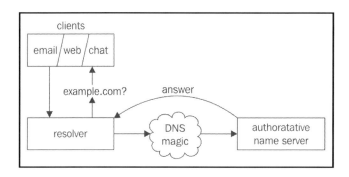

Figure 5.1: Clients use resolvers to query authoritative nameservers. The DNS Magic cloud is described in the next section.

Before those resolvers can query your nameservers, they have to find out which authoritative nameservers they should query for each hostname, **resource record** (**RR**), or domain that they need to look up. We'll look at that process in the *Anatomy of a DNS* query next.

# Differences between stub resolvers, caching resolvers, and full resolvers

Throughout this book, we use the term "resolvers" to denote the entire logical side of the DNS lookup process that is "asking" or "querying" the authoritative nameservers on the other side of the lookup who are answering them.

## Stub resolvers

Stub resolvers reside on a device, host, or computer and process DNS queries for the operating system. Applications themselves typically don't need to worry about where the responses for their DNS lookups will come from or how they will obtain them. They simply make a call using a library function, such as `gethostbyaddr()` or `gethostbyname()`.

The operating system then hands the query off to the local stub resolver, which is a minimal DNS stack that knows enough to find a full resolver (sometimes called a recursor) configured for the network, and forwards its query there.

## Caching resolvers

This is a resolver that has an onboard cache to store queries to minimize repeated lookups. This can minimize queries out to the wider internet and improve the performance of local applications. Home routers are frequently equipped with caching resolvers.

## Full resolvers

In contrast with stub resolvers, the full resolver can follow referrals and, when completed, it hands the final response back to the stub resolver. The stub resolver then makes that response available to the application that called it.

Full resolvers are nameservers that find out answers to DNS queries that applications need answered, and they report those answers back to those applications. This can mean anything that is conducting DNS lookups on behalf of other applications. Some devices may have their own full resolvers onboard, as opposed to using a local stub resolver forwarding to a separate full resolver.

If a resolver encounters a reference or a query for a record it already knows because it asked the same question recently and cached it, it can speed the process up by simply reusing the value it already has in that local cache.

The resolver will (or should) cache the response locally for the value defined in the record's **time to live** (**TTL**). On the authoritative nameserver side, the TTL may be defined globally in the domain's zone or per **Resource Record** (**RR**) but the resolver only sees the end result.

In the following `dig` command, it will use whatever the local system has configured as a caching resolver. This is because it is not specifying a nameserver to query via @nameserver (see `Chapter 9`, *Debugging Without Tears – DNS Diagnostic Tools*).

```
$ dig packtpub.com
;; QUESTION SECTION:
;packtpub.com. IN A


;; ANSWER SECTION:
packtpub.com. 600 IN A 83.166.169.231
```

The local resolver will cache this response for 600 seconds. Now when we repeat this command, we will see that the TTL now shows us how much time the local resolver will keep reusing this cached response:

```
$ dig packtpub.com
;; QUESTION SECTION:
;packtpub.com. IN A


;; ANSWER SECTION:
packtpub.com. 320 IN A 83.166.169.231
```

When it hits zero, it will refresh the query from the `https://www.packtpub.com/` authoritative nameservers (which turn out to be easyDNS nameservers, by happy coincidence).

# Negative caches

When a resolver sends a query for a name that doesn't exist (or if the name exists but not with the requested query type), it will receive a "negative response" containing the **start-of-authority (SOA** ) record of the zone in the authority section of the response. What this means is if no-such-`host.example.com` is queried, the authority section of the response will contain the SOA for example.com (again, we break down the various sections of the DNS query and response in the *Anatomy of a DNS query* section, and we look at SOA and the other various record types in `Chapter 5`, *DNS Queries in Action*).

A negative response can be received if the queried name does not exist (NXDOMAIN) or if the name exists but not with the requested RR type. In the latter condition, the response code will be NOERROR but the presence of the SOA RR in the response implies NODATA.

The negative cache TTL is the amount of time a resolver should remember that the queried record doesn't exist before it goes back to the authoritative nameservers and asks the same question again. The TTL value used (the amount of time the resolver caches this for) should be the lower value of the SOA TTL or the "minimum" field SOA record. (We look at the structure of the SOA Resource Record in `Chapter 7`, *Types and Uses of Common Resource Records*.)

Resolvers are often effectively invisible to many end users. Full resolvers are often assigned via DHCP from your network administrator or upstream connectivity provider. On the server side, they are defined in `/etc/resolv.conf` and whatever is in there will be used to answer nearly all queries any application on a given server will originate. Stub resolvers are part of the device itself.

In other words, DNS resolution is often so far abstracted from both end users and application layers that, until quite recently, hardly anybody ever thought much about them, unless they were DNS geeks or hapless sysadmins who had to debug resolution issues.

This has been changing, in 2006 OpenDNS launched DNS resolution as a service. OpenDNS was eventually acquired by Cisco, and there have been a few other entrants into the space since, including Google's Public DNS, Quad9 and Cloudflare's 1.1.1.1.

# Authoritative nameservers

The other component of the magical lookup process that results in a successful DNS query is the authoritative nameservers. These nameservers actually hold the zone data for the names being queried and they respond to those queries for all zones that they are authoritative for.

Much of this book is specific to operating authoritative nameservers, which is why this section may seem relatively scant, compared to our look at resolvers.

Suffice it to say here that in broad terms, authoritative nameservers are often split into two subcategories, "masters" and "slaves" or "primaries" and "secondaries" (and sometimes even "tertiaries," which really just means, "additional secondary").

# Primary Nameserver

The primary nameserver is the authoritative nameserver that contains the actual zonedata from which all other authoritative nameservers obtain their copy. Traditionally, since the vast majority of nameservers still run BIND, this means the nameserver is the source of the zonedata being served. Secondary or slave nameservers typically have local storage for the zonedata they are mirroring from their masters.

Today, increasingly more production platforms are using PowerDNS or other nameservers, where the distinction may be further blurred when using a database backend. However, even in those cases, the secondaries will typically have a local replication of the database.

## Hidden primaries

In this day and age, especially when running DNS for large numbers of domains, it is common to run what are called "hidden primaries" or "hidden masters."

These are primary authoritative nameservers that are not listed in the various domain delegations in those domains' parent TLDs. A zone's delegation is the nameservers for a specific zone that are published in that zone's parent. The "delegated nameservers" are the ones that will receive any DNS queries for the zone.

Hidden primaries typically don't receive DNS queries from resolvers out in the world. They are just there to feed the zonedata out to the other secondary nameservers.

There are a few reasons you would want to do this, especially as the number of domains under management goes up:

- Your hidden primary could be inside a DMZ.
- It may employ some proprietary methods of organizing its zonefiles (for example, enjoy close access to internal databases).
- You don't want your source repository of live zonedata taking actual queries from the outside world.
- You don't want to expose the location (IP address) of your hidden primary to the outside world.
- Your zones are DNSSEC-signed and you are using offline-signing (see the *DNSSEC* section in `Chapter 12`, *Nameserver Considerations.*)

In practical terms, what ends up happening with more regularity is that all of the public-facing authoritative nameservers end up being secondary nameservers obtaining their data from hidden primaries:

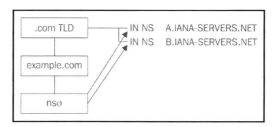

Figure 5.2: The publicly visible nameservers load data from a hidden master

## Hidden primary considerations

For reasons consisting (seemingly to me) of bureaucratic puritanism, some TLDs do not play nicely with domains utilizing hidden primaries.

Some of them insist that, as per RFC 1035, the `mname` field of the SOA record (which we'll look at in `Chapter 6`, *DNS Queries in Action*) contain. The `<domain-name>` of the name server that was the original or primary source of data for this zone.

The problem is when you're employing a hidden primary, you might put something else in the MNAME field or put a host there with an internal IP because, it's y'know, hidden. Some ccTLD's will not delegate a domain to your nameservers unless the MNAME field contains the hostname of a nameserver that is also defined among your NS records for the zone and that they can query directly (because some ccTLDs will actually want to test of your nameservers that the domain is set up ahead of time before they will delegate to it).

If you run into this, you have to adjust your systems to accommodate it (here at easyDNS, we have a data structure called `$FINICKY_CCTLDS`, which has the country codes for all the ccTLDs that enforce this and we rewrite the SOAs in those zones accordingly).

The other problem (when dealing with BIND, at least) is if you're dealing with a ccTLD that needs to be able to query your `MNAME` (master) and if you then rewrite the MNAME with the value of one of your published secondaries, your primary will stop sending NOTIFY packets to that specific secondary whenever the zone is updated. This is because the master will now surmise that since it is the master, the MNAME specified in the SOA must be itself, so there is no need to waste a NOTIFY packet on itself. One needs to work around this with an also-notify, which we cover in `Chapter 12`, *Nameserver Considerations*.

## Secondary nameservers

Secondaries are authoritative nameservers that obtain their copy of the zonedata from the primary nameserver or master.

If you are running BIND, they typically do this via a zone transfer (known as an "AXFR", defined in *RFC 5936*) or an **Incremental Zone Transfer** (**IXFR**, defined in *RFC 1995*). When a zone is reloaded on the primary or master nameserver, it will send a NOTIFY packet to each of the listed NS records for the zone, those are the secondary nameservers.

The zone transfer mechanisms built into the DNS protocols themselves owe their origins to the early days of the DNS and were developed in lieu of reliable, portable methods for syncing data across servers, of which many exist today. Not the least of which are SQL-based backends.

It is not surprising then, that there are alternative methods for handling zonedata syndication across nameservers that blur the distinctions between primaries and secondaries.

As hinted, you could use a nameserver with a database backend (that is, MySQL), such as PowerDNS with a MySQL, PostgreSQL, or other SQL backend. In those cases, your zone-modifying processes would update the database backend, which may be a completely disparate server or storage cluster, and they may transmit those changes to their secondaries via database replication.

There have also been implementations where all nameservers use file-based methodologies, such as rsync, to incrementally copy zonefiles across to the secondary nameservers. This is the preferred methodology used by djbdns (also known as "tinydns") and is sometimes used in BIND implementations. Zonefiles can even be managed across nameservers by using source code repository tools, such as Git.

# Summary

While there are other nameserver roles (such as forwarders, which sit inside internal networks and pull queries from the outside world), we've seen that there are two kinds of nameservers that correspond to the two sides of the DNS query: a question (resolver) and a response (authoritative).

Resolvers are the ones asking the questions. They may be separate servers or they may be an onboard application. There are privacy implications of public resolvers. (I personally expect a growing trend toward personal resolvers on one's own device or under one's control, but I could easily be wrong. These days, people seem content to post their entire lives on Facebook, so maybe nobody will care if every single website, address, or hostname they look up turns out to be vacuumed, logged, cross-referenced, analyzed, repackaged, retargeted, rehypothecated, and sold.)

Authoritative nameservers are the ones answering the questions for their respective zones. But before you can actually get to an authoritative nameserver to ask it *The Query*, you have to somehow figure out which authoritative nameserver to query, which we'll look at next in *Anatomy of a DNS Query*.

# References

1. https://tools.ietf.org/html/rfc2308
2. There are exceptions to this: when a daemon is running chrooted, it may make its own copy of /etc/resolv.conf, for example, the postfix mailer daemon.

# 6
# DNS Queries in Action

By the time we're done with this chapter, you will understand how queries are formed and why they matter.

You will know how those queries originate from a resolver and find their way to the ultimate authoritative nameserver that will send back the response, and you will understand how nameservers are selected in the course of a query/response cycle.

Then, we'll look inside those queries so that you can see what the contents of those queries mean.

In this chapter, we will look at:

- Top-level domain nameservers (DNS)
- Nameserver order
- The anatomy of a DNS lookup
- When DNS uses TCP instead of UDP
- How nameserver selection works

Let's start at the top of the DNS tree.

## Top-level domain nameservers

The DNS hierarchy flows from an inverted tree that begins at the internet root, which is signified by the . . As we'll see, each . in a hostname or domain name signifies another layer in the tree.

All hostnames terminate with an inferred  .; however, they are frequently written without them. Take a look at this diagram:

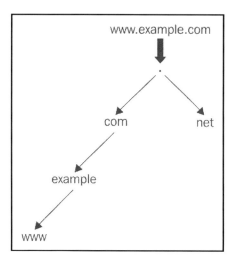

From right-to-left, each dot in a hostname corresponds to the next level in the inverted DNS tree

The root and top-level domain nameservers are required for resolvers to discover which authoritative nameservers to send any given query to. Now look at this diagram:

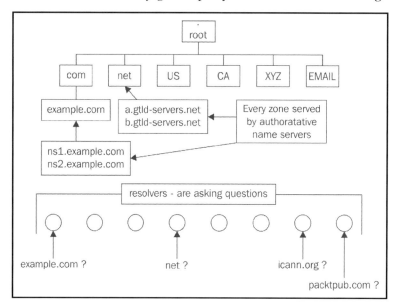

The DNS system forms an inverted tree hierarchy with the internet root "." at the top

The root nameservers refer to the internet root, that is, the "." that terminates the entire inverted tree that forms the DNS. The nameservers for a given **top-level domain** (**TLD**) immediately below the root are TLD/TLD nameservers.

TLD nameservers are authoritative nameservers for TLD, the labels to the right of the . . In the case of example.com, the relevant TLD nameservers would be the .com nameservers:

```
$ dig +short -t ns com
f.gtld-servers.net.
m.gtld-servers.net.
d.gtld-servers.net.
e.gtld-servers.net.
j.gtld-servers.net.
h.gtld-servers.net.
i.gtld-servers.net.
c.gtld-servers.net.
a.gtld-servers.net.
b.gtld-servers.net.
g.gtld-servers.net.
k.gtld-servers.net.
l.gtld-servers.net
```

Every TLD has its associated top-level nameservers:

```
$ dig +short -t ns ca
c.ca-servers.ca.
any.ca-servers.ca.
j.ca-servers.ca.
k.ca-servers.ca.
tld.isc-sns.net.
e.ca-servers.ca.
l.ca-servers.ca.
```

Here is one of the original specialized TLDs, .mil for the US DoD:

```
$ dig +short -t ns mil
EUR2.NIPR.mil.
PAC1.NIPR.mil.
CON2.NIPR.mil.
PAC2.NIPR.mil.
CON1.NIPR.mil.
EUR1.NIPR.mil.
```

Here's an example of one of the new gTLDs:

```
$ dig +short -t ns website
d.nic.website.
```

```
a.nic.website.
b.nic.website.
c.nic.website.
```

Here is another one:

```
$ dig +short -t ns wtf
demand.gamma.aridns.net.au.
demand.beta.aridns.net.au.
demand.delta.aridns.net.au.
demand.alpha.aridns.net.au.
```

And, as noted, the top node of the inverted-tree structure that forms the DNS is simply the root or .:

```
$ dig +short -t ns .
b.root-servers.net.
d.root-servers.net.
a.root-servers.net.
m.root-servers.net.
l.root-servers.net.
e.root-servers.net.
f.root-servers.net.
i.root-servers.net.
j.root-servers.net.
k.root-servers.net.
g.root-servers.net.
h.root-servers.net.
c.root-servers.net.
```

# Nameserver order

One thing you may notice when you look at these results is that, even though a lot of these nameserver delegations appear to be named in alphabetical or numerical order, they are not necessarily returned in that order. It's a commonly held fallacy that nameservers are queried in listed order; they are not. We'll learn more about why they are not in this chapter.

TLD nameservers are authoritative for their own TLD, but for the most part they are populated with delegations. Delegations are nameserver records for all the child zones, otherwise known as a nameserver delegation, a DNS delegation, or a zone cut. It used to be referred to as "sub-delegation," although this is now thought to be confusing and is largely redundant.

Looking at `example.com` again, we see the following:

```
$ host -t ns example.com
example.com name server b.iana-servers.net.
example.com name server a.iana-servers.net.
```

It means that the authoritative nameservers for `example.com` are `b.iana-servers.net` and `a.iana-servers.net`. How did we find that out? By asking the `.com` top-level nameservers. Take a look at this:

```
$ dig -t ns @a.gtld-servers.net example.com
; <<>> DiG 9.8.5-P1 <<>> -t ns @a.gtld-servers.net example.com
; (1 server found)
;; global options: +cmd
;; Got answer:
;; ->>HEADER<<- opcode: QUERY, status: NOERROR, id: 58516
;; flags: qr rd; QUERY: 1, ANSWER: 0, AUTHORITY: 2, ADDITIONAL: 4
;; WARNING: recursion requested but not available

;; QUESTION SECTION:
;example.com.                   IN      NS

;; AUTHORITY SECTION:
example.com.            172800  IN      NS      a.iana-servers.net.
example.com.            172800  IN      NS      b.iana-servers.net.

;; ADDITIONAL SECTION:
a.iana-servers.net.    172800  IN      A       199.43.135.53
a.iana-servers.net.    172800  IN      AAAA    2001:500:8f::53
b.iana-servers.net.    172800  IN      A       199.43.133.53
b.iana-servers.net.    172800  IN      AAAA    2001:500:8d::53

;; Query time: 80 msec
;; SERVER: 192.5.6.30#53(192.5.6.30)
;; WHEN: Tue Jun  5 10:47:38 2018
;; MSG SIZE  rcvd: 165
```

How did we know that a.gltd-servers.net was a top-level nameserver for .com? Because our resolvers went out and queried the root "." first and received a referral to the .COM nameservers. They then went and queried those nameservers and received a referral to the nameservers for example.com.

The process repeats until they hit a set of nameservers that send back a response with an answer section (see below) that contains the authoritative answer for the query itself.

The following `dig` command shows us how a resolver will recursively start at the internet root and successively follow each referral to the next level in the DNS tree until it reaches the authoritative nameservers for the name being queried:

```
$ dig +trace -t ns example.com
; <<>> DiG 9.8.5-P1 <<>> +trace -t ns example.com
;; global options: +cmd
.  517845  IN  NS  g.root-servers.net.
.  517845  IN  NS  f.root-servers.net.
.  517845  IN  NS  i.root-servers.net.
.  517845  IN  NS  b.root-servers.net.
.  517845  IN  NS  l.root-servers.net.
.  517845  IN  NS  k.root-servers.net.
.  517845  IN  NS  d.root-servers.net.
.  517845  IN  NS  a.root-servers.net.
.  517845  IN  NS  j.root-servers.net.
.  517845  IN  NS  h.root-servers.net.
.  517845  IN  NS  m.root-servers.net.
.  517845  IN  NS  e.root-servers.net.
.  517845  IN  NS  c.root-servers.net.
;; Received 496 bytes from 64.68.200.205#53(cns3.easydns.com) in 2678 ms

com.  172800  IN  NS  b.gtld-servers.net.
com.  172800  IN  NS  l.gtld-servers.net.
com.  172800  IN  NS  c.gtld-servers.net.
com.  172800  IN  NS  k.gtld-servers.net.
com.  172800  IN  NS  f.gtld-servers.net.
com.  172800  IN  NS  j.gtld-servers.net.
com.  172800  IN  NS  g.gtld-servers.net.
com.  172800  IN  NS  m.gtld-servers.net.
com.  172800  IN  NS  a.gtld-servers.net.
com.  172800  IN  NS  d.gtld-servers.net.
com.  172800  IN  NS  h.gtld-servers.net.
com.  172800  IN  NS  e.gtld-servers.net.
com.  172800  IN  NS  i.gtld-servers.net.
```

```
;; Received 489 bytes from 192.112.36.4#53(g.root-servers.net) in 3804 ms
example.com. 172800 IN NS a.iana-servers.net.
example.com. 172800 IN NS b.iana-servers.net.
;; Received 165 bytes from 192.26.92.30#53(c.gtld-servers.net) in 110 ms

example.com. 172800 IN NS b.iana-servers.net.
example.com. 172800 IN NS a.iana-servers.net.
;; Received 165 bytes from 199.43.133.53#53(b.iana-servers.net) in 131 ms
```

It bears repeating: To find the authoritative nameservers for any given name, your resolver has to start from the closest point in the DNS tree for which it already knows the answer (such as the authoritative nameservers for the target name's parent) and iteratively receives a reference to the next level (the chunk before the preceding dot), until the resolver arrives at a set of nameservers that are "authoritative" for the original name being queried.

If the resolver doesn't have anything cached (like the NS records for the top-level domain of the name being queried) to shorten this path then it has to start the process all the way back at the root . domain. Take a look at this diagram:

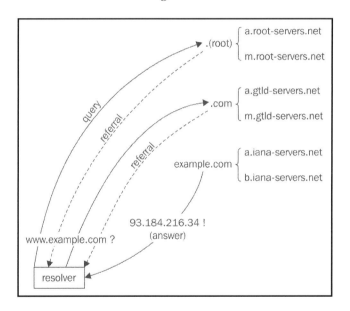

The resolver iteratively queries each level of nameserver in the tree until it gets to a level that responds with an authoritative response to the query

DNS lookups generally occur over UDP, but there are notable exceptions, which we will discuss now.

# How does a resolver know where the "." nameservers are?

That's an excellent question. If the internet root . is the DNS equivalent of a "Buck Stops Here" plaque on the President's desk, how does one know where to find the desk in the first place?

It's called `root hints`, usually a flat file that sits on a resolver's local storage, or it is sometimes compiled into the nameserver itself. The `root hints` contains the initial set of hostname to IP address mappings for the . zone:

```
$ cat /var/named/named.ca
; This file holds the information on root name servers needed to
; initialize cache of Internet domain name servers
; (e.g. reference this file in the "cache . <file>"
; configuration file of BIND domain name servers).
;
; This file is made available by InterNIC
; under anonymous FTP as
; file /domain/named.cache
; on server FTP.INTERNIC.NET
; -OR- RS.INTERNIC.NET
;
; last update: Jun 17, 2010
; related version of root zone: 201006170
;
; formerly NS.INTERNIC.NET
;
.                         3600000      IN NS A.ROOT-SERVERS.NET.
A.ROOT-SERVERS.NET.       3600000      A 198.41.0.4
A.ROOT-SERVERS.NET.       3600000      AAAA 2001:503:BA3E::2:30
;
; FORMERLY NS1.ISI.EDU
;
.                         3600000      NS B.ROOT-SERVERS.NET.
B.ROOT-SERVERS.NET.       3600000      A 192.228.79.201
;
; <snipped>  (c thru m.root-servers follow...)
;
.                         3600000      NS M.ROOT-SERVERS.NET.
M.ROOT-SERVERS.NET.       3600000      A 202.12.27.33
M.ROOT-SERVERS.NET.       3600000      AAAA 2001:DC3::35
; End of File
```

# Anatomy of a DNS lookup

The full loop of a DNS lookup occurs when a query is originated by a resolver and, after traveling through the DNS hierarchy discussed previously, receives a response from the authoritative nameserver responsible for the resource record being queried.

Resolvers send packets with questions, and authoritative servers send back packets with responses.

# Format of a DNS query

The DNS message format looks like this:

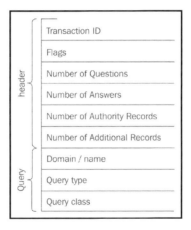

Structure of a DNS query message

# Transaction ID

The transaction ID is a random number generated by the nameserver initiating the query. When the answering nameserver responds with an answer, it will set the same transaction ID. DNS cache poisoning can occur if the transaction is non-random or predictable (along with other preconditions, see the **What is DNS Cache Poisoning?** sidebar).

What is DNS cache poisoning?

DNS cache poisoning can occur when an attacker can trick a resolver into accepting faked data for a given query and then having the "poisoned" resolver hand that faked data out to its clients.

The risk is if somebody managed to, for example, poison your resolver into accepting forged responses from a fake authoritative nameserver for your bank. They could redirect you to a fake online banking login page and potentially capture your authentication credentials.

Several things need to happen for this to work. The attacker must do the following:

- Calculate or predict the value of the transaction ID.
- Discover the source port and the source address of the real master nameserver being queried.
- Send their fake responses back, crafted accordingly with their own values in the Answer section.
- Those responses must arrive at the querying nameserver before the real responses do (perhaps they can nudge this race in their favor by using DDoS to send the actual authoritative name servers for the query).

An absent DNSSEC-aware resolver querying DNSSEC-signed zones is more than a theoretical security risk given that several proof-of-concepts as well as real-world attacks have been documented over the years (see *DNS Security: In Depth Vulnerability and Mitigation Solutions, Anestis Karadis).*

Most recently, a new approach to conducting a type of cache poisoning has emerged, where attackers use BGP hijacks to take over the address space of the target domain nameservers, and then erect their own nameservers to serve up fake responses. In this manner, resolvers affected by the route hijacks query the wrong nameservers altogether. This was achieved in April, 2018, in an attack on the `MyEtherWallet` cryptocurrency platform by hijacking the address space of their DNS provider, Amazon Route 53.

For more information, refer to the following:

`https://www.theregister.co.uk/2018/04/24/myetherwallet_dns_hijack/`

This type of attachment underscores the relevance of DNSSEC, which we looked at in `Chapter 1`, *The Domain Name Ecosystem.*

In the flags section, various bits are set or not set and thus guide the flow of processing a query. These will be of interest when we want to debug issues. We can use the `dig` command to see these packet responses in more detail than is available via other diagnostic tools such as the default `host` lookup or `nslookup`. (We look at diagnostic tools more closely in `Chapter 10`, *Debugging without Tears- DNS Diagnostic Tools*). Take a look at the following diagram:

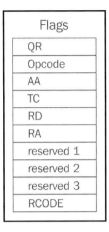

The DNS flags section

The flags are as follows:

- **QR (query response)**: This is set to zero in a packet that is a question, and one in a response packet that is an answer.
- **AA (authoritative answer)**: This flag is set in a response by the nameserver when it is answering authoritatively for the hostname that was queried. An authoritative answer means that the nameserver responding is a primary or secondary nameserver for the domain or hostname in question; it is not a resolver answering out of the cache.
- **TC (truncated content)**: This will be set to one if the response packet is larger than the reply size limit. See the Large responses section below.
- **RD (recursion desired)**: If set to one, the querying nameserver is asking the remote nameserver to resolve the query recursively. It is important to understand that if the nameserver being queried is an authoritative nameserver for the hostname being queried, it wouldn't (or shouldn't) do recursion. In any case, the RD response will be the same as the RD bit in the query.
- **RA (recursion available)**: This will be set to one in a response if recursion is available (as in a resolver). Authoritative nameservers will ideally not be enabled for recursion and set this to zero.

- **RCODE (response code)**: In a query response, this is the status of the query:

| Value | Mneumonic | Meaning |
|---|---|---|
| 0 | NOERROR | Everything went fine. |
| 1 | FORMERR | Format error. |
| 2 | SERVFAIL | An error condition on the nameserver itself prevented a response; this could include a problem within the zone queried as opposed to an issue with the nameserver. |
| 3 | NXDOMAIN | The requested name does not exist. |
| 4 | NOTIMP | Nameserver does not support requested query type. |
| 5 | REFUSED | Nameserver refused the query for policy reasons. Typically, this happens when an authoritative nameserver receives a query for a name for which it is *not* authoritative. |

# Number of questions

This will be the number of questions the resolver is asking. The protocol allows for more than one, but I have never been able to come up with a scenario where it's set to a value greater than one.

# Number of answers

This will be set to zero by the resolver asking the question, and it will be set in response to the number of records being returned in the answer section of the response. It will be zero if the response is a referral.

# Number of authority records

This will also be set to zero in the query and to the number of entries in the authoritative section of the response. The authoritative section should list each authoritative nameserver for the query (if returned by the authoritative nameserver). If the nameserver is configured with minimal responses enabled, the authoritative nameserver will only populate the authoritative section in the case of referrals or when the data is otherwise required. The rationale behind this is to optimize performance.

# Number of additional records

In EDNS queries, this is set to one; otherwise, it is set to zero on questions.

On answers, the additional section contains information that may be required for the resolvers to complete their lookups, such as nameserver hints.

# Query name

The query name (`QNAME`) is the name that was actually queried, such as `example.com`, `"www.example.com"`, `_xmpp-client._tcp.example.com`, and so on.

# Query type

This is the type of **resource record** (**RR**) requested: "A", "MX", "NS" (we look at these in `Chapter 7`, *Types and Uses of Common Resource Records*).

The following QTYPES have special meanings and do not correspond to DNS resource record types:

- **ANY**: When a nameserver receives an ANY query, it should respond with all known records for the QNAME that it has within its cache.
  A lot of DNS operators hate ANY queries because they can be used in DNS amplification attacks. At various points in time, more than one managed DNS provider has attempted to unilaterally deprecate the ANY query by announcing they would no longer respond to them. Typically, this ignites a theological schism amongst the DNS-ops community. One vendor (Cloudflare) now refuses ANY queries with a specially crafted response
  (`https://tools.ietf.org/html/draft-dnosp-refuse-any-00`).
  Personally, I think it's OK to drop ANY queries if they're being used against you during a DDoS. We'll show you how in the chapter on mitigating DDoS attacks.

  The only public-facing application that I know of that uses ANY is qmail, and there's a patch for that to work without it.

  PowerDNS does make extensive use of ANY; however, it does so internally, in its communications with its own backends, which we look at in `Chapter 8`, *Quasi-Record Types*.

- **AXFR** and **IXFR**: These are QTYPES that signal that the querying server is requesting a zone transfer for QNAME. This should only be permitted from valid secondary nameservers for QNAME, all others should receive a REFUSED.
- **OPT**: A pseudo-Qtype for use in EDNS, including DNSSEC.

## Query class

For our purposes, QCLASS will always be "IN" (which is the "INternet" class). Other classes exist; we'll touch on them briefly in the next chapter.

## Additional section responses in queries

As we learned previously, the number of additional records section tells us how many records to expect here as part of the response.

While the answer section and even the authority section probably seem pretty straightforward, you may wonder what exactly happens within the additional section of query responses.

Consider the following:

```
$ dig -t ns easydns.com @dns1.easydns.com
; <<>> DiG 9.8.3-P1 <<>> -t ns easydns.com @dns1.easydns.com
;; global options: +cmd

;; Got answer:
;; ->>HEADER<<- opcode: QUERY, status: NOERROR, id: 4400
;; flags: qr aa rd; QUERY: 1, ANSWER: 4, AUTHORITY: 0, ADDITIONAL: 6
;; WARNING: recursion requested but not available
;; QUESTION SECTION:
;easydns.com. IN NS


;; ANSWER SECTION:
easydns.com. 300 IN NS dns1.easydns.com.
easydns.com. 300 IN NS dns3.easydns.org.
easydns.com. 300 IN NS dns2.easydns.net.
easydns.com. 300 IN NS dns4.easydns.info.


;; ADDITIONAL SECTION:
dns1.easydns.com. 300 IN A 64.68.192.10
dns1.easydns.com. 300 IN AAAA 2001:1838:f001::10 dns2.easydns.net. 600 IN A
```

```
198.41.222.254
dns3.easydns.org. 60 IN A 64.68.196.10
dns4.easydns.info. 43200 IN A 194.0.2.19
dns4.easydns.info. 43200 IN AAAA 2001:678:5::13


;; Query time: 625 msec
;; SERVER: 64.68.192.10#53(64.68.192.10)
;; WHEN: Mon May 9 18:35:45 2016
;; MSG SIZE rcvd: 259
```

# When does DNS use TCP instead of UDP?

Most of the time, DNS happens over UDP. It's lightweight and faster than TCP. There have been trade-offs as a result of the design decision. It's easier to spoof UDP packets, so you have to worry about things like cache poisoning or DDoS attacks involving forged packet headers.

But nameservers still need to be available on TCP as well as UDP. The following will explain why.

## Zone transfers happen over TCP

The AXFR and IXFR methods of transferring updated zone data from the master to its secondaries occur over TCP.

In some cases, when a slave queries the master to check whether an update is required, it may happen over TCP (for example, NSD nameservers do this).

## EDNS and large responses

EDNS stands for "extension mechanisms" for DNS, and it specifies methods to enable additional capabilities that were not present in the original DNS specification.

Originally, nameservers expected responses to fit within a 512-byte message, but, as DNS evolved, there became situations where this limit was exceeded. EDNSo can specify a response limit larger than the default.

The TC flag is set when the response is either larger than this EDNS0 receive buffer, or, in the absence of EDNS0, greater than the default of 512 bytes. This signals the client/resolver to retry the query over TCP.

For example, it is possible in this context to have "too much redundancy" in your nameserver delegation by simply adding so many nameservers to your domain delegation that the response to a query is larger than the receiving side allows.

When running a lookup via `dig` or `host`, you will see a warning that the retry over TCP will occur, as shown here:

```
$ dig -t ns managingmissioncriticaldomains.com @dns1.easydns.com
;; Truncated, retrying in TCP mode.
...
;; Query time: 38 msec
;; SERVER: 64.68.192.210#53(64.68.192.210)
;; WHEN: Thu Dec 11 10:52:30 EST 2014
;; MSG SIZE rcvd: 589


Note the last line of the output:
;; MSG SIZE rcvd: 589
```

Furthermore, use cases exist where the TC bit is set even if the response is under 512 bytes and doesn't involve EDNS extensions.

During a DDoS attack against your nameservers, one possible mitigation strategy is to reply to all queries with the TC bit set so that all clients are signaled to retry over TCP. The logic behind this is that only the real/legitimate resolvers will actually retry their queries. If participants in the attack also retry, that will occur over TCP and be easier to filter. Usually, the first response forcing the retry is sent by a firewall or other mitigation appliance, and not the nameserver itself. This may sound similar to **response rate limiting** (**RRL**), but it isn't. We will look at RRL in `Chapter 13`, *DNS and DDoS Attacks*.

Another case is to always set the TC bit in all responses to ANY queries, whether there is an attack in progress or not. This is to pre-empt DNS amplification attacks that make use of the ANY query.

# The anatomy of a DNS query – how nameserver selection actually works

One of the more commonly held fallacies about nameservers concerns what order nameservers in a given delegation are queried in.

Take our archetypical `example.com`, posited to have a delegation as follows:

```
ns1.example-dns.co
mns2.example-dns.com
ns3.example-dns.com
ns4.example-dns.com
```

A commonly held misunderstanding is that the nameservers will be queried in that literal order, and redundancy comes about when and if the first listed nameserver is unavailable (`ns1.example-dns.com`), then the next one is queried (`ns2.example- dns.com`), and so on. In other words, it is not uncommon to assume that nameserver selection works as MX record selection is supposed to work, in that they are ostensibly used in order of preference and availability. (I say "ostensibly" because anybody operating mail servers knows that mail can and will arrive at backup mail spoolers even when the primary handlers are online and available.)

But that isn't what happens.

What really happens varies between nameserver implementations. But, in one way or another, the queries are distributed across any of the available nameservers, and they do not go "in order" of the delegation list.

Some nameservers will keep track of **round-trip times** (**RTTs**) of their queries to each of the authoritative nameservers, and then favour the ones with the shortest RTTs with subsequent queries (this is the method historically employed by BIND). Among nameservers that distribute based on RTT, differing approaches are used. For more information, see Authority Server Selection of DNS Caching Resolvers.

Others, such as Unbound, DNS Cache, and Windows DNS, will evenly distribute their queries between all the nameservers in the set, regardless of the RTTs.

# Summary

Now that you have an understanding of how DNS queries are formed and answered, as well as the meaning of the various flags and component parts of a DNS message, you will better understand various diagnostic outputs from utilities we're going to look at in `Chapter 10`, *Debugging without Tears- DNS Diagnostic Tools*.

Furthermore, you now have an understanding of the distinction between UDP and TCP as it relates to DNS and why your nameservers are required to respond to both.

Finally, we've dispelled any misconceptions around how nameserver selection works, and we also know how DNS queries progress from the root servers through to the authoritative servers.

# References

1. I can also tell you from experience that the phrase "sub-delegation" is often used. I have it on good authority (namely, every single tech reviewer of this book) that this phrase is redundant and confusing. I should also admit to having used it until now.
2. Anestis Karasaridis, DNS Security: In Depth Vulnerability and Mitigation Solutions.
3. `https://www.theregister.co.uk/2018/04/24/myetherwallet_dns_hijack/`
4. If the nameserver is configured with minimal-responses enabled, the authoritative nameserver will only populate the AUTHORITATIVE SECTION in the case of referrals or when the data is otherwise required. The rationale behind this is to optimize performance.
5. `https://tools.ietf.org/html/draft-dnsop-refuse-any-00`
6. What we are talking about here may sound similar to Response Rate Limiting (RRL), but it isn't. We will look at RRL in `Chapter 14`, *DNS and DDoS Attacks*.
7. I say "ostensibly" because anybody operating mail servers knows that mail can and will arrive at backup mail spoolers even when the primary MX handlers are online and available.
8. See `Authority Server Selection of DNS Caching Resolvers` for a deep dive into this.

# 7
# Types and Uses of Common Resource Records

In Chapter 1, *The Domain Name Ecosystem*, we constructed the analogy that you could break down a domain's Whois record into logical chunks, such as Registrant, Admin Contact, Registrar Status, and Nameservers, which comprise the logical anatomy of a domain name.

The DNS **Resource Records (RRs)** are what comprise the actual data values that nameservers exchange. A DNS zone can be broken down into RRs, and RRs have specific formats, functions, and uses.

We won't list them all here; we'll cover the common ones and some not-so-common ones that may see growing usage in the years to come.

This section does not purport to deconstruct and define the RR types in minute RFC-compliant detail. *Cricket Liu* and Paul Ablitz's *DNS and Bind*, as well as Ron Aitchison's *Pro DNS and Bind 10*, do superb jobs of this.

What we will concentrate on here are the "things to know" when using these record types, including the considerations when managing large portfolios of domains and how they affects a given record type.

In this chapter, we will cover the following:

- Format of an RR
- Construction of a DNS zone
- The Start of Authority record (SOA)
- Nameserver (NS)
- A record
- CName/Alias
- The Mail Exchanger (MX) record

- TXT/Text Records
- The Service record (SRV)
- Naming Authority Pointer (NAPTR)
- The Delegation Name record (DNAME)
- Reverse Pointer (PTR)
- IPv6 addresses
- Certificate Record (CERT)
- TLSA certificate association
- Certificate Authority Authorization (CAA)
- DNSSEC Record types

# Format of an RR

In our examples, the syntax will be described in generic DNS record format/zone file format:

```
<OWNER-NAME> <TTL> <CLASS> <TYPE> <DATA>
```

- **OWNER-NAME** (or ONAME): The domain or hostname of the *current resource record*. This is distinct from the Registrant (the "owner" of a domain name registration). If the ONAME does not end in a ".", the current $ORIGIN zone will be appended to it. The @ special character denotes the current $ORIGIN (explained next). The first record of a zone *must* have an OWNER-NAME; it is optional in all subsequent records. When omitted, the last used OWNER-NAME will be used.
- **TTL**: (optional) The **Time to Live** (**TTL**) of the current record. This governs how long resolvers will keep this answer in their local cache before refreshing from an authoritative nameserver for the domain being queried. If no TTL is specified per record, the value specified in the global $TTL directive will be used, and if there isn't a global $TTL, it will use the minimum value from the SOA RR.
- **CLASS**: This is pretty well always "IN" for "internet". It can be omitted.

Other classes do exist. The CH (chaos) class, which is still (mis)used in special queries to query server versions and locally configured hostnames (as in the *Debugging under anycast* section in Chapter 10, *Debugging Without Tears – DNS Diagnostic Tools*), and the old stand-by query to garner a server version:

```
dig @192.168.1.1 version.bind txt chaos
```

There is also the HS (Hesiod) class, which could be used to put user and group data into your DNS:

- **TYPE**: The RR type, and that is what the rest of this chapter looks at
- **DATA**: Contains the record-specific values for the current <ONAME>

# Constructing a zone

Different nameservers have differing representations of the DNS data being served, but for simplicity and because of its ubiquity, we'll use a traditional zone file format commonly used by BIND to display the components of a DNS zone:

```
;
; This is an example zone file
;
; example.com
;
; generated: 02-Sep-2016 06:08:26 local time
; 02-Sep-2016 10:08:26 GMT
;
$ORIGIN example.com.
$TTL 86400
@          IN SOA          sns.dns.icann.org. noc.dns.icann.org. 2016110710
7200 3600 1209600 3600
@          IN NS           a.iana-servers.net.
@          IN NS           b.iana-servers.net.
@          IN MX           0 mail.example.com.
@          IN A            93.184.216.34
@          IN AAAA         2606:2800:220:1:248:1893:25c8:1946
www        IN CNAME        example.com.
```

The zone may have more than one $ORIGIN. The first $ORIGIN usually corresponds to the domain we are constructing the zone for. If there is no $ORIGIN, it will default to the zone name from the configuration that loaded the zone.

If the OWNER-NAME or ONAME on the left-hand side does not end in a period, ., then the current $ORIGIN will be appended to the name.

In the case of the @ sign, the current $ORIGIN is substituted. Each zone must have one SOA RR.

Each zone must have one NS RRSet (at least two nameservers—you can get away with having one, but it's not recommended).

None of the remaining RR types (A, MX, CNAME, TXT, SRV, and so on) are mandatory within a zone. But they all have their rules for use and many come with their own set of "things to know."

Let's begin.

# Start of Authority (SOA)

The SOA record is the "start-of-authority record." There must be one SOA RR present in every zone at the apex. It signals basic information about the zone to other name servers, such as (ostensibly) who the responsible party for the zone is, at what intervals secondaries should refresh their zones, and how long resolvers should cache negative lookups.

Here is the SOA RR Syntax:

```
<OWNER-NAME> IN SOA <MNAME> <RNAME> <SERIAL> <REFRESH> <RETRY> <EXPIRE>
<MINIMUM>
```

It can also be written as:

```
<OWNER-NAME IN SOA <MNAME> <RNAME> (
<SERIAL>
<REFRESH>
<RETRY>
<EXPIRE>
<MINIMUM>
)
```

The **Right-Hand Side (RHS)** or "rdata" of an SOA record consists of seven fields:

- Originating nameserver (MNAME)
- The responsible person (RNAME)
- Serial
- Refresh
- Retry
- Expire
- Minimum

```
$ dig +short packtpub.com -t soa
dns1.easydns.com. zone.easydns.com. 1524487408 43200 10800 604800 300
```

# MNAME (Originating Nameserver)

This is supposed to be the hostname of the originating master nameserver, the primary nameserver from which the secondaries slave the zone. Some country code registries will complain if this hostname is not part of your nameserver delegation, as will some DNS diagnostic tools.

# RNAME (Point of Contact)

This looks like a host name, but if you translate the first unescaped dot as an @ sign, you're supposed to wind up with the email address of the person responsible for the zone. In our example SOA for packtpub.com, the point-of-contact address would then be dns1@easydns.com.

# Serial

The Serial number is the most important field here because when the serial number increases, it means that the zone has been updated. It's the value in this field being higher than what the secondaries have locally that signals to the slaves that there has been an update on the master and that they need to refresh. This becomes irrelevant if you are using a nameserver implementation that employs alternate methods of data-syncing, such as PowerDNS using MySQL replication.

There are a few different methods of formatting the serial number:

### Date-based

YYYYMMDDNN This is perhaps the most popular method of specifying the serial among hand-edited zones. It corresponds to the current date with the last field, NN, being the numeric iteration of a zone being loaded for that day.

A common mistake (when hand-editing zones) is to make changes to your zone file but neglect to increment the serial number. After reloading your primary nameserver, the secondaries never reflect the updates.

### Unix timestamp

This is my preferred method, where you simply use the 32-bit Unix timestamp of the moment you generate the `zone` file from whatever process you have doing so.

# Raw count

Alluded to in the original *RFC 1035*, this just starts at 1 and simply increments a raw count whenever the zone is updated.

Again, some DNS diagnostic systems have an opinion on this and if you get enough DNS geeks in a room and add alcohol you can ignite vigorous debates around the "best format" for this one field. In reality, it's pointless. Make sure it increments every time you update the zone. That's it.

## When the format of the Serial actually matters

Aside from every time you update the zone, conflicting formats of the serial number can become an issue when you are moving domains between nameserver delegations, moving masters or adding secondaries. If your master is using one format (for example, Unix timestamp) and your secondaries already have a copy of your zone with a date-based serial, you can wind up with the latter neglecting to refresh the zone because it thinks its current copy is more recent than the master:

```
10-May-2018 11:21:43.848 client 64.68.198.83#13014: received notify for
zone 'example.com'
May1011:21:43 mia named[4404]: zone example.com/IN: notify from
64.68.198.83#13014: zone is up to date
```

The remedy in these situations is to force an unconditional retransfer to the secondaries.

You can do this in most nameservers by using their command utilities to force a retransfer.

BIND:

```
rndc retransfer example.com
```

PowerDNS:

```
powerdns_control retrieve example.com
```

NSD:

```
nsd_control force_transfer example.com
```

# The Refresh interval

This is how long your own secondary nameservers should wait before they check their master for an updated serial. This number should err on the side of longer, especially if the number of zones under management is large. If you have thousands, or hundreds of thousands, of zones under management and this interval is too short, you may end up with a bottleneck as at any given time you have a lot of SOA queries in progress for zones checking whether they have been updated.

Since the DNS NOTIFY transaction came along, we don't have to be so rigorous about polling. The master will let the slaves know when an update happens. If we are using an alternative nameserver, such as PowerDNS with database replication or tinydns copying zones to secondaries via rsync, it becomes largely moot.

# The Retry interval

This next value controls how soon a secondary should retry a refresh if the refresh didn't work the first time.

Again, both of these values, in practice, are becoming increasingly superseded now that master nameservers send NOTIFY messages (if they aren't using some other method of syncing data entirely).

# The Expire interval

The next value is the expire interval; this is how long an *authoritative* nameserver should hang on to the zone and keep answering authoritatively for queries about it even if it can't check to see whether the master has been updated. Again we err to the side of longer, most of the time. 10 days to 2 weeks are common values, sometimes even a month. It means that if the master nameserver is down or unreachable, the remote secondaries will keep answering authoritatively out of their local copy of the zone until that expire interval elapses.

After that interval, the secondary will make a fateful assumption that the copy of the zone it has is now stale or out-of-date, and it will drop its local copy and cease answering queries about the zone.

# Minimum

This meaning of this field has changed.

Originally this was how long resolvers (also known as recursors, non-authoritative nameservers) would keep a reply from an authoritative nameserver in its local cache, and answer subsequent queries for those records from its local cache before it will refresh those records from one of the authoritative nameservers. In other words, this value used to specify the default **Time-to-Live** (**TTL**) for each record within a zone that did not have an explicit TTL setting.

It later became the Negative Cache TTL (as per RFC 2308); the interval resolvers would cache a lookup with a negative result (unless the SOA's TTL is lower, in which case *that* would be used).

*RFC2308* also described the $TTL directive, which governs the global TTL for a zone that will apply to all RRs that do not have their own TTL specified.

Having said all that, if one omits a $TTL directive from their zone file, the nameserver will use this value as the default TTL.

However the Minimum is derived, contrast Expire with Minimum; Minimum controls how long *resolvers* answer subsequent queries from their local cache before refreshing that record from one of the zone's authoritative nameservers. Expire governs how long a *slave* will continue replying from its local cache while it is unable to refresh from its master before discarding it as stale.

When planning migrations, cutovers, and maintenance windows, be mindful that any adjustments to the Minimum/TTL or individual RR TTLs have to be done ahead of the event. (See Chapter 9, *Common Nameserver Software*, Section *DNS Use Cases*)

## Can't You Just Set Your $TTL To 0?

One may wonder whether you could have your DNS changes visible across the internet instantly by setting your TTLs to 0.

You could do that. By doing that you are telling all client resolvers and recursors to not cache your zone (or specific RRs within the zone) and come back and ask one of your authoritative nameservers every single time they get a query for it.

It's expensive to do that–not only in the engineering-speak meaning of "expensive"–in that every query has to go through the entire lookup process every time (see `Chapter 6`, *DNS Queries in Action*)

But since many commercial DNS providers *charge by the query* (usually in terms of cost-per-million), it can be literally, *expensive.*

# Nameserver (NS)

The NS RR provides a list of the authoritative nameserver hostnames for the current owner-name. They appear both in the current zone and in the parent zone.

NS RR Syntax:

```
<OWNER-NAME> IN NS <nameserver hostname>
```

For example.com's namservers, they would be in the .COM TLD (the parent):

```
$ORIGIN com.
example IN NS a.iana-servers.net.
example IN NS b.ianaservers.net.
```

And then within the child zone:

```
$ORIGIN example.com.
IN NS a.iana-servers.net.
IN NS b.iana-servers.net. ; authoritative nameservers for the current zone
```

Within any zone, you can further specify authoritative nameservers for another delegation (create a zone cut) by entering NS records for the child zone:

```
$ORIGIN example.com.
IN NS a.iana-servers.net.
IN NS b.iana-servers.net. ; authoritative nameservers for the current
origin (example.com)
subzone  IN NS dns1.example.net.
subzone IN NS dns2.example.net. ; delegation of subzone.example.com to
other nameservers
```

If the NS RRs are within the current zone (in bailiwick), there must be corresponding A (and optionally AAAA) records for the nameserver hostnames to their appropriate IP addresses in the current zone. If the NS RR hostnames are in-bailiwick then there must also be A or AAAA records for the nameserver hostnames in the *parent zone* (known as glue records). When you update a zone, NOTIFY packets will be sent to each listed NS RR in the current zone, along with any other IPs listed either in a global configuration option or in each zone's also-notify option.

In our preceding example, the nameservers for example.com are in bailiwick, while those for subzone.example.com are out of bailiwick (because the nameservers for subzone.example.COM are both under a different example.NET domain). We'll look more at in bailiwick versus out of bailiwick considerations in the *Nameserver TLD redundancy* section.

# A/IPv4 Address

IPv4 Address/A records could very well be the most commonly used RR in DNS. These records map a hostname to its IPv4 address (IPv6 addresses are mapped via "AAAA" records).

An RR Syntax:

```
<OWNER-NAME> IN A <hostname>
```

The OWNER-NAME of the record specifies the hostname. If the name is not terminated with a trailing dot, the current $ORIGIN is appended to it. (This is one of the more common DNS configuration errors, leading to records seemingly disappearing inexplicably, only to resurface in the form of www.example.com.example.com).

In other words, given:

```
$ORIGIN example.com.
www IN A 192.168.1.1
;
; maps www.example.com to 192.168.1.1
www.example.com. IN A 192.168.1.1
;
; also maps www.example.com to 192.168.1.1
; but
;
www.example.com IN A 192.168.1.1
;
; creates an hostname called www.example.com.example.com!
```

It is legal to specify multiple labels as A records with different IP addresses. Doing so creates a **Resource Record Set** (**RRSet**) for the label. Nameservers are commonly configured to return RRSets in round-robin order, creating Round Robin DNS records (see the *Round Robin* section in `Chapter 11`, *DNS Operations and Use Cases*).

It is also legal to have additional RR types with the same name as an A record (and in some cases, a requirement).

If your nameservers are in bailiwick, there must be corresponding A records for each NS record within the zone.

When creating Mail Exchangers (MX records), the data section on the Right-Hand Side (RHS) will need an accompanying A record, whether it's inside the current zone or an external one. It cannot be a CNAME nor can it be a naked IP address.

TXT records frequently correspond to a matching A record, such as SPF data or validation strings for third-party integrations.

Your SOA record will most usually have a matching A record, often corresponding to the zone's apex.

# CNAME/Alias

*"I am reliably informed that CNAME was intended as a transition mechanism when renaming internet resources, and that the way we use them today (www, etc), is crazy."*

*- Paul Vixie*

*"I recommend that all CNAME records be eliminated. DNS should have been designed without aliases."*

*- Dr. Daniel J. Bernstein.*

Here is the CNAME syntax:

```
<OWNER-NAME> IN CNAME <cname target>
```

The CNAME or Alias is a "canonical name"–the easiest way to understand it is as an alias for "the actual name".

Given:

```
web.example.com.  IN CNAME www.example.com.
```

It would mean that *web.example.com* is another identifier for `www.example.com`. In practical terms, when a resolver does a lookup on web.example.com and gets a CNAME in response, it will restart the query process using the alias (`www.example.com`).

The most important thing to know about CNAMEs is that there can be no other RRs with the same owner-name as a CNAME. That is, the owner-name of a CNAME RR *must* be unique and there can be no other RRs with the same name using it. (The only exception to this rule is in the case of DNSSEC-signed zones, see the section on DNSSEC where you CNAME would have a matching RRSig.).

In other words, this will hose your DNS:

```
www.example.com.   IN CNAME example.com.
www.example.com. IN MX 5 mail.example.com.
```

This also means you cannot create multiple CNAME RRSets:

```
ca.example.net. IN CNAME ca1.example.com.
ca.example.net, IN CNAME ca2.example.net.
```

When it comes to DNS, this "CNAME cannot have other data" rule is probably the one rule that most people want to be able to break. The most common reason why is because a lot of people really wish that they could alias their domain apex to another hostname. The preceding example of a multiple-CNAME RRSet is a real-world use case, which we'll cover more in the *Geo DNS* section of DNS Use Cases.

The motivations for doing this are often credible, such as hosting your domain on a third-party application platform or on a **content-delivery network** (**CDN**). Life would be so easy if you could just do this:

```
; quick and dirty point your domain at your Content Delivery Network (CDN)
; too bad it will blow up your zone
example.com. IN CNAME example.com.some.network.cdn.
```

Demand for these capabilities has become so widespread that more than one DNS provider (including easyDNS) has come up with ways to delicately bend or even break this rule. At least one nameserver daemon (PowerDNS) has come out with native support for domain apex aliasing. Given this reality, there is an entire section on **Domain Apex Aliasing** in `Chapter 11`, *DNS Operations and Use Cases*.

# When to use Aliases vs Hostnames

This is hotly debated. Within a single zone, it's often customary to create the zone apex as an A record and then alias `"www.<domain>"` to the apex. That way, if the IP address ever changes, you only need to update one record in the zone.

This begins to make a bigger difference as you start to scale your portfolio. Suppose you're running a content-delivery network or a web hosting farm, and you're stacking up hundreds or thousands of domains per IP address or hostname for your application.

Strategic use of CNAMEs can make your life a lot easier, and in extreme cases, save your butt. Consider the scenario where you have 5,000 client hostnames on a shared hosted application on a single IP address.

If you've set up your application on an IP:

```
voip.voips-r-us.dom. IN A 198.51.113.89
```

If you have each record setup as a hostname:

```
$ORIGIN example.com.
voip.example.com. IN A 198.51.113.89
```

and...

```
$ORIGIN thosegermans.de.
voip.thosegermans.de. IN A 198.51.113.89
```

Before long, you have thousands of these out there, business is good!

What would you do if `198.51.113.89` has a serious problem and you end up having to renumber onto `198.51.113.30`?

Imagine that you're not even in control of the DNS zones for a sizeable portion of these client domains. You've got a serious problem on your hands.

Through the strategic use of CNAMEs, you can handle it all in one update; instead for each client, use a naming convention along these lines:

```
; each client provisions via a CNAME to your endpoint
;
$ORIGIN example.com.
voip.example.com. IN CNAME voipstack.voips-r-us.dom.
```

Then in the zone for your application that is under your control, use the following:

```
; The underlying endpoint has a single RR (or even a single RRSet)
;
$ORIGIN voips-r-us.dom.
voipstack IN A 198.51.113.89
```

Now you are in a position to move your entire client base around without updating each individual zone that you are maintaining for your clients, or requiring all the ones outside your control to update their DNS settings.

From experience, I can tell you that once you have your clients initially provision their DNS records to you, those records have a tendency to ossify that way. Making end users update their own DNS zones is a time-consuming and laborious prospect. Doing it in bulk is a painstaking one. Usually, the only time you can motivate everybody to make a change quickly is in under the impetus of a complete failure condition. But once that happens, you also run the risk that they are also just as likely to simply provision off to another provider. It's best that you set things up so that *you* can control the DNS and move your end users around without waiting on them. That way, your users don't have to pay much attention to their DNS records once they've pointed them to your application.

# The Mail Exchanger (MX) record

The mail exchanger record (also known as "MX record "or "MX handler") was first defined in RFC 1035.

If you look at an email address, you can see it has two parts divided by an `@sign`. The left-hand side sign is the recipient and the right-hand side is the hostname or a domain name of that recipient's logical mailbox. So `markjr@easydns.com` means that you are sending an email to the recipient `markjr` (that's me) `@easydns.com`.

The MX record tells other **Mail Transport Agents (MTAs)** where to send that email destined for any `easydns.com` addresses.

In common zone-file format, it would look like this:

```
easydns.com.    IN MX 5 mail.easydns.com.
easydns.com.    IN MX 10 backupmx.easydns.com.
```

The mail server itself sorts out what to do with the email it receives addressed to the recipient and how to process those messages. They may get forwarded somewhere; their destinations may get expanded out into multiple recipients or sent through a program. They may be dropped into an email box or they may be silently discarded:

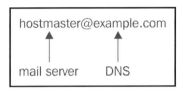

Figure 7-1: Who cares about what part of an email address

At the DNS level, we are concerned with the right-hand side of the address, the hostname. That is what MX records describe. When an MTA sends an email, it does a DNS lookup for the hostname part of the email address and will get back one or more mail exchangers as a result. Then it should try delivering the email to the mail exchanger with the *lowest* preference number first.

# Preferences, Priorities, and Delivery Order

You'll notice that MX records have a field for Preference, which is also known as Priority in some circles (PowerDNS, for example, usually refers to it as the latter).

Mail servers are supposed to attempt delivery to the MX handlers in *ascending order* of the preference. In other words, the lower the preference number, the higher its priority is. This is also sometimes described as distance, which does make it somewhat more intuitive if you think in terms of MTAs preferring to attempt delivery to the shortest-distanced MX handler.

If the originating (or intermediary) mailserver cannot deliver the email to the most preferred MX handler, either because it cannot connect or if it receives a soft error, it will attempt deliver it to the next highest preference, and those are known as the **backup mail spool**, or **backup MX**.

# Backup MX handler considerations

When we define a backup MX, it is going to end up receiving a certain amount of email for your destination *even if the main mail handler is up and functional*. It's just one of those things that could be caused by nearly anything, like any kind of transient network glitch. Also spammers may try to use the backup mail exchanger to inject spam "through the backdoor" into a given mail host.

Defining a backup mail exchanger in the DNS for a zone doesn't magically convey backup MX capabilities onto the server that is designated as the backup MX. That server actually has to be configured to accept mail for those domains. This is outside the scope of DNS, but it's something you need to be aware of. You can't just define a backup MX record in your DNS zone and expect it to work.

# Special case MX records

If there is no MX record present, the protocol is to try to deliver the email to the A or AAAA record in the destination. For example, an email is sent to markjr@antisocial.dom but antisocial.dom has no MX records. The MTA will then do an A-record lookup for antisocial.dom and attempt delivery there.

There is also the special case of the **null MX** (formalized in RFC7505) which is defined as a ".", preference 0 and that means no email is expected nor accepted for this domain. MTAs are supposed to hard fail and return a **Non-Delivery Notifcation** (**NDN**) when encountering email addressed to a domain with the null MX set.

You would probably define that in conjunction with the SPF record in the domain that disavows all email that is claimed to originate from it and between the two you can signal to the world that a given domain has absolutely no email associated with it at all:

```
antisocial.dom. IN MX 0 .
; Translation: Don't talk to me!
antisocial.dom. IN TXT "v=spf1 -all"
; Translation: I'm not saying anything to anybody!
```

# Managing many MX domains

If you are managing large numbers of domains, perhaps as a domain registrar or web-hosting provider, it's a good practice to make something similar to the preceding snippet a standard component of your default DNS zone template. That way your users are not receiving random spam directed at newly minted domains, and those same domains are insulating themselves from any autobot spam that may forge them into their envelopes. In other words, turn on your email signalling within the DNS when your end user specifically wants it on, don't enable it by default.

# TXT/Text Records

The TXT Resource Record Syntax is:

```
<OWNER-NAME> IN TXT <free form data>
```

The data section of TXT records contain freeform text data that were historically comments, but have since evolved into specialized add-on purposes that take on a type of pseudo-record functionality or contain metadata.

Examples include:

- **Sender Policy Framework** data (**SPF**)
- DKIM and Domain Keys (the latter is now deprecated)
- DMARC data

The TXT data can be any length, however if it is larger than 255 characters, it must be chunked into multiple strings of 255 chars or fewer. Further, care should be taken on the size, if it is over the maximum packet size, then you will force queries into TCP retry mode, which incurs additional overhead.

# SPF records

We mention SPF records here because the use of Sender Policy Framework (SPF) data became so widespread it eventually received its own RTYPE (defined in RFC 4408), alas that SPF RR was later deprecated in RFC 7208.

The important thing to know is that SPF-aware MTAs will *always* look for and process SPF data found in the applicable TXT records, while only *maybe* look for it in an SPF record. In practical terms, the SPF RR Type is an evolutionary dead-end.

Keep your SPF data within TXT records, and if you haven't already made provisions for SPF RR Types in your architecture, you can safely ignore them. They are mentioned here because it is not widely known that the SPF RR Type has been deprecated.

We look closer at employing SPF, DKIM and DMARC records in `Chapter 10`, *Debugging Without Tears – DNS Diagnostic Tools*.

# SRV

SRV records are like a Swiss-Army Knife for DNS. They can be thought of as an all purpose MX-*ish* record that can convey preferences and weightings of hostnames that are available to provide specific services beyond SMTP.

Here is the SRV RR Syntax:

```
<_service>.<_protocol>.<OWNER-NAME> <TTL> IN SRV <priority> <weight> <port>
<target>
```

In this syntax:

- `_service` is the symbolic name of the service, such as `_sip`, `_ldap` or `_autodiscover`, taken from IANA service names list (formerly Assigned Numbers STD-2) or a local label.
- `_protocol` is the protocol, most often `_tcp` or `_udp` (case insensitive) but can contain other values, such has `_http` or `_ldap`.
- Underscores are precluded from use in hostnames. It is legal to use underscores in `_service` and `_protocol` fields, where they are prefixed with an underscore to avoid name collisions with other names within the zone. (Refer back to `Chapter 1`, *The Domain Name Ecosystem*, for descriptions of hostnames and syntax.)
- **owner-name** is the hostname of the service you are defining, that is, `voip.example.com`.
- **TTL** is the Time-to-Live as in any other record.
- **priority** functions the same as that of an MX handler's priority (or preference). The lower this number, the sooner it will be used (the shorter the distance).

- **weight** is something SRV records provide, which MX handlers do not. SRV records being applicable to an open-ended set of use cases, we have here the ability to facilitate load-balancing from within the DNS. The difference between priority and weight is that the former stipulates in what order each set of RRs are to be used (lowest-numbered priority first), while the weight is intended to distribute the load within a set of RRs for that given priority.
- **port** lets us define the port for the given service, and could thus facilitate running well-known services on non-standard ports. If the major web browsers supported SRV, it would make it lot easier to run web endpoints on non-standard ports.
- **target** is the hostname that will ultimately fulfill the service requests.

The following SRV record publishes information about an XMPP (jabber) server for the `example.com` domain:

```
_jabber._tcp               IN SRV 0 5 5269 sipster.example.com.
_xmpp-client._tcp          IN SRV 0 5 5222 sipster.example.com.
_xmpp-server._tcp          IN SRV 0 5 5269 sipster.example.com.
_xmpp-server._tcp.chat     IN SRV 5 10 5269 sipster.example.com.
_xmpp-server._tcp.notify   IN SRV 5 10 5269 sipster.example.com.
```

# NAPTR

NAPTR stands for Naming Authority Pointer.

NAPTRs are primarily used in IP telephony applications in conjunction with SRV RR records within the context of ENUM.

ENUM provides a mechanism for mapping e164-format telephone numbers into the DNS. The full mechanism is described in RFC6116, but it is basically any telephone number in the form of +A.BBBBBBBBBBBB, where + is a literal "+" character, A is the NPA Country Code, and BBBBBBBBBBBB is the telephone number with all non-numerals and any leading zeros stripped out.

The process works by reversing the digits of the phone number and then putting a "." between each digit, finally (in the case of public ENUM) appending the special domain, e164.arpa.

For example, the phone number `1-(416)-535-8672` would map as follows:

```
e164: +1.4165553231 ENUM: 2.7.6.8.5.3.5.6.1.4.1.e164.arpa
```

It is within the `2.7.6.8.5.3.5.6.1.4.1.e164.arpa` zone then, where we can use NAPTR records to set up some IP telephony magic for this phone number:

```
$ORIGIN 2.7.6.8.5.3.5.6.1.4.1.e164.arpa.
IN NAPTR 100 10 "u" "E2U+sip" "!^.*$!sip:phoneme@example.net!" .
IN NAPTR 102 10 "u" "E2U+mailto" "!^.*$!mailto:myemail@example.com!" .
```

Here is the NAPTR RR Syntax:

```
<OWNER-NAME> IN NAPTR <PREF> <WEIGHT> <FLAG> <SERVICE> <REGEX>
<destination>
```

The format of a NAPTR record is as follows:

- **Preference**: This functions in the same manner as the SRV records priority field.
- **Weight**: The weight of the record, can be used to differentiate records of the same preference.
- **Flag**: Double quoted and can be any alphanumeric digit (case insensitive). Its meaning is defined by the application, but there a few that are conventionally used. My personal shorthand for them is to mentally think of them as "what comes next" indicators.
- **"U"**: The result of processing this NAPTR record will be an URN.
- **"A"**: The result of processing this NAPTR will be a hostname that can be queried via A or AAAA lookups.
- **"S"**: The result of processing will be a SRV record.
  - U, A, and S flags are all terminal rules in that they signify the end of processing NAPTR records *within the current origin* (because a "U" flag will yield a URN, which may query a NAPTR record in the parent zone of the URN's DNS hostname). An additional "P" flag is available, which means there are no more NAPTR records to process, but that the application may continue processing other RR types along its own rules.

- **Service**: Additional parameters to be passed to the application. The parameters and format are not defined by the NAPTR specification but by the workings of the application itself. The format is:

```
<resolution service>+<protocol>
```

Commonly used resolution services include:

- **E2U**: Enum to URI (defined in RFC 3671), such as e2u+sip or e2u+mailto.
- **SIP**: Session Initiation Protocol, sip+d2t (SIP over TCP), sip+d2u (SIP over UDP). If the flag in the current record is terminal, then a protocol must be present. If there is a protocol present, but the flag is not terminal, then the next lookup ("what happens next") is another NAPTR lookup.
- **Regex**: A POSIX-extended regular expression that will be applied to LHS of the NAPTR record. This is the mechanism that rewrites the current record in a format that can be used by the application in the transformation. In other words, for ENUM processes that are mapping telephone numbers to URIs. These regexes are how we get from the former to the latter. Any character that would *not* ordinarily be used in a DNS hostname may be used as the regex delimiters. Convention commonly has them as exclamation marks (!) but you may also use forward-slashes (/), which may be more familiar to you when working with regexes.
- The i flag is also available to denote case insensitive matching:
  - `"!^.$!mailto:myemail@example.com!i"` or
  - `"/^.$/ mailto:myemail@example.com/i"`
- **Destination** (or replacement): The next value to look up in non-terminal NAPTR records. The process of starting with an old-world telephone number and winding up with a VOIP call, or a fax or some other internet telephony application is commonly a two-step or multi-step process utilizing NAPTR records, depending on the value of the flag. First, we map the telephone number to a URN, as in our example in the ENUM sidebar:

```
$ORIGIN 2.7.6.8.5.3.5.6.1.4.1.e164.arpa.
IN NAPTR 100 10 "u" "E2U+sip" "^.*$!sip:phoneme@example.net!"
IN NAPTR 102 10 "u" "E2U+mailto" "!^.*$!mailto:myemail@example.com!"
```

The "U" flag means weare going to end up with a URN, in our case, we start with the first NAPTR record (lowest preference) and we end up with the `sip:phoneme@example.net` URN.

Within the example.net zone, we will have another NAPTR record that will catch this query and provide the application with the rest of the information it will need to complete the construction of an SIP session:

```
$ORIGIN example.net.
IN NAPTR 100 10 "S" "SIP+D2U" "!^.*$!!" _sip._udp.example.com.
IN NAPTR 102 10 "S" "SIP+D2T" "!^.*$!!" _sip._tcp.example.com.
```

Here, the "S" flag means that processing will lead us to an SRV record lookup, after we've applied the regex search/replace to the final destination.

In other words:

1. Our application dialed `+1-(416)-555-3231`
2. It did a NAPTR lookup under `1.3.2.3.5.5.5.6.1.4.1.e164.arpa.` to find the URN `sip:phoneme@example.net`
3. It did another NAPTR lookup under example.net and was given an SRV record to look up
4. It did an SRV lookup at `_sip._udp.example.com` to get the location of the relevent SIP server or gateway

NAPTRs, and their close cousins the SRV record, provide a powerful toolset for underpinning internet telephony. As more of the world moves to VOIP, incorporating SIP and ENUM, you can expect to be working with these RR types a lot more.

# DNAME

The **Delegation Name Record** (**DNAME**) provides a way to map an entire DNS tree to another namespace.

Here is the DNAME RR Syntax:

```
<OWNER-NAME> IN DNAME <destination>
```

As in:

```
example.com. IN DNAME example.net.
```

Each node in the mapping behaves as a logical CNAME expansion, so in our case:

`www.example.com` will be treated as a CNAME lookup to `www.example.net`. However, there are certain things to know about DNAME's:

Absent an explicit record (such as an A, MX or AAAA), a lookup on the Left-Hand Side of the DNAME will not match anything.

The mapping takes place below the record. In other words:

```
example.com. IN DNAME example.net.
; maps *.example.com to their respective lookups under example.net,
; but NOT example.com itself.
```

Contrary to how a wildcard record would behave, any other hostname records (A or AAAA) within the scope of a DNAME *will not work*. The DNAME mapping will take precedence:

```
example.com. IN DNAME example.net. foo.example.com. IN A 192.68.143.3
; a lookup on "foo.example.com" will NOT return 192.68.143.3
; but rather trigger another lookup on foo.example.net
; contrast with a wildcard DNS entry
*.example.com. IN A 10.1.1.4 foo.example.com. IN A 192.168.143.3
; a lookup on "foo.example.com" WILL return 192.168.143.3
```

It is important to note the differences between DNAME and wildcards:

A wildcard maps the entire namespace below the label to a *single* value (be it a hostname or a CNAME), while the DNAME maps *each value* under the label to its corresponding value under the target zone.

The former is multiple-to-one, the latter is multiple instances of one-to-one.

# PTR

Think of a PTR record as the flipside of an A record or a hostname lookup. A records specify IP addresses of a hostname, while PTR records go the opposite direction: they look up the hostname of a given IP address.

Here is the PTR RR Syntax:

```
<OWNER-NAME> IN PTR <hostname>
```

In PTR records, the OWNER-NAME will be an IP address, expressed in reverse or inverted notation, relative to the current $ORIGIN of the zone; while the **Right-Hand Side (RHS)** will be a hostname.

What people often miss is that we are actually talking about two completely different branches of the DNS tree when we discuss a forward and a reverse lookup.

Consider the following:

```
www.example.com.    IN A    192.168.13.56
```

We are looking at this branch:

- Level 0:  (the internet root)
- Level 1: com (the .COM TLD)
- Level 2: example (the "example.com" domain delegated from .COM)
- Level 3: www (the subdomain, subhost, or `www.example.com` hostname)

Now let's break down the IP address assigned to `www.example.com` in the same fashion. Notice in the sequence, when we broke down `www.example.com`, we actually went in reverse order, starting at the internet root (".") and proceeding from right to left. Each "." was a subdomain of the label before it.

The reverse mapping will work in the same way, so the IP address will be represented in reverse-octet form under the infrastructure TLD below arpa (described in `Chapter 1`, *The Domain Name Ecosystem*):

```
56.13.168.192.in-addr.arpa
```

Because this is an IPv4 address, it is within the in-addr.arpa tree. If we were looking at an IPv6 address, it would be under `ip6.arpa`:

- Level 0: . (the internet root)
- Level 1: `arpa`
- Level 2: `in-addr` (the branch under which IPv4 addresses are mapped)
- Level 3: `192` ("192" would be a /8 netblock)
- Level 4: `168` ("192.168" would be a /16 netblock)
- Level 5: `13` ("192.168.13" would be /24 netblock)
- Level 6: `56` ("192.168.13.56" is a single IPv4 address, a /32)

What is important to understand is that the reverse mapping for an IP address is under a completely different branch of the naming tree than its forward mapping:

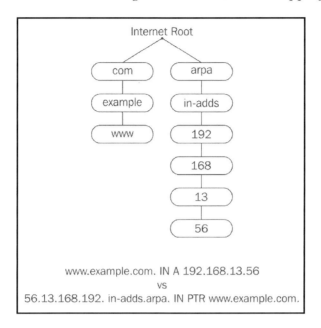

Figure 7-2: The difference between the forward and reverse lookups for a hostname resides along two different paths in the DNS tree.

When you define this in a zonefile:

```
$ORIGIN example.com.
www IN A 192.168.12.56
```

You will *never* put the PTR record in this same zone because the PTR for `192.168.12.56` belongs in a completely different zone, namely one under the `12.168.192.in-addr.arpa` zone:

```
$ORIGIN 12.168.192.in-addr.arpa.
56 IN PTR www.example.com.
```

But what you *can* do is have the PTR point at CNAMEs in the forward zone so that you can edit the ultimate values for both the forward and reverse lookups in that forward zone:

```
$ORIGIN 12.168.192.in-addr.arpa.
56 IN PTR 56.ptr.example.com.
Then in your forward zone:
$ORIGIN example.com.
www IN A 192.168.12.56
$ORIGIN ptr.example.com.
56 IN CNAME www.example.com.
```

Also important to know is that the authoritative nameservers for example.com are not necessarily the same nameservers that will be authoritative for `12.168.192.in-addr.arpa`, in fact that is probably not the case more often than it is.

This is because the domain names are delegated from the registry of its parent TLD, while address space is delegated from regional numbering authorities. It is possible, and not uncommon, to have forward and reverse nameservers coincide, but it involves obtaining the relevant delegations from two separate upstream entities.

We'll look at setting up reverse DNS for your address space in `Chapter 11`, *DNS Operations and Use Cases*.

# IPv6

IPv6 addresses are supported by all modern nameservers, and as the Internet of Things (IoT) and other similar initiatives gain momentum, expect to be doing more over IPv6.

Many of the DNS records will continue to function as is, CNAMEs will still reference Hostnames, as will MX handlers and NS records, but going forward, those hostnames will themselves be IPv6-enabled and thus have one or more IPv6 addresses. For the foreseeable future, such devices will likely be dual-stacked with both IPv4 and IPv6 addresses, but eventually we should see at least some devices moving exclusively to IPv6. While that statement may elicit vigorous debate, you'll still have to play nice with IPv6 even if you don't believe it.

# AAAA

Given that IPv4 addresses are mapped via A records (hostnames), it makes sense that IPv6 addresses, which are four times as many bits, are represented by AAAA (also known as "quad-A") addresses.

Here is the AAAA RR Syntax:

```
<OWNER-NAME> IN AAAA <ipv6 address>
```

IPv6 addresses 128-bits segmented into 8 groups of hexadecimal (base-16) numbers separated by colons:

```
2001:db8:5:0000:0000:0000:0000:13
```

Segments consisting of all zeros can be omitted to save keystrokes: `2001:678:5::13`.

The double-colon signifies the missing 0-padded chunks. The double-colon can only appear once in an address.

The AAAA record then takes the same format as the A (Hostname) record, and the two can happily co-exist (and must in the case of dual stacked services):

```
dns1.example.com. IN A 192.168.1.78
dns1.example.com. IN AAAA 2001:678:5::13
```

# A6

The A6 record was an alternate method of specifying IPv6 addresses that has since been deprecated. A6 enabled one to split the IPv6 address across multiple A6 RRs to better capture the hierarchical structure of the DNS.

Here is the A6 RR Syntax:

```
<OWNER-NAME> IN A6 <TTL> <PREFIX> <IPV6> [NEXTNAME]
```

For example:

```
dns1    IN A6    64 ::4    ipv6ns.example.com.
```

The prefix specifies the number of bits out of the 128-bit IPv6 address that will be specified in the next record. The next record will be a subsequent A6 query on the label specified by the optional [next-name] (`ipv6ns.example.com`). The IPv6 value in the current RR will specify the remaining bits of the address in the current record.

The A6 record has been deprecated and is mentioned here for historical reasons.

# CERT

The CERT RR type allows you to publish public key certificates (and their revocation lists) over DNS.

Here is the CERT RR Syntax:

```
<OWNER_NAME> IN CERT <TYPE> <KEY-TAG> <ALGORITHM> <cert-crl>
```

The type field is either an unsigned decimal (column 1) or a mnemonic (column 2) that corresponds to the following values:

```
The following values are defined or reserved:

    Value   Mnemonic  Certificate Type
    -----   --------  -----------------
        0             Reserved
        1   PKIX      X.509 as per PKIX
        2   SPKI      SPKI certificate
        3   PGP       OpenPGP packet
        4   IPKIX     The URL of an X.509 data object
        5   ISPKI     The URL of an SPKI certificate
        6   IPGP      The fingerprint and URL of an OpenPGP packet
        7   ACPKIX    Attribute Certificate
        8   IACPKIX   The URL of an Attribute Certificate
    9-252             Available for IANA assignment
      253   URI       URI private
      254   OID       OID private
      255             Reserved
  256-65279           Available for IANA assignment
65280-65534           Experimental
      65535           Reserved
```

Table 7-1. CERT RR Type Field Values (via RFC 4398)

The **key-tag** field is a 16-bit value derived from the key in the certificate/crl.

The **algorithm** field uses the same encryption algorithm values/mnemonics as used in DNSSEC.

The **certificate** or **crl** itself is base64-encoded and can be broken up by whitespaces or span multiple lines that are then concatenated into the full signature, the following CERT RR advertises my public GPG key for my email address, `mark@thirteen.ca`:

```
$ORIGIN jeftovic.net.
mark IN CERT 0003 0000 00
2D2D2D2D2D424547494E20504750205055424C4943204B455920424C4F434
```

When you put a CERT RR into a zone, be prepared for the response to be greater than 512 bytes, and thus cause a retransmission over TCP:

```
$ dig +short -t cert mark.jeftovic.net.
;; Truncated, retrying in TCP mode.
PGP 0 0 2D2D2D2D2D424547494E20504750205055424C4943204B455920424C
4F434B2D2D2D2D2D0A5665727
(etc...)
```

# TLSA

**DNS-based Authentication of Named Entities (DANE)** is a relatively new method for authenticating the identity of internet endpoints using DNS. It lets you map X.509 certs used in TLS encryption to domain names. DANE can obviate the need to use a central **Certificate Authority (CA)**, however it can still be used in conjunction with one.

This is accomplished via the TLSA RR, which is described in RFC 7671.

The format of the TLSA RR is:

```
<PORT>.<PROTOCOL>.<OWNER-NAME> IN TLSA <USAGE> <SELECTOR> <TYPE> <DATA>
```

- **Port**: The port corresponding to the service to be secured
- **Protocol**: Usually `_tcp`
- **Usage**: This is **certificate usage** and has one of the following values:

| | |
|---|---|
| 0 | CA Constraint or PKIX-TA. There must be a trust path to a trusted third-party CA. |
| 1 | Service Certificate Constraint and PKIX-EE. A certificate that must match the TLSA record and pass PKIX validation. |
| 2 | DANE-TA/Trust Anchor Assertion. The certificate has a valid certification path to the certificate mentioned in the record but PKIX is not required. |
| 3 | DANE-EE/Domain-issued certificate. A self-signed record that is not tied to a CA. |

- **Selector**: Determines which part of the certificate should be checked:

| 0 | The entire certificate |
|---|---|
| 1 | Just the public key |

- **Type**: What type of data in the cert should be matched when checking:

| 0 | the entire information in the certificate |
|---|---|
| 1 | a SHA-256 hash of the data |
| 2 | a SHA-512 hash of the data |

For example, the following code would present TLSA validation for mx.example.com, a mail server on port 25 using TCP, with a self-signed TLS certificate that is not connected to a third-party CA, which should be compared to a SHA-256 hash of the public key portion of the certificate:

```
$ORIGIN example.com.
_25._tcp.mx IN TLSA 3 1 1
5af9bc735736d0351a68819684960b8404299ef1b56d9db04cc6ffb68a28a6a9
```

# CAA

The **Certification Authority Authorization** (CAA) RR specifies a mechanism in the DNS to assert which CAs are valid ones to issue any TLS certificates on that domain (think of it as akin to an SPF for TLS certs).

This is a relatively new RR, but CAB (CA Browsers Forum) recently made CAA checks mandatory for CA issuers. What this means is that when CAs receive a request to issue a cert, they will start checking DNS zones for CAA RRs and if they exist, abide by the policy they encode. Said policy is transmitted via the CAA record.

CAA RRs are supported as of BIND 9.10.1, PowerDNS 4.0, NSD 4.0.1, and Knot DNS 2.2.0.

Here is the CAA RR syntax:

```
<owner-name> IN CAA <flag> <tag> <value>
```

- **Owner-name**: The address for which certs in question can be issued for
- **Flag**: Takes on specific values as per the RFC

- **Tag**: Will take on possible values:

| | |
|---|---|
| **issue** | The CA specified in `<value>` is authorized to issue a certificate for this name (`www.example.com`). |
| **issuewild** | The specified CA can issue a wildcard certificate under the name (`*.example.com`). |
| **iodef** | A value in Incident Object Description Exchange Format (IODEF)[12] for reporting policy violations. (Not yet supported by all CAs.) |

Only one tag value would be used within a record, but multiple CAA RRs are permitted per owner-name.

- **Value**: This specifies which CA can issue certificates for the owner-name and with what conditions. Additional descriptors are permitted in `name=value` pairs, as described in *Section 5.2* of the RFC. Multiple `name=value` pairs are permitted in the `<value>`:

```
$ORIGIN example.com.
CAA 0 issue "ca.example.net; account=230123".
CAA 0 iodef "mailto:security@example.com".
CAA 0 iodef "http://iodef.example.com/"
```

The preceding example (from RFC 6844) illustrates that the "CA.EXAMPLE.NET" CA is allowed to issue a certificate for "`example.com`".

# DNSSEC-specific RR Types

There are several RRTypes that are specific to DNS Security Extensions (DNSSEC), namely **DNSKEY**, **RRSIG**, and **DS**. We will cover the DNSSEC RR Types in `Chapter 13`, *Securing Your Domains and DNS*.

# Summary

A working knowledge of the mechanics of these commonly used RR Types should now be yours and we now have some appreciation of the subtleties that creep in when the number of RRs (either within a single zone or across numerous collections of zones) becomes very large.

These principles can be applied to make managing complex portfolios of domains somewhat easier, especially with respect to the two DNS biggies: outages and changes.

# References

1. Also available online as DNS For Rocket Scientists: `http://www.zytrax.com/books/dns/`

2. For a good introduction to Chaos and Hesiod DNS classes, see: `https://miek.nl/2009/July/31/dns-classes/`, `https://cr.yp.to/djbdns/notes.html`

3. Ron Aitchison's Pro DNS & Bind 10 explains "canonical" as "the genuine or expected name"

4. Soft errors mean that the failure is temporary and should be retried later, whereas a hard error means the error is permanent and a non-delivery announcement should be returned to the sender (the email bounces).

5. HOW TO Define an SPF Record `http://www.zytrax.com/books/dns/ch9/spf.html`

6. There are also private ENUM islands, in which case the organization would define its own private ENUM namespace Yes, you can wildcard CNAMES, but it's your funeral

7. Classless Inter-Domain Routing or CIDR

8. The "make-dns-cert" command can create a CERT RR from your exported GPG key. For a couple of good tutorials that walk you through how to generate these RRs and how to configure your GPG to look for keys over DNS, see `http://www.gushi.org/make-dns-cert/HOWTO.html` and `http://www.initd.net/2010/12/adding-gpg-public-keys-to-your-dns.html`.

9. `https://tools.ietf.org/html/rfc6844`

# 8
# Quasi-Record Types

This chapter was originally called *Pseudo-Record Types* but that might cause confusion with **OPT** pseudo RR, which nameservers use to communicate the ability to convey EDNS.

There are some who think that this section shouldn't even be in here, because a lot of what's covered here is outside the actual DNS protocol. That said, this book is about managing DNS *and* domains. What happens under the umbrella "quasi-records" I put here because they are use cases or functionalities that frequently get bundled together under domain management.

In this vein, Quasi-Record Types is a phrase coined to denote record types commonly identified by their function that do not actually have true corresponding RR types within the DNS protocol.

For example, you may be familiar with the terms URL forward, Stealth Redirect, or some other derivations of them. All registrar or DNS provider user interfaces will have sections or modules that correspond to these URL-forwarding records. People expect them.

But there is no actual DNS RR type that signifies a URL Forwarder. By the time one makes it into your DNS zone, it will be an A record or a CNAME that points to some resource, such as a server, a CDN, or a load balancer. It just so happens that that endpoint will be configured to manipulate and forward HTTP requests, and thus you have a URL forwarder.

In other words, these quasi-record types often derive their meaning from some process that happens outside the DNS protocol, but usually get managed from within the same system where the DNS is managed. We'll run through them in this chapter, as follows:

- URL Forwards and Redirects
- The Zone Apex/ANAME
- Multiple CNAME POOL records
- Dynamic DNS/DYN records
- Email forwarders

# URL Forwards and Redirects

A URL forwarder is simply a hostname configured to redirect to an actual *URL*, as opposed to being aliased to some other hostname (CNAME) or set to resolve to an IP address.

An example would be:

```
example.com → http://www.example.net/something/goes.html
```

There is no DNS-protocol-specific method to redirect a URL in this way. It's accomplished by standing up a web server somewhere that does nothing but redirect incoming requests, and then pointing your DNS records at it using a host record or a CNAME. The redirect server then needs to maintain a database with the mappings, including the full request URI of the remote destination. It will then need to key on the incoming "Host" header of client browser requests and redirect those requests to the remote destination.

You may hear forwarder or redirect versus stealth or cloaked. The difference is that forwarders or redirects will simply redirect the browser to the remote destination by sending a `Location: <URI>` HTTP response header. That causes the URI displayed in the browser's location bar to change to the remote destination:

```
$ lynx -head http://blog.example.com
HTTP/1.1 302 Found
Date: Thu, 22 Jan 2015 19:01:23 GMT
Server: Apache/2.2.22 (Debian)X-Powered-By: PHP/5.4.360+deb7u3
Location: http://blog.example.org
```

Contrast that with cloaking, stealth forwarding, or other variants that will preserve the initial hostname being forwarded within the browser's location bar. It usually does so by outputting an HTML frameset to the requesting client with an invisible frame and another frame, sized to be 100% of the browser canvas whose source is set to the remote destination:

```
<html>
<head>
<title></title>
<meta name="EASYDNS-FORWARDER" content="easydns.caprica_v2.webfwd2" />
</head>
<frameset rows="100%,*" border="0" frameborder="0" framespacing="0">
<frame name="top" src="http://easytest.tripod.com" noresize />
<frame name="easydns.caprica_v2.webfwd2" src="about:blank"
marginwidth="0" marginheight="0" scrol
<noframes>
<body>
<h1>Doh!</h1>
<p>Your web-browser does not support frames. You will need to <A
```

```
HREF="http://easytest.tripod.
<BR>Click for <A
HREF="http://easytest.tripod.com">http://easytest.tripod.com</A> </body>
</noframes>
</frameset>
</html>
```

It should be noted that one cannot stealth-forward SSL/TLS (`https://`) requests without a certificate for the forwarded domain being installed at the forwarder. Without such a certificate, that is precisely what SSL and TLS were created to prevent. The presence of the TLS cert validates that your browser is really connected to the server specified in the destination URL.

# The Zone Apex Alias (ANAME)

This is the Big Kahuna of protocol violations. If there were just one rule in the DNS most people wish they could break with impunity, it would be the dreaded "CNAME can't contain other data" rule, which we also examined in the *CNAME* section of `Chapter 7`, *Types and Uses of Common Resource Records*.

Once you create a record as a CNAME, it can't exist next to other data of the same name. The only exception to this rule being DNSSEC RRs (see `Chapter 13`, *Securing Your Domains and DNS*).

It precludes being able to do this:

```
$ORIGIN example.com.
example.com. IN CNAME example.com.cdn-networks-r-us.dom.
```

Why? Because `example.com` is the domain's apex, which means there must also be present both an SOA record and accompanying NS records:

```
; this will not work.
$ORIGIN example.com.
IN SOA dns0.example.com. ops.example.com. 2015040113 16384 2048 1048576
2560
IN NS dns1.example.com.
IN NS dns2.example.net.
IN NS dns3.example.org.
example.com. IN CNAME example.com.cdn-networks-r-us.dom.
```

Rules against multiple CNAME data aside (see sidebar), the use case remains and with the emergence of third-party application platforms (such as Google Apps and Heroku) and CDNs (such as Amazon Cloudfront and Cachefly), the demand is stronger than ever.

Thus methods have been created to effectively create "Aliases at the apex", under various names (such as ANAMEs and CNAME Flattening) by various DNS providers. The PowerDNS (v4) nameserver daemon supports this natively with the **ALIAS** record.

What it entails is simply interpolating the destination hostname of the apex into its corresponding hostname record/A and AAAA record(s).

Logically, the process goes as follows:

End user:

```
example.com. (CNAME | ANAME) to example.com.cdns-r-us.dom.
```

Middleware process:

```
example.com.cnds-r-us.dom lookup = IN A 192.168.2.1
```

Result in nameserver /zonefile:

```
example.com. IN A 192.168.2.1
```

The **right-hand side** (**RHS**) of the apex alias is abstracted away from the user. When a resolver queries `example.com`, it will **never** see `example.com.cdns-r-us.dom`, but only the resulting IP address(es) that the record resolves to.

There are several considerations when implementing this kind of scheme.

# Updates

It's not enough to simply have your middleware interpret the apex target into its constituent A/AAAA records and put them into your zone. The apex target has to be monitored for changes and when they occur, the zone needs to be republished with the new values for the apex record.

This is akin to a reverse-dynamic DNS, where instead of a remote endpoint monitoring its own IP address and triggering an update in the DNS system when it changes, the DNS system is monitoring the values of the remote target and initiating an update in its local client zone when it sees a change.

# Multiple A records (RRSets)

The destination of the apex alias might turn out to be an RRSet of multiple A records functioning as a round-robin. Your middleware has to be prepared to receive a multiple-hostname result for a single apex alias lookup and be able to store them all as multiple A records.

# CNAME chains

It is also very possible that your apex alias itself points at another CNAME.

That is, `example.net` is apex-aliased to `www.example.com`:

```
$host www.example.com
www.example.net is an alias for example.net.wp.cdns-r-us.dom.
example.net.wp.cdns-r-us.dom is an alias for ips3.ca.cdns-r-us.dom.
ips3.ca.cdns-r-us.dom has address 64.68.201.251
```

In this case, you cannot simply store the first result (`example.net.wp.cdns-r-us.dom`), as you're just substituting one CNAME for another CNAME and thus still breaking the rule.

The middleware process needs to follow all CNAME chains to their terminations and store the resulting A record, which may also be a multiple-record RRSet.

# POOL records (multiple CNAME RRSet)

Multiple CNAME RRSets, which is having multiple CNAMEs for the same name, are not as in-demand as apex aliases, but there are use cases for them. To make matters more confusing, these actually used to work back in the BIND4 days, then optionally worked later under BIND8 (with the **allow- multiple-cnames** option enabled) and were discontinued as of BIND 9.1.

Now most people will simply point at the "CNAME cannot coexist with other data" rule and leave it at that.

The POOL record would then implement multiple CNAMEs, such as:

```
us.example.com.IN CNAME us1.provider.example.
us.example.com. IN CNAME us2.contributed.dom.
us.example.com. IN CNAME www4.example.net.
```

The nameserver would be responsible for cycling through the available results, just as in the case of a round-robin of A or AAAA records. However, instead of returning all available RRs, as with A or AAAA records, you must only return a single record. Otherwise, any additional CNAME results would appear to be allowing a zone with multiple CNAME RRs for a single name, breaking the "CNAME contains other data" rule. The preceding use case is borrowed from an implementation we did for PHP.net to geo-distribute their download mirrors (see the *Geo DNS* section in `Chapter 11`, *DNS Operations and Use Cases*), where they wanted to take their user-contributed mirrors, group them by country code, and create a CNAME RRSet for each country code to each hostname of the contributed mirror.

Most stock nameservers don't support this out of the box. In our case, we used a PowerDNS pipe backend, which we constructed for a Geo DNS implementation.

One has to internally store and rotate the order of results to be handed back, and return the next RR in the order, and only that record. It then moves to the next record in rotation upon reciept of the next query.

# Why can't you have a CNAME with other data?

From RFC 1034:

> *"If a CNAME RR is present at a node, no other data should be present; this ensures that the data for a canonical name and its aliases cannot be different. This rule also insures that a cached CNAME can be used without checking with an authoritative server for other RR types.*

> *CNAME RRs cause special action in DNS software. When a name server fails to find a desired RR in the resource set associated with the domain name, it checks to see if the resource set consists of a CNAME record with a matching class. If so, the name server includes the CNAME record in the response and restarts the query at the domain name specified in the data field of the CNAME record. The one exception to this rule is that queries which match the CNAME type are not restarted."*

> *RFC 1912 (Common DNS Errors) goes on to state quite simply:*

> *"A CNAME record is not allowed to coexist with any other data. In other words, if suzy.podunk.xx is an alias for sue.podunk.xx, you can't also have an MX record for suzy.podunk.edu, or an A record, or even a TXT record. Especially do not try to com- bine CNAMEs and NS records like this!:*

> *podunk.xx. IN NS ns1*

*IN NS ns2*

*IN CNAME mary*

*mary IN A 1.2.3.4*

*This is often attempted by inexperienced administrators as an obvious way to allow your domain name to also be a host. However, DNS servers like BIND will see the CNAME and refuse to add any other resources for that name. Since no other records are allowed to coexist with a CNAME, the NS entries are ignored. Therefore all the hosts in the podunk.xx domain are ignored as well!"*

The easiest way I explain this restriction to people is to imagine a CNAME as akin to the Unix filesystem symbolic link.

In our apex-aliasing case, a query for the SOA or the NS recs of example.com would never return the defined SOA for example.com, but they would be translated into queries for the SOA or NS records of `example.com.cdn-networks- r-us.dom` (the value the CNAME for `example.com` points at).

The authoritative nameserver answering for `example.com` would never return the SOA or NS recs for `example.com.cnd-networks-r-us.dom` because they are outside its zone.

The symbolic link analogy also works well when explaining this in relation to MX handlers:

```
$ORIGIN example.com.
mail IN MX 5 example.com.mailfiters.dom.
mail IN CNAME example.com.mailfilters.dom.
```

In our analogy, the easiest way to visualize why this will not work is because when you then send email to `postmaster@mail.example.com` your MTA will never, in effect, see that address, let alone figure out where the MX handler for `mail.example.com` is. This is because it will instead be looking for the MX for `postmaster@example.com.mailfilters.dom`.

# DYN (Dynamic DNS records)

DYN is a pseudo-record type for handling dynamically updated hostnames that are triggered via `http` or `https` requests (as opposed to *RFC 2136*-style dynamic updates).

They may not be called DYN, they may not be called anything, but rather be managed through a component of a management panel specific to dynamic updates or specific API methods.

The main motivation for doing it this way is to put some logical separation between records that can be modified remotely and other records within the zone that you may want to protect from any possible remote modification.

By doing this, if the authentication credentials on a remote dynamic device are ever compromised, it cannot be used to hijack other records within the domain.

Best practices also dictate using a separate authentication string for the device password instead of the actual password corresponding to the domain user's login credentials. Again, this mitigates total compromise by preventing update credentials on a remote device from being used to log in to the control panel should the device be compromised.

The actual implementation of a DYN record simply creates an A or AAAA record/hostname.

Also see the *Dynamic DNS* section in `Chapter 11`, *DNS Operations and Use Cases*, where we look at the different methods of accomplishing dynamic DNS updates.

# Email forwarders

Email delivery and email forwarding are outside the actual DNS protocol once the MTAs have used DNS to determine where to attempt delivery on a given message.

We mention email forwarders here because, when working with DNS and domain names, this often ends up being your problem. Many registrars, web-hosting providers, and DNS operators provide email forwarding and backup spooling as part of the overall service.

# Generic email forwarding

This means you are providing a mechanism for your users to map or forward messages at their own domain names to addresses at other domains. From a DNS standpoint, when somebody enables this on a domain you manage, you need to set that domain's MX handler to a mail server you control, which has access to the database of mail mappings your users will create.

There are a multitude of methods you can use to store the forwarding data, including:

- Any kind of SQL database
- LDAP
- DBM, DB, btree, cdb, or other kinds of hash files
- Flat files

Most **mail transport agents** (**MTAs**) support reading their tables from any of these formats.

# Separating forwarders from backup spooling via MX records

Your user interface has to be able to discern between domains that are going to be using email forwarding, in which case the MX handler of your mail forwarder has to be the lowest preference MX handler; and those using your system for backup MX.

If you are also providing backup MX spooling/backup MX, you need to be able to detect when that is being invoked. Enter the MX handler of your spoolers as higher numbered preferences than the domain's main MX handler.

As we noted earlier, simply numbering MX handlers as a primary or backup MX does not magically imbue them with these abilities. They must still be configured to either forward or relay mail for the domains for which they are to fulfill those duties.

If you are both forwarding and backup spooling, you should think about your mail pool architecture before you provide this functionality for hundreds or thousands of domains.

Ideally, you would separate mail forwarders and backup spoolers into separate pools. Even if you aren't running separate pools in the early stages (both functions provided by same set of servers), you should still set up separate *logical* paths via your naming scheme:

```
forwardingcustomer.dom.      IN MX .    0 mailfwd.registrarco.dom.
....
backupcustomer.dom.          IN MX      0 mx.backupcustomer.com.
                             IN MX      5 backupmx.registrarco.dom.
```

When the time comes, all you need do is create the separate mail pool (or server) and renumber the appropriate record. In the early stages, `backupmx.registrarco.dom` and `mailfwd.registrarco.dom` may be the same server or server pool, but as the operations and the mail load scales, it is a lot easier to separate these functions later because the naming scheme has set it up in advance.

# How to handle a large volume of email – where to cluster?

As the mail volume increases, you may hit the point where you need to cluster several servers (or hundreds!) to handle the load. Because load balancing can be "sort of " achieved via DNS round-robin and a round-robin is quite easy to set up, one option is to go this route:

```
mailfwd.registrarco.dom.  IN A 205.210.42.40
mailfwd.registrarco.dom.  IN A 205.210.42.41
mailfwd.registrarco.dom.  IN A 205.210.42.42
```

This lets the DNS balance the load between your mail servers. If you do this, be sure to keep low TTLs on the records in case you need to remove an overloaded server from the pool:

```
mailfwd.registrarco.dom.  120 IN A 205.210.42.41
mailfwd.registrarco.dom.  120 IN A 205.210.42.42
mailfwd.registrarco.dom.  120 IN A 205.210.42.43
```

If one of the members of your mail pool becomes overloaded or degraded, you can remove its DNS entry from the RRSet, and then use a firewall rule (or a kernel rule on the server via ipchains or iptables, for example) to block port 25 inbound while the server runs down its remaining queue.

You could also spread the load using multiple MX handlers with the same preference:

```
registrarwebmail.dom 120 IN MX 5 mail1.registrarco.dom.
registrarwebmail.dom 120 IN MX 5 mail1.registrarco.dom.
registrarwebmail.dom 120 IN MX 5 mail1.registrarco.dom.
```

Another approach, and my preferred method, is to use a load balancer in front of your mail pool. If the cost of commercial load-balancing hardware is prohibitive to your organization, there are several open source load balancers that can be run on commodity hardware.

# Summary

In this chapter, we learned about what is involved in managing the operational functions associated with use cases, that they are not DNS per se, but frequently managed from within the same scope as the DNS operations.

On their own, providing these functions for a single or small number of domains is not rocket science. Subtle issues begin to emerge when scaling into the higher orders of magnitude, such as migrating the IP address on a couple of hundred thousand URL forwarders, or relaying millions of email messages per day across thousands of domains.

# References

1. This used to be unheard of, but with initiatives such as the **Internet Security Research Group's (ISRG)**(`https://en.wikipedia.org/wiki/Internet_Security_Research_Group`) LetsEncrypt, TLS certificates are now much more accessible.
2. Historically, PowerDNS earlier versions used to support a native email forwarding record called MBOXFW, but it has since been discontinued.

# Common Nameserver Software

**9**

In this chapter, we will look at various nameserver daemons that are available to run on your authoritative nameservers. In the `Chapter 12`, *Nameserver Considerations*, we look at using more than one type of nameserver daemon and whether you would want to.

It never hurts to be familiar with more than one type of nameserver, and depending on your use case, you may find that one of the alternatives suits your organization better than the common default of a BIND server.

Further, you may be in a position where you are managing multiple zones and some may be mirroring from external masters while others may be allowing third-party mirrors or both. In these cases, it is not uncommon to be interfacing with nameservers different than your own, so it's always good to understand how to integrate with them.

An excellent resource that dives deep into the various options out there is Jan-Piet Mens "Alternative DNS Servers" (`https://jpmens.net/2010/10/29/alternative-dns-servers-the-book-as-pdf/`), which is now available for free as a PDF.

Because the material in this chapter could easily fill a book on its own, I've tried to keep the scope limited to the basic issues. In some cases I used the following format:

- A brief overview of it (who created it, where it came from, essential concepts)
- Things to know about this server (considerations factoring into a decision to deploy it)

And then I'm making an assumption that most readers are operating out of a BIND environment. We look at things such as:

- Basic quick-start configuration
- How to convert your bind format data into the nameserver's native format
- How to have this type of nameserver slave from a bind master

- How to have a bind secondary slave from this type of master
- Logging
- Resources/where to get more information

In that context, we will cover the following in this chapter:

- BIND
- BIND-DLZ
- PowerDNS
- NSD
- Tinydns
- Knot DNS

# BIND

Originally created by students at UCB, Paul Vixie took over BIND maintenance in 1988 and it is still the most popular authoritative nameserver in existence. It remains the default nameserver in most *nix and Windows environments, and is one of the first nameservers ever written.

Because there is so much existing material on BIND, we're not going to rehash it all here. Readers wishing to learn about setup and configuration specific to BIND nameservers should check out Cricket Liu and Paul Albitz's **DNS and Bind** (O'Reilly), or Ron Aitcheson's **Pro DNS & Bind** (Apress) or his free online version, DNS ForRocket Scientists (`http://www.zytrax.com/books/dns/`).

What we will briefly go over here is the current status of BIND and where it will go next.

BIND 9 is maintained by **ISC** (originally the **Internet Software Consortium**, now the Internet Systems Consortium), which also operates the "F" root server, `f.root-servers.net`.

The successor to BIND 9 was intended to be BIND 10; a complete rewrite of the nameserver. After a version was released in April 2014, the initiative was suspended by the ISC.

The successor project has been renamed **Bundy** and work continues as an integrated authoritative DNS and DHCP server. See: `https://github.com/bundy-dns/bundy`.

BIND 9 is still very much alive and continues to be actively developed and maintained.

# BIND-DLZ

http://bind-dlz.sourceforge.net/

BIND DLZ is a patch for BIND 9 that enables **DLZ (Dynamically-Loaded Zones)**. This project was an effort to make it easier to manage large-scale DNS environments with respect to adding new zones on the fly and maintaining existing ones.

Until BIND 9 added dynamic zone additions and deletions (version 9.7.2), this could become a problem when operating at scale. See the **Adding new zones to busy BIND servers** below.

BIND-DLZ remained relevant after the advent of BIND 9's dynamic adds and deletions because it made it possible to run a BIND 9 nameserver using alternative backend data stores for the zone data, such as MySQL, PostgreSQL, and LDAP. However, BIND has also since added its own DLZ drivers, accomplishing much of the same functionality.

Those considering a method to enable database storage for DNS zonedata may be better off looking at PowerDNS, which was built for this from the outset and comes in at much higher performance benchmarks than BIND-DLZ.

At the time of writing, the sourceforge project seems to still be alive, but it remains to be seen what will happen to BIND-DLZ.

# Adding new zones to busy BIND 9 servers (in the olden days)

Traditionally when operating under BIND, a new zone would not be available until the server was at least reconfigured. Doing so would cause a momentary hang in nameerver responsiveness, lasting a fraction of a section to a few seconds, or even longer when serving many zones on slower machines.

This necessitated some thought around how to approach adding new zones to large-scale production environments. There are two approaches: spooling new addition for periodic reloads or processing right away in a non-disruptive manner.

Spool new additions for periodic reloads, for example, once per hour. However since most Top-Level Domains now update in real-time, it's desirable (and frequently expected) that a newly registered domain, or a newly added zone, is available on the designated new nameservers right away as well.

Further, there are numerous country code TLDs that will not update their zone with a child zone's nameservers until those nameservers have been tested and confirmed to be operational and answering authoritatively for it. This is technically how new zones are intended to be delegated.

In these cases, the parent TLD will not delegate until after this spool of new additions is processed.

Process right away in a non-disruptive manner. One could add new domains as they come in and run reconfigs as required. However, you would then be faced with minor "outages" on each nameserver node for the few seconds it takes to reload. You could just live with that (after all, the remote resolver is just going to retry the next authoritative nameserver, it'll be fine–unless they're *all* reconfiguring at the same time!).

In an anycast environment, you could automate a process where the local node's BGP announcement is dropped while the reconfig runs and then re-announced once it's finished. On the surface it seems an elegant solution, however if this happens often enough, your upstream transit providers may view your constant "route-flapping" as a problem and start ignoring or dampening your route announcements.

If each POP in your nameserver deployment is a cluster of nameservers, behind a load balancer, you could simply remove the backend node being reconfigured from the distribution.

None of the solutions was optimal, especially the busier your environment got. Ideally, you would be able to dynamically add new zones to busy nameservers and not have to worry about reconfigging them in order to start answering authoritatively for them.

BIND-DLZ enabled this reality before BIND 9 added dynamically-added zones in version 9.7.2.

Other nameservers, such as PowerDNS, made this a non-issue from the outset.

# PowerDNS

PowerDNS is an authoritative nameserver (distinct from the PowerDNS Recursor) that can be described as a core nameserver engine that utilizes one or more backends. Those backends support a myriad of database platforms and different nameserver emulators.

For example, there is a BIND backend to PowerDNS, which lets you run your server with native BIND-style zonefiles.

You can specify multiple backends and a query will be attempted in each backend, in order, until a match is found.

Finally, the end user can code their own custom backends for PowerDNS, making it one of the most versatile of the prime-time-ready nameservers we've ever worked with.

# Things to know

The ANY qtype has special importance to powerdns.

Assume that the ANY qtype is used internally on essentially *every* inbound query. That is, when PowerDNS receives a query from the outside world, when it relays that query to a given backend, the qtype the backend sees is almost always ANY.

The backend will process the ANY query and send back all relevant records. It is at that point that the PowerDNS core engine will extract the records, matching the initial inbound qtype and return those records to the querying resolver.

# The Supermaster (auto-adding new zones to secondaries)

You can configure various powerdns **supermasters** for slave/secondary nodes. A supermaster means that when the slave nameserver received a NOTIFY packet for a given domain, it will automagically add the domain to its local config and go ahead and do an initial zone transfer for it.

For example, using the **gmysql** backend, you do this by adding an entry to the **supermasters** table:

```
mysql> select * from supermasters;

+--------------+----------------------+---------+
| ip           | nameserver           | account |
+--------------+----------------------+---------+
| 64.68.198.91 | ns1.mainserver.dom   | xfr0    |
```

You need to make sure that the hostname listed in the nameserver field matches one of the NS RRSet for a given domain being added as a slave.

If it doesn't, you will see an error along the lines of:

```
Oct 13 13:54:54 pdns0 pdns[16247]: Unable to find backend willing to host
example.dom for potential potential supermaster 64.68.198.91
```

The reason why, is because:

```
$ dig +short -t ns example.dom @64.68.198.91 ns1.example.dom
ns2.example.dom ns3.example.dom
```

There is no matching hostname in the supermasters nameserver column. We need to add an additional supermaster entry:

```
mysql> select * from supermasters;

+--------------+----------------------+---------+
| ip           | nameserver           | account |
+--------------+----------------------+---------+
| 64.68.198.91 | ns1.mainserver.dom   | xfr0    |
| 64.68.198.91 | ns1.example.dom      | xfr0    |
```

This means that in a large-scale nameserver environment, where you may be hosting hundreds or thousands of zones from disparate third party hosts, where they may be using unique NS records (such as **vanity nameservers**), you may end up with multiple entries in the supermasters table with the same IP address, but each having a unique nameserver value.

When the stars do align, we see the magic happen:

```
Oct 14 19:55:09 pdns0 pdns[16247]: Created new slave zone 'example.dom'
from supermaster 64.68.198.91
```

# Installation

Use your favorite package manager to install `pdns-server`, you can update your package managers to use `repo.powerdns.com` to obtain the latest versions.

# Lua integration

You don't need Lua to run PowerDNS, but perhaps the reason you are running it is because you want something a little beyond the standard.

Enter Lua (http://www.lua.org/), which PowerDNS integrates with; it is a lightweight, portable scripting language. It was invented in Brazil and originally intended to be used in embedded systems, it lends itself well to the function of providing inline processing and scripting of DNS responses within PowerDNS. From there, one can add enhancements and compliments, such as load balancing, hostname failover, and GeoDNS.

You can install the various backend plugins via your package manager, in this case pdns-backend-lua (you may need to install the readline-dev package for your o/s).

In version 4.2, PowerDNS introduced a LUA record, which takes the integration to the level of a DNS record with inline LUA scripting:

```
www     IN LUA A      "ifportup(443, {'192.0.2.1', '192.0.2.2'})"
```

It can get quite sophisticated:

```
www IN LUA A ("ifportup(443, {'192.0.2.1', '192.0.2.2', '198.51.100.1'}" ",
{selector='closest'}) ")
```

Anything scriptable in LUA can be used in these records to output a DNS RRtype like an **A** or **CNAME** .

# Configuring powerdns

The main configuration file is pdns.conf, most often found in /etc/powerdns.

Convention has an include directive in the config, which specifies a subdirectory where you can put configurations for each powerdns backend:

```
include-dir=/etc/powerdns/pdns.d
```

If we look in that directory, we'll see it would include the following:

```
$ ls pdns.d
pdns.local pdns.local.gmysql.conf pdns.simplebind.conf
```

Most of the main configuration is well documented within the comments and straightforward.

Of importance are your **launch** directives, which specify which backends to launch on startup, and in what order a query will traverse these backends:

```
####################################

# launch Which backends to launch and order to query them in
#
launch=mypipe,gmysql

pipe-command=/usr/local/mybackend-py/run_dns.sh
```

In this example, we are launching the **gmysql** backend and our own custom backend specified via `pipe-command` (custom pipe backends are described in later in this section).

When the core PowerDNS engine receives a query, it will then pass it to the `gmysql` backend, then if no responses are returned from it, it will send the query to the next available backend: `run_dns.sh`.

# Converting BIND-style zone data into powerdns

The **zone2sql** utility bundled with PowerDNS can convert BIND-style zonefiles into (nearly) all of the generic SQL backends.

That said, the easiest way to migrate your zones, especially when you have a lot of them, is to leverage the supermaster capability.

If you have lots of zones to transfer, remember to adjust your bind config to allow a lot of concurrent transfers to the powerdns server:

```
options {
        transfers-out 1024;
        transfers-per-ns 200;
        serial-query-rate 1000;
        allow-transfer {
                104.236.6.173; // pdns1.zoneedit.com
        };
};
```

# Slaving PowerDNS from BIND masters

Most of the PowerDNS backends can act as a secondary to a BIND master out of the box.

Using **gmysql**, you simply need to add the domain as a "SLAVE" type to the domains table with the IP address of the master nameserver:

```
+--------+-------+--------------+------------+-------+-----------------+
| id | name | master | last_check | type | notified_serial | account |
+--------+-------+--------------+------------+-------+-----------------+
| 141397 | x9.to | 64.68.198.91 | 1446574889 | SLAVE | NULL | NULL |
+--------+-------+--------------+------------+-------+-----------------+
1 row in set (0.00 sec)
```

PowerDNS will respond to incoming NOTIFY packets like any other bind secondary nameserver.

Recall that if the master nameserver is a designated **supermaster** and the domain does not yet exist within PowerDNS, it will add it to its configuration upon receiving its first NOTIFY from the master.

# Using a PowerDNS master to BIND secondaries

When running in **master** mode, PowerDNS can send NOTIFY packets when a zone is updated, so that a BIND secondary will treat that as any other inbound NOTIFY and transfer the zone from its configured master.

This is controlled from within the PowerDNS **domainmetadata** table.

To set up a given zone to be mirrored by a remote BIND slave, or any other nameserver daemon that can respond to a NOTIFY packet and initiate a zone transfer, you first need to find out its internal `domain_id`:

```
mysql> selectid fromdomains wherename='tap.ca';

+--------+

| id     |

+--------+

| 141135 |

+--------+

1 row in set(0.01 sec)
```

Use this ID when you add rows to **domainmetadata**, to allow the transfer:

```
mysql> insert into domainmetadata (domain_id, kind, content)
values(141135,'ALLOW-AXFR-FROM',' 64.68.198.97');
Query OK, 1 row affected (0.00 sec)
```

(You can also set the global `allow-axfr-ips` in `pdns.conf`, be sure to turn off `disable-axfr` if you do).

PowerDNS will send NOTIFY packets to all NS RRs in the zone, if there are any others you want notified (such as warm spare nameservers not in your active delegation), you would also add `also-notify`:

```
mysql> insert into domainmetadata (domain_id, kind, content)
values(141135,'ALSO-NOTIFY',' 64.68.196.18');
Query OK, 1 row affected (0.00 sec)
```

At this point, your remote nameserver is now ready to mirror this zone, while any other remote PowerDNS servers that were mirroring it via the gmysql backend database replication will continue to do so.

The capabilities added via `domainmetadata` go beyond configuring your `axfr-allow` and `also-notify` equivalents.

Both TSIG and GSS-TSIG are supported to secure your zone transfers and securely facilitate the associated key exchange.

This is also another point where one could bolt in the Lua integration to add scripts which can further operate on a zone as it transfers in.

# Adding custom backends to PowerDNS

The design premise of PowerDNS is a core nameserver engine that proxies DNS queries to one or more backends, takes those responses back, optionally processing them further via Lua hooks, before serving the results back to the resolver originating the query.

There are already numerous pipe backends (`https://doc.powerdns.com/md/authoritative/`) ranging from various nameserver backends such as BIND, and an experimental TinyDNS backend to database backends such as MySQL, Oracle, PostgreSQL, and even GeoIP–a geodns backend.

It's a powerful approach made even more so by the ability to add one's own backend to the PowerDNS core engine.

In my very first attempt to do so, I made a simple md5 backend, which would respond to TXT queries with their MD5 hash, and if given a query of an MD5 hash, would attempt to decode it by looking into a local database of MD5 hashes. It had no practical use, but it was a good way to experiment with the backend capabilities of PowerDNS, and demonstrates that you are only limited by your own imagination when it comes to thinking up non-standard use cases for customized backends.

Since then, we've used custom PowerDNS backends to create:

- **Wildcard/NXDOMAIN server**: Domains whose registrations have expired are delegated to special purpose nameservers, which use a custom backend to wildcard the domains to send traffic to a "This domain has expired" page.
- **geoDNS server**: The easyDNS geoDNS implementation (version 2) uses a custom backend to map the IP address of the originating resolver IP to a Maxmind geoIP database and then serves back any corresponding records in place for the querying region.

A pipe backend (or "coprocess") can be written in any language, it reads queries on a file handle, default STDIN, and will reply via another file handle, defaulting to STDOUT.

The PowerDNS core will provide an initial handshake to the coprocess, which is simply the HELO string followed by a space and an integer describing in what format it will use pipe-abi-version:

```
pipe-abi-version = 1 [ default ]

Q qname qclass qtype id remote-ip-address

pipe-abi-version = 2

Q qname qclass qtype id remote-ip-address local-ip-address

pipe-abi-version = 3

Q qname qclass qtype id remote-ip-address local-ip-address edns-subnet-
address
```

Check out this extremely simplified adaptation of the powerdns perl example:

```perl
#!/usr/bin/perl -w
# sample PowerDNS Coprocess backend
#

use strict;


$|=1;                                      # no buffering

my $line=<>;
chomp($line);

unless($line eq "HELO\t1") {
        print "FAIL\n";
        print STDERR "Received '$line'\n";
        <>;
        exit;
}
print "OK      Sample backend firing up\n";        # print our banner

while(<>)
{
        print STDERR "$$ Received: $_";
        chomp();
        my @arr=split(/\t/);
        if(@arr<6) {
                print "LOG     PowerDNS sent unparseable line\n";
                print "FAIL\n";
```

```
                next;
        }


        # note! the qname is what PowerDNS asks the backend. It need not be
what the internet asked PowerDNS!
        my ($type,$qname,$qclass,$qtype,$id,$ip)=split(/\t/);

        if(($qtype eq "SOA" || $qtype eq "ANY") && $qname eq "example.com")
{
                print STDERR "$$ Sent SOA records\n";
                print "DATA     $qname $qclass SOA     3600     -1
ns1.example.com ahu.example.com 2008080300 1800 3600 604800 3600\n";
        }
        if(($qtype eq "NS" || $qtype eq "ANY") && $qname eq "example.com")
{
                print STDERR "$$ Sent NS records\n";
                print "DATA     $qname $qclass NS     3600     -1
ns1.example.com\n";
                print "DATA     $qname $qclass NS     3600     -1
ns2.example.com\n";
        }
        if(($qtype eq "TXT" || $qtype eq "ANY") && $qname eq "example.com")
{
                print STDERR "$$ Sent NS records\n";
                print "DATA     $qname $qclass TXT    3600     -1
\"hallo allemaal!\"\n";
        }
        if(($qtype eq "A" || $qtype eq "ANY") && $qname eq
"webserver.example.com") {
                print STDERR "$$ Sent A records\n";
                print "DATA     $qname $qclass A     3600     -1
1.2.3.4\n";
                print "DATA     $qname $qclass A     3600     -1
1.2.3.5\n";
                print "DATA     $qname $qclass A     3600     -1
1.2.3.6\n";
        }
        elsif(($qtype eq "CNAME" || $qtype eq "ANY") && $qname eq
"www.example.com") {
                print STDERR "$$ Sent CNAME records\n";
                print "DATA     $qname $qclass CNAME  3600     -1
webserver.example.com\n";
        }


        print STDERR "$$ End of data\n";
        print "END\n";
}
```

Here, it is important to reiterate that $qtype will almost *always* be ANY. Return all records that match the query for all RR types, then let PowerDNS core sort out what gets sent back to the client.

Also see `https://doc.powerdns.com/md/authoritative/backend-pipe/`.

# PowerDNS wrap-up

I consider PowerDNS the "Swiss Army knife" of nameservers. If you have some outlier use case that absolutely nobody else supports (or all other implementations are proprietary), you can do it with PowerDNS either via Lua hooks or with a designer pipe-backend.

It also lends itself well to upgrading from almost any dilapidated environment because of the various backends available; in the same vein, it is great for custom integrations into your own environments because of the myriad choices one has for database backends.

Because of the numerous backends, including the BIND backend, PowerDNS is one of the easiest drop-in replacements for BIND, for example when seeking to implement nameserver heterogeneity.

# NSD

Written by **NLnet Labs**, the same team behind the Unbound resolver and OpenDNSSEC. NSD stands quite simply for name server daemon. Several of the global internet roots run using NSD, thereby affording the root servers of the internet **nameserver heterogeneity** (which we cover in the `Chapter 12`, *Nameserver Considerations*).

# Things to know

NSD is one of the easier nameservers to set up. It uses BIND-style zonefiles, which it transparently imports and compiles into a native format.

## No native support for RFC 2136 dynamic DNS

There is no native support for dynamically updating records via the "UPDATE" operation. As we see in `Chapter 11`, *DNS Operations and Use Cases*, most dynamic DNS offerings don't happen via this method anyway.

## Notifies to slaves

In contrast with BIND, which will send a NOTIFY to each listed NS RR in the zone when updated, NSD does not. It will only send NOTIFY packets to the `notify:` entries in the config file.

# Installation and setup

Once you've used your system's preferred package manager install NSD, make sure your control channel is set up:

```
root@nsd1:/etc/nsd# nsd-control-setup setup in directory /etc/nsd
generating nsd_server.key

Generating RSA private key, 3072 bit long modulus

......++

...................................++ e is 65537 (0x10001)

nsd_control.key exists

create nsd_server.pem (self signed certificate) create nsd_control.pem
(signed client certificate)

Signature ok subject=/CN=nsd-control Getting CA Private Key

Setup success. Certificates created. Enable in nsd.conf file to use
```

Create a `db dir`:

```
root@nsd1:/etc/nsd# mkdir -p /var/db/nsd root@nsd1:/etc/nsd# chown nsd.nsd
/var/db/nsd root@nsd1:/etc/nsd# nsd-control start
```

And edit `/etc/nsd/nsd.conf` for your setup. Most of the config is somewhat self-explanatory.

What is unique to nsd are the **pattern** sections of the configuration, where you can define a label that will apply the subsequent configuration to zones attached to that label:

```
pattern:

name: "foo"

zonefile: "foo/%s.zone"

request-xfr: 64.68.198.97 NOKEY

request-xfr: 64.68.198.91 NOKEY

allow-notify: 64.68.198.83 NOKEY

allow-notify: 64.68.198.183 NOKEY

pattern:

name: "bar"

zonefile: "bar/%s.zone"

request-xfr: 64.68.198.97 NOKEY

request-xfr: 64.68.198.91 NOKEY

allow-notify: 64.68.198.83 NOKEY

allow-notify: 64.68.198.183 NOKEY
```

# nsd wrap-up

I enjoyed working with NSD immensely while writing this section, and was very impressed with its speed and ease of configuration. At the time of writing we are running one NSD nameserver as a beta in our test environment (130,000+ domains) and it was the simplest nameserver variant to set up, import our data, and get into realtime sync with our environment.

NSD supports commonly used features that BIND does, such as DNSSEC and IPv6. Other than the need to convert one's config file format, it becomes, in my mind, one of the easiest drop-in replacements for BIND nameservers when seeking to implement nameserver heterogeneity.

# djbdns/tinydns

Written by the colorful and sometimes controversial Dr. Daniel J. Bernstein, who also created the qmail program, djbdns is a package of modular DNS programs created out of a dissatisfaction with what Dr. Bernstein felt were incessant and overly frequent security flaws found in BIND (then in version 4 and later 8).

The authoritative nameserver component of the package is **tinydns**. The recursor is **dnscache**. This is unlike BIND, which can be configured to run as authoritative, or configured as a resolver, or misconfigured to run as both.

djbdns is a nice, tight modular package and is generally secure. It doesn't typically use BIND-style zone transfers (AXFR or IXFR) but recommends to sync its data across nodes via rsync over ssh.

There are components to execute AXFR zone transfers to facilitate inter-operations with BIND and other nameserver types.

## Things to know

No native support for RFC 2136 dynamic DNS.

As with NSD, there is no native support for dynamically updating records via the UPDATE operation.

In this case, there is a patch available (`https://sites.google.com/site/dmoulding/dns-update-djb`) to add support.

## No native support for DNSSEC

There is no native support for DNSSEC security extensions in tinydns. Dr. Bernstein publicly doubts its efficacy and instead approaches DNS security a different way: **dnscurve**

A third party project, `http://www.tinydnssec.org/`, has been created to add DNSSEC to tinydns.

# No responses for non-authoritative domains

When tinydns receives a query for record in a zone for which it is not authoritative, it does not respond at all. It leaves it to the querying server (the resolver) to time out on its own schedule.

# TCP not supported in main daemon

The tinydns server does not listen on TCP, it responds only to UDP queries. Operations requiring TCP are handled by the separate **axfrdns** program.

There are real-world situations where we need TCP. Some ccTLDs will not delegate a domain unless its nameservers respond to TCP queries, and in cases where the TC bit is set in a response, the retry happens over TCP.

# Supports IPv6, SRV, NATPR, etc, natively, out-of-box (mostly)

You may find references around the interweb that djbdns doesn't natively support IPv6 AAAA records (or SRV, or NAPTR) without a patch.

The fact is tinydns supports all the DNS RR types, if it does not have an explicit nomenclature for it, then it will use the genericsyntax with the RR type integer code:

```
$ grep marco.example.net data

+marco.example.net:205.210.42.111:7200
:marco.example.net:35:00d00201P07SIP53D2U0004137sip04137udp11joinvideo03net
:marco.example.net:35:00Z00201P07SIP53D2T0004137sip04137tcp11joinvideo03net
```

When we do a lookup:

```
$ dig +short -t naptr marco.example.net @tdns1.zoneedit.com
100 50 "P" "SIP+D2U" "" _sip._udp.example.net. 90 50 "P" "SIP+D2T" ""
_sip._tcp.example.net.
```

In our data conversion benchmarks with tinydns, when we axfr-ed in every zone, all RR types were suitably imported and query-able, including **IPv6**, **SRV**, and **NATPR**.

# All zones in a single datafile

All zones are compiled into a single datafile in .CDB format (`data.cdb`) which is recompiled by `tinydns-data` when there are updates.

data.cdb is a type of hash where the keys are the queries and the values are the responses.

In the following example snippet, the bolded hostnames are the record keys, the remainder of the record, and the values:

```
+www.example.com:198.51.100.4:0:4000000038af1379
+www.example.com:198.51.100.7::4000000038af1379
```

# How time is handled

Timestamps in data records arc in **TAI64** format and they have some interesting properties based on how you use them.

If you create a record with a timestamp in the future but a TTL of zero, that record will *expire* when the timestamp elapses.

Conversely, if you create a record with a non-zero TTL and a timestamp in the future, that means it will *not* resolve until *after* the timestamp passes.

This provides some nifty mechanisms to schedule maintenance windows and migrations.

# Installation from source

The other nameservers in this chapter can simply be installed via your system's package manager. Not tinydns. There is a **dbndns** package for Debian and Ubuntu, which is a fork of the djbdns suite that includes the IPv6 patch otherwise required to add support for tinydns to listen via IPv6 addresses.

The project homepage is at `http://cr.yp.to/djbdns/` and installation instructions are at `http://cr.yp.to/djbdns/install.html`

Before you can install djbdns, you need to install two other packages first:

- daemontools: `http://cr.yp.to/daemontools/install.html`
- ucspi-tcp: `http://cr.yp.to/ucspi-tcp/install.html`

## daemontools

Create /packages and download the package into it (the installer and startup scripts will expect this path to be here):

```
$ mkdir -p /package chmod 1755 /package cd /package

$ wget http://cr.yp.to/daemontools/daemontools-0.76.tar.gz

--2015-08-01 18:20:57-- http://cr.yp.to/daemontools/daemontools-0.76.tar.gz

Resolving cr.yp.to (cr.yp.to)... 131.155.70.13, 131.155.70.11 Connecting to
cr.yp.to (cr.yp.to)|131.155.70.13|:80... connected. HTTP request sent,
awaiting response... 200 OK

Length: unspecified [application/x-gzip] Saving to:
?daemontools-0.76.tar.gz?

daemontools-0.76.tar [ <=> ] 36.11K 115KB/s in 0.3s

2015-08-01 18:20:58 (115 KB/s) - ?daemontools-0.76.tar.gz? saved [36975]
```

Then build the package with a simple:

```
./package/install
```

Different *nix systems use different startup methodologies.

On my debian install, it is implemented by appending /etc/rc.local to the following:

```
csh -cf '/command/svscanboot &'
```

You can also just run it straight as /command/svscanboot & because it is just a symbolic link to /package/admin/daemontools/command/svscanboot, which is a bourne shell script. Whichever method you use, be sure to adjust your system's startup process (in my case, /etc/rc.local) accordingly.

The instructions then recommend rebooting in order to activate svscan.

### ucspi-tcp

First download and unpack the package:

```
$ wget http://cr.yp.to/ucspi-tcp/ucspi-tcp-0.88.tar.gz

--2015-08-01 18:53:02-- http://cr.yp.to/ucspi-tcp/ucspi-tcp-0.88.tar.gz

Resolving cr.yp.to (cr.yp.to)... 131.155.70.13, 131.155.70.11

Connecting to cr.yp.to (cr.yp.to)|131.155.70.13|:80... connected. HTTP
request sent, awaiting response... 200 OK

Length: unspecified [application/x-gzip] Saving to: ?ucspi-tcp-0.88.tar.gz?

ucspi-tcp-0.88.tar.g [ <=> ] 51.78K 111KB/s in 0.5s 2015-08-01 18:53:02
(111 KB/s) - ?ucspi-tcp-0.88.tar.gz? saved [53019]

gunzip ucspi-tcp-0.88.tar tar -xf ucspi-tcp-0.88.tar cd ucspi-tcp-0.88
```

Then make and install the following:

```
$ make
...
$ make install check
```

Now we're ready to build djbdns...

Download and unpack http://cr.yp.to/djbdns/djbdns-1.05.tar.gz:

```
$ make setup check
```

# Getting your bind data into tinydns

The two main approaches for getting your bind data into this format remains the same:
either write or use a parser that will do the conversion, or if your target nameserver
supports AXFR (which tinydns does) and you have the ability to open the BIND master for
transfers to your tinydns client, then you can zone-transfer each zone and let the
nameserver itself do the work of converting the data into its native format.

The preferred method in tinydns is to use the axfr method.

# axfr each zone

You can import your data from your bind servers by allowing transfers to your tinydns server from the bind master:

```
options {
        allow-transfer {
        104.236.132.147; // tdns1.zoneedit.com
        };
};
```

Then from your tinydns client, you simply axfr each zone:

```
$ cd /etc/tinydns/root

# foreach domain you would do:

$ tcpclient -v  53 axfr-get  zones/.zone tmp/.tmp
```

Once you've transferred all of your zones, you aggregate them into your `data` file and compile it:

```
$ sort -u zones/* > ./data
$ make
```

This generates your `data.cdb`, which tinydns reads its data from, and the good news is the update to the new file is atomic. It can occur while tinydns is running and it won't miss a beat.

The other good news is that this method also takes care of mapping all the RR types tinydns doesn't have explicit native formatting for, such as NAPTR and AAAA.

# Using a parser

There are not a lot of actively supported parser utilities to covert BIND format zonefiles into tinydns format data.

The one I tested with was Daniel Erat's `bind-to-tinydns` (`https://github.com/derat/bind-to-tinydns`).

Again, we run each zonefile through the parser. `bind-to-tinydns` takes the zone's origin and output filename as its arguments and then reads the input zonefile from STDIN:

```
$ for i in `cat domainlist`; do

> echo $i
> ./bind-to-tinydns $i zones/$i.zone
> ./tmp/$i < /zones/primary/$i.zone
> done
```

It coverted our test suite of 130,000 zones in a little under 2 hours on a commodity VPS with 6 GB RAM and dual-core Xeon E5440@2.83 GHz CPUs. We could split this up into multiple jobs running concurrently to cut that time down.

Once we have all our data in tinydns format, we would again aggregate them into our **data** file and compile it for tinydns.

# Slaving from a Bind master

There are various mechanisms to slave a zone from a bind master (or any other master that supports AXFR). We used the **axfr-get** command to initially populate a tinydns server with zones from a master. (Recall, the preferred way to keep tinydns instances in sync with other is via a secure file sync, such as rsync over ssh.)

Russ Nelson wrote axfr.pl (`http://koansys.com/tech/use-djbdns-to-slave-a-zone-from-a-master`), which will traverse a directory structure that corresponds to the various master IPs and transfer the zones.

However, there is no native mechanism for tinydns to listen for NOTIFY packets and then transfer the zone when it gets one, nor are there any third-party utilities to do this. The consensus among the tinydns community is that on-demand zone transfers add additional complexity and that syncing between servers is best accomplished via methods such as rsync.

This isn't terribly practical in a situation where you're managing a lot of domains from a disparate set of external masters, you don't have control over many of the masters, or you are trying to implement nameserver heterogeneity.

# Slaving bind from a tinydns master

djbdns has a separate service called **axfrdns**, which listens for tcp queries and provides zone transfers for authorized clients.

First you would set up axfrdns as a service at which point you will then have the ability to allow remote nameservers to slave all or specific zones on the local tinydns master. It can get just as granular as any bind config.

Imagine your master IP address is `10.0.4.56`:

```
axfrdns-conf Gaxfrdns Gdnslog /etc/axfrdns /etc/tinydns 10.0.4.56
ln -s /etc/axfrdns /service
```

The following entry disallows `axfers` by default:

```
echo ':allow,AXFR=""' > /etc/axfrdns/tcp
```

Now we can add specific entries.

To allow a remote nameserver with IP address `192.168.23.45` to mirror all of the locally configured zones, simply add the following line to your database (as configured in the preceding step):

```
echo '192.168.23.45:allow' >> /etc/axfrdns/tcp
```

To allow another nameserver with `10.0.45.200` to mirror `foo.dom`:

```
echo '10.0.45.200:allow,AXFR="foo.dom"' >> /etc/axfrdns/tcp
```

Multiple zones can be specified by separating them with slashes, or you could enter multiple lines:

```
echo '10.0.45.200:allow,AXFR="example.com/example.net/example.org"' >>
/etc/axfrdns/tcp echo '10.0.45.200:allow,AXFR="example.ca"' >>
/etc/axfrdns/tcp
echo '10.0.45.200:allow,AXFR="example.io"' >> /etc/axfrdns/tcp
```

The server will allow these transfers when you rehash your database:

```
cd /etc/axfrdns make
```

The only thing left is that axfrdns doesn't have inherent support for sending NOTIFY packets when a local zone is updated.

There are standalone utilities and scripts which can simply send a NOTIFY packet for you, such as a tinydns version of Joe Backus' **dnsnotify**.

Whatever process you are using to update your tinydns master, you need only add a hook to invoke your dnsnotify to send a packet to your remote BIND (or any other nameserver that supports it).

# tinydns wrap-up

Dr. Bernstein is a colourful figure within the DNS community, and some may say that the limitations or omissions in tinydns preclude it from being considered in many environments. That said, I am reliably informed that Facebook's DNS infrastructure is run using tinydns, albeit a heavily customized version, which means this software is holding up one of the busiest platforms in existance.

Also see `http://www.lifewithdjbdns.com/`.

# Knot DNS

The `Knot DNS` server is a relatively recent entrant into the space. There is not even a chapter on Knot DNS in Jan-Piet Men's **Alternative DNS Servers** as that was published before it existed. It was created by CZ.NIC, the team that operates the .CZ Top-Level Domain and Knot DNS also powers the .CZ TLD.

Parenthetically, the team that made Knot DNS also created `FRED`, an EPP-compliant domain and ENUM registry that is also open source, something which may be of great value to those seeking to operate a Top-Level Domain.

## Installation

Download the source from `https://www.knot-dns.cz/download/` or using your favorite package manager, add the `https://deb.knot-dns.cz/knot/` repository:

```
su -
wget -O - https://deb.knot-dns.cz/knot/apt.gpg | apt-key add -
echo "deb https://deb.knot-dns.cz/knot/ $(lsb_release -sc) main" >
/etc/apt/sources.list.d/knot.list
apt-get update
apt-get install knot
```

# Configuration

The configuration is straightforward and self-explanatory, as we can see from the example bare-bones setup:

```
# Example of a very simple Knot DNS configuration.

server:
    listen: 0.0.0.0@53
    listen: ::@53

zone:
  - domain: example.com
    storage: /var/lib/knot/zones/
    file: example.com.zone

log:
  - target: syslog
    any: info
```

(Via https://www.knot-dns.cz/docs/2.6/html/configuration.html#simple-configuration)

Knot DNS provides user-definable zone templates, where you can set up initial values for varying situations and any new zones will assume those values upon initial addition to the system:

```
# Configuration export (Knot DNS 2.6.7)

server:
    listen: [ "0.0.0.0@53", "::@53" ]

log:
  - target: "syslog"
    any: "debug"

acl:
  - id: "acl_master"
    address: "64.68.198.83"
    address: "64.68.198.91"
    action: "notify"

remote:
  - id: "xfr0"
    address: "64.68.198.83@53"
    address: "64.68.198.91@53"
```

```
template:
  - id: "default"
    storage: "/var/lib/knot"
acl:
  - id: "acl_master"
    address: "64.68.198.83"
    address: "64.68.198.91"
    action: "notify"

remote:
  - id: "master"
    address: "64.68.198.83@53"
    address: "64.68.198.91@53"

template:
  - id: "default"
    storage: "/var/lib/knot"

zone:
  - domain: "example.org."
    master: "master"
    acl: "acl_master"

  - domain: "example.ca."
    master: "master"
    acl: "acl_master"
```

Any setting within a default template can be overridded within a specific zone's configuration.

# knotc – the Knot DNS controller

The nameserver daemon is `knotd`, while `knotc` is the command interpreter interface to control operations. Using `knotc` most configuration options and normal course operations can be run dynamically, without the need to edit the configuration file and reload the server.

If you do that, you must first configure and then initiate the configuration database, otherwise your state changes will be lost between restarts:

```
$ knotc     config-init
$ knotc     config-import <your.conf>
```

The command interpreter is actually in Lua (remember the Lua integration from PowerDNS), so you can write elaborate configuration rules with events, loops, and conditionals.

## Slaving zones

Knot supports NOTIFY so it is an easy candidate for slaving to a BIND master, one can use the dynamic configuration ability to add new zones on the fly:

```
$ knotc conf-begin
OK
$ knotc conf-set zone[example.com]
OK
$ knotc conf-set zone[example.com].master  xfr0
OK
$ knotc conf-commit
OK
```

The preceding sequence of commands adds example.com as a secondary zone from the master previously defined as xfr0 in our sample configuration file.

There is also a rollback option to back out of a configuration transaction:

```
$ knotc conf-abort
OK
```

## DNSSEC support

It also takes a lot of the headaches out of DNSSEC and is a great candidate for implementing it if your requirements include it (see Chapter 13, *Securing Your Domains and DNS*):

```
root@knot:/etc/knot# knotc conf-begin
OK
root@knot:/etc/knot# knotc conf-set zone[easybrand.ca].dnssec-signing on
OK
root@knot:/etc/knot# knotc conf-set zone[easybrand.ca].dnssec-policy rsa
OK
root@knot:/etc/knot# knotc conf-commit
OK
```

And we see what happened from our logs:

```
Jun 14 18:59:34 knot knotd[27097]: info: [easybrand.ca.] DNSSEC, signing
zone
Jun 14 18:59:34 knot knotd[27097]: info: [easybrand.ca.] DNSSEC, key, tag
43879, algorithm RSASHA256, KSK, public, ready, active
Jun 14 18:59:34 knot knotd[27097]: info: [easybrand.ca.] DNSSEC, key, tag
44623, algorithm RSASHA256, public, active
Jun 14 18:59:34 knot knotd[27097]: info: [easybrand.ca.] DNSSEC, signing
started
Jun 14 18:59:34 knot knotd[27097]: info: [easybrand.ca.] DNSSEC,
successfully signed
Jun 14 18:59:34 knot knotd[27097]: info: [easybrand.ca.] DNSSEC, next
signing at 2018-06-21T18:59:34
Jun 14 18:59:34 knot knotd[27097]: notice: [easybrand.ca.] DNSSEC, KSK
submission, waiting for confirmation
Jun 14 18:59:34 knot knotd[27097]: info: [easybrand.ca.] zone file updated,
serial 1528838942 -> 1528838943
```

Originally, I ran out of time before my deadline and I had to leave Knot DNS out of the first drafts with an "honourable mention" as an up-and-coming authoratative nameserver. But then as the book was delayed, I took the opportunity to learn a bit more about it and am glad I did. It's another great option in our quest for nameserver diversity.

# Conclusion

In this chapter, we took at look at the more common alternative nameservers to the default BIND. Because we consider nameserver diversity a best practice, we considered these alternatives from the perspective of using them in tandem with BIND or with each other, as opposed to deciding between them.

Of the nameservers we looked at, PowerDNS, NSD, and KnotDNS look to be the easiest drop-in replacements for BIND. PowerDNS is attractive because of its ability to automagically add new domains from trusted masters a way to more easily import large numbers of zones, and the versatility to be obtained from combining multiple, programmable backends.

Knot DNS' dynamically scriptable configuration took a while to get my head around, but it's powerful and lends itself well to complex environments and portfolios.

PowerDNS, NSD, and Knot have all done well to simplify DNSSEC implementation, something that I think will be considered more important as the future unfolds.

Tinydns may seem unweidly and the odd man out, but its adherents swear by it in near—religious zeal. I am informed that Facebook runs its entire DNS infrastructure on tinydns (albeit a heavily customized one), but there you have an instance where tinydns is holding up one of the largest and busiest platforms in existence.

# References

1. Shane Kerr: The Decline And Fall of Bind 10 `https://ripe68.ripe.net/presentations/208-The_Decline_and_Fall_of_BIND_10.pdf` `https://www.isc.org/?faqs=dynamically-loadable-zones`

2. The easyDNS implementation of GeoDNS was initially accomplished using custom PowerDNS backends

3. There are ways to get the original `qtype` to the backend, but for now, if you are not aware of this, you *will* go insane when you try to code a backend that expects to have visibility into the original `qtype`.

4. `https://blog.powerdns.com/2017/12/15/powerdns-authoritative-lua-records/` and `https://doc.powerdns.com/authoritative/lua-records.html`

5. `https://doc.powerdns.com/md/manpages/zone2sql.1/`

6. There isn't actually a defined "BIND-style" file format, rather BIND was the first to use the Master File Format specified in `RFC 1035`

7. `https://doc.powerdns.com/md/authoritative/domainmetadata/`

8. Script from `https://raw.githubusercontent.com/PowerDNS/pdns/master/modules/pipebackend/backend.pl`

9. See: `https://www.nlnetlabs.nl/svn/nsd/trunk/doc/NSD-FOR-BIND-USERS`

10. Full disclosure: our "test environment" is Zoneedit.com, a DNS provider we quietly acquired in 2014, which runs on a freemium model–free DNS with premium add-ons. Because it has a lot of free users, Zoneedit is somewhat of a mad scientist's lab. The adage states, "If you aren't paying for the product, you *are* the product," except at Zoneedit, you're not paying for the product because you're a lab rat, sorry. The flip-side is that many of the really neat things happen on Zoneedit before they happen on our core commercial business, easyDNS. If we roll out a feature that causes hair loss, we want it to happen to the free users, not the paying customers.

11. See his comments at `http://cr.yp.to/djbdns/forgery.html`

12. `https://dnscurve.org/`

13. See `https://cr.yp.to/djbdns/tcp.html`

14. The .CDB ("Constant Database") format was invented by Dr. Bernstein. It is a type of hash that allows multiple values per key. The only operations are "create" and "read". Modifications and deletions are effected by replacing the database with a new version. This can happen on the fly when used by tinydns.

15. `https://cr.yp.to/djbdns/tinydns-data.html`

16. See `http://cr.yp.to/djbdns/tcp.html`

17. `https://github.com/bradpeczka/tinydns-notify`

# 10
# Debugging Without Tears – DNS Diagnostic Tools

Debugging DNS issues can be tricky. There are numerous moving parts to any given DNS lookup, and because they occur under the hood and are abstracted away from the user-facing network functions, you have to know exactly where to look and what to look at to figure out what is happening.

Furthermore, it is not uncommon for users to suspect DNS problems when facing symptoms that are *not* related to DNS. Getting a "404 Not Found" page when you navigate to a website is *not* a DNS issue. Yet it is frequently reported as one.

What follows are various tools that can be used to isolate and diagnose issues. First, we'll look at command-line tools, and then at web-based ones.

In this chapter, we will cover the following topics:

- Command-line-based tools:
    - Whois
    - dig
    - named checkzone and named checkconf
    - dnstop
- Web-based debugging tools:
    - DNSstuff
    - whatismydns
    - dnsviz
    - easyWhois
    - domaintools

# Command line-based tools

I don't know whether I'm old school (or just old!), but it just seems easier, faster, and better to debug DNS problems from the command line. The most commonly used DNS-related diagnostic commands can be counted on to be present on most systems and, if not, they are usually easy to install using your favorite package manager, or, given the nature of DNS, you can just quickly log into another shell where you know they are installed and run your commands from there.

# whois

Regardless of the issue being reported regarding any zone, the first thing I always do is a quick whois lookup for the domain (or parent domain) for the hostname involved.

The are several things I look for in the result, such as the following:

- Are we looking at the correct domain?
- Has the domain expired at the registry?
- What is the registry/registrar status of the domain?
- Is the zone even delegated to the nameservers we expect it to be?
- Is it DNSSEC-signed?

While we covered the components of a Whois record in detail in `Chapter 1`, *The Domain Name Ecosystem*, it is helpful to expand on some of the preceding points, as these points comprise my initial checklist for debugging any problem related to DNS.

# Are we looking at the correct domain?

This may not be as obvious as it seems for a few reasons. First, there is the straightforward case of whether you're looking at the correct domain, absent typos, relevant TLD, hyphens, no hyphens, and all the other mistakes you can make relating a domain name from one party to another.

The not-so-obvious cause is that the domain that may be failing may not actually be the one being reported. This happens in the case of a hostname whose destination points to a CNAME at some other domain, and *that* domain has failed. The rest of this checklist would help you get there.

# Has the domain expired at the registry?

This is a leading cause of all unplanned DNS outages right here. It happens so often, it is the very first thing I check, and I train my staff to check it after they've made sure they are looking at the correct domain.

# What is the Registry/Registrar status of the domain?

Is the domain in clientHold status? That means the Registrar has suspended the domain, and then we need to figure out why. It could be a **Whois Accuracy Process (WAP)**, such as the one we covered in Chapter 3, *Intellectual Property Issues*.

# Is the domain using the expected nameservers?

It is not uncommon, after a domain transfer between registrars, to see trouble tickets wondering why the new DNS settings aren't taking effect. This check reveals when the domain is still delegated to the old nameservers, or to some other nameservers entirely.

There are also circumstances when the nameservers displayed in the Whois record aren't reflecting what is actually happening to the domain.

An example would be when the domain is on **clientHold** status, in which case the nameservers will be listed in the Whois record, but the actual nameserver delegation for the domain will be absent of the TLDs nameservers. This is an important distinction: The nameservers listed in the Whois record don't always absolutely correspond to the delegation in the TLD zone.

Furthermore, if the domain *is* delegated in the parent zone, but both the Whois record and the delegation are showing completely different than the expected nameservers, it could be because the domain is in an expired state and the Registrar has switched the delegation pending a renewal or eventual deletion of the zone, as per *The Domain Expiry Cycle* section in Chapter 1, *The Domain Name Ecosystem*.

Finally, it could also be the case that the Whois server itself has not yet updated to reflect a change that took place in the zone's nameserver delegation.

You would compare your findings here with what is actually present in the TLD zone, using a tool such as **dig**, which is covered next.

## Is it DNSSEC-signed?

The whois output for TLDs that are DNSSEC-signed will show the DNSSEC status for the domain queried. If the zone is signed, one avenue of inspection is the validity of the DNSSEC chain-of-trust and keys.

# How to look at a Whois record for a new TLD

As I write this, a common problem when debugging a new TLD zone is that many command-line whois clients sometimes cannot find the whois server for the new zone. Take a look at the following:

```
$ whois newage.guru
No whois server is known for this kind of object.
```

You can solve this by adding the whois server for all known TLDs to `/etc/whois.conf`; however, that would be subject to revision (as I reviewed this section, I saw a news article that the 1,300th new TLD has been delegated to the root today).

You can also specify `-h <whois_host>` on the command line. All new TLD operators are required to operate their port 43 whois using this format:

```
whois.nic.<TLD>
```

This is what they change it to:

```
$ whois -h whois.nic.guru newage.guru
```

# dig

**Domain Information Groper** (**dig**) is possibly the most-used DNS diagnostic in existence. It is dnssec-aware, can lookup over udp or tcp, and has options to manipulate nearly every aspect of a query packet and then allows the detailed unpacking and examination of the responses.

# Understanding dig responses

The output of a dig command can be split into four main sections (not all of which will be present in all responses). The HEADER and QUESTION sections will always be present. Then there will be ANSWER, ADDITIONAL, and AUTHORITY sections, if their corresponding COUNT header fields are non-zero. Under some circumstances, there may also be an OPT PSEUDOSECTION. These sections correspond to the format of DNS query packets, as outlined in Chapter 5, *A Tale of Two Nameservers*.

In the following sections, we look at the response to the dig lookup. Take a look at the code line:

```
$ dig -t mx easydns.com @dns1.easydns.com
```

# The HEADER section

This is a representation of the DNS response packet. It will contain status codes, flags, and sometimes additional diagnostic output. Look at this code block:

```
; <<>> DiG 9.8.5-P1 <<>> -t mx easydns.com @dns1.easydns.com
```

The first line of the output displays the version of the dig tool itself followed by the command-line arguments it was invoked with.

```
; <<>> DiG 9.8.3-P1 <<>> -t mx easydns.com @dns1.easydns.com
;; global options: +cmd
;; Got answer:
;; ->>HEADER<<- opcode: QUERY, status: NOERROR, id: 20714
;; flags: qr aa rd; QUERY: 1, ANSWER: 1, AUTHORITY: 4, ADDITIONAL: 9
;; WARNING: recursion requested but not available
```

It then unpacks the answer received. Here we can see, from status: NOERROR, that the query was answered without a problem.

Status values are as follows, and are as described in the *Format of a DNS Query* section in Chapter 5, *A Tale of Two Nameservers*.

The **flags** present may include one or more of the following:

- **qr (Query Response):** This bit is set when the packet is a query response.
- **aa (Authoritative Answer):** The response is authoritative, which means it came from one of the authoritative nameservers for the domain. It did not come from a resolver or DNS cache. You should only see this flag when you directly query an authoritative nameserver using @nameserver.

- **ra (Recursion Available)**: The nameserver that responded to this query is available for recursion. Typically ra and aa are mutually exclusive, as authoritative nameservers are generally deliberately configured to not offer recursion.

- **rd (Recursion Desired):** The query was sent requesting recursion; this is the default behavior for dig, and most of the time it doesn't make a difference. If the client (dig) requests recursion and is answered by a server that isn't offering it, there will be no `ra` flag. You can override sending rd using the `+norecurse` flag; this becomes a factor when debugging certain CNAME chains

- **cd (Checking Disabled):** Do not check the DNSSEC-signed responses for validity.

- **ad (Authenticated Data):** A zone is DNSSEC-signed, and all RRs germane to the query have been validated.

- **tc (Truncated):** This signals the client to retry over TCP.

After the flags, dig will display the four main section names, including the counts of how many records are present in each section, followed by each section, as shown here:

```
;; flags: qr aa rd; QUERY: 1, ANSWER: 1, AUTHORITY: 4, ADDITIONAL: 9
;; WARNING: recursion requested but not available

;; QUESTION SECTION:
;easydns.com.                    IN      MX

;; ANSWER SECTION:
easydns.com.            300      IN      MX      0 mx.easymail.ca.

;; AUTHORITY SECTION:
easydns.com.            300      IN      NS      dns4.easydns.info.
easydns.com.            300      IN      NS      dns1.easydns.com.
easydns.com.            300      IN      NS      dns3.easydns.org.
easydns.com.            300      IN      NS      dns2.easydns.net.

;; ADDITIONAL SECTION:
mx.easymail.ca.         300      IN      A       64.68.200.59
dns1.easydns.com.       300      IN      A       64.68.192.10
dns1.easydns.com.       300      IN      AAAA    2400:cb00:2049:1::a29f:1835
dns2.easydns.net.       600      IN      A       198.41.222.254
dns2.easydns.net.       600      IN      AAAA    2400:cb00:2049:1::c629:defe
dns3.easydns.org.       60       IN      A       64.68.196.10
dns3.easydns.org.       360      IN      AAAA    2620:49:3::10
dns4.easydns.info.      300      IN      A       64.68.197.10
dns4.easydns.info.      300      IN      AAAA    2620:49:4::10
```

We'll step through each section.

# The ANSWER section

The answer section contains the actual response to the lookup. The dig equivalent of "cutting straight to the chase" is to use the **+short** flag and only output the answer data. Take a look at this:

```
$ dig +short easydns.com
205.210.42.135
```

# The AUTHORITY section

This section will return the list of nameservers that should be authoritative for the query. It is derived from the list of NS RRs in the published zone, not from the set of nameservers that may be delegated for the zone in the TLDs rootzone. Take a look at these:

```
;; AUTHORITY SECTION:
easydns.com.            300     IN      NS      dns4.easydns.info.
easydns.com.            300     IN      NS      dns1.easydns.com.
easydns.com.            300     IN      NS      dns3.easydns.org.
easydns.com.            300     IN      NS      dns2.easydns.net.
```

This is an important distinction to be aware of, because there are frequently circumstances when the nameserver delegation in the zone's TLD is not the same as the ones listed within the NS RRSet.

# The ADDITIONAL section

Finally, the ADDITIONAL section will provide references that have been deemed useful for completing the query. Details about nameserver glue records would be conveyed here:

```
;; ADDITIONAL SECTION:
mx.easymail.ca.         300     IN      A       64.68.200.59
dns1.easydns.com.       300     IN      A       64.68.192.10
dns1.easydns.com.       300     IN      AAAA    2400:cb00:2049:1::a29f:1835
dns2.easydns.net.       600     IN      A       198.41.222.254
dns2.easydns.net.       600     IN      AAAA    2400:cb00:2049:1::c629:defe
dns3.easydns.org.       60      IN      A       64.68.196.10
dns3.easydns.org.       360     IN      AAAA    2620:49:3::10
dns4.easydns.info.      300     IN      A       64.68.197.10
dns4.easydns.info.      300     IN      AAAA    2620:49:4::10
```

Tech reviewer Matt Pounsett also adds the finer detail that "the OPT PSEUDOSECTION is a part of the ADDITIONAL data, but dig will display it separately, while still giving an accurate ADCOUNT value in the header. So an OPT record will make it look like the ADCOUNT doesn't agree with the number of ADDITIONAL RRs displayed."

# Using dig

You can specify which server to query directly using **@nameserver**, as shown here:

```
$ dig -t mx easydns.com @dns1.easydns.com
; <<>> DiG 9.8.3-P1 <<>> -t mx easydns.com @dns1.easydns.com
;; global options: +cmd
;; Got answer:
;; ->>HEADER<<- opcode: QUERY, status: NOERROR, id: 20714
;; flags: qr aa rd; QUERY: 1, ANSWER: 1, AUTHORITY: 4, ADDITIONAL: 9
;; WARNING: recursion requested but not available

;; QUESTION SECTION:
;easydns.com.                   IN      MX

;; ANSWER SECTION:
easydns.com.            300     IN      MX      0 mx.easymail.ca.

;; AUTHORITY SECTION:
easydns.com.            300     IN      NS      dns4.easydns.info.
easydns.com.            300     IN      NS      dns1.easydns.com.
easydns.com.            300     IN      NS      dns3.easydns.org.
easydns.com.            300     IN      NS      dns2.easydns.net.

;; ADDITIONAL SECTION:
mx.easymail.ca.         300     IN      A       64.68.200.59
dns1.easydns.com.       300     IN      A       64.68.192.10
dns1.easydns.com.       300     IN      AAAA    2400:cb00:2049:1::a29f:1835
dns2.easydns.net.       600     IN      A       198.41.222.254
dns2.easydns.net.       600     IN      AAAA    2400:cb00:2049:1::c629:defe
dns3.easydns.org.       60      IN      A       64.68.196.10
dns3.easydns.org.       360     IN      AAAA    2620:49:3::10
dns4.easydns.info.      300     IN      A       64.68.197.10
dns4.easydns.info.      300     IN      AAAA    2620:49:4::10

;; Query time: 1415 msec
;; SERVER: 64.68.192.10#53(64.68.192.10)
;; WHEN: Sat Jun  9 11:33:40 2018
;; MSG SIZE  rcvd: 361
```

If the nameserver to query is omitted, dig will simply use the configured resolvers. Notice the absence of the aa flag from the HEADER and the TTL field within the ANSWER SECTION when we leave off the nameserver to directly query:

```
$ dig -t mx easydns.com

; <<>> DiG 9.8.3-P1 <<>> -t mx easydns.com
;; global options: +cmd
;; Got answer:
;; ->>HEADER<<- opcode: QUERY, status: NOERROR, id: 15863
;; flags: qr rd ra; QUERY: 1, ANSWER: 1, AUTHORITY: 0, ADDITIONAL: 0

;; QUESTION SECTION:
;easydns.com.                    IN      MX

;; ANSWER SECTION:
easydns.com.            14      IN      MX      0 mx.easymail.ca.

;; Query time: 832 msec
;; SERVER: 127.0.0.1#53(127.0.0.1)
;; WHEN: Sat Jun  9 12:00:21 2018
;; MSG SIZE  rcvd: 59
```

In our case, **14** means that this response was answered out of our local resolver's cache and that this cached response is valid for a further 14 seconds. We can repeat the process after the cached response has expired, like this:

```
$ dig -t mx easydns.com

; <<>> DiG 9.8.3-P1 <<>> -t mx easydns.com
;; global options: +cmd
;; Got answer:
;; ->>HEADER<<- opcode: QUERY, status: NOERROR, id: 15863
;; flags: qr rd ra; QUERY: 1, ANSWER: 1, AUTHORITY: 0, ADDITIONAL: 0

;; QUESTION SECTION:
;easydns.com.                    IN      MX

;; ANSWER SECTION:
easydns.com.            300     IN      MX      0 mx.easymail.ca.

;; Query time: 832 msec
;; SERVER: 127.0.0.1#53(127.0.0.1)
;; WHEN: Sat Jun  9 12:00:21 2018
;; MSG SIZE  rcvd: 59
```

We can see that it has received its response fresh from one of the authoritative nameservers and will once again cache it for the specified TTL.

# DNSSEC

The +dnssec switch tells dig to request DNSSEC data if available:

```
$ dig +short easydnssec.com 7
2.8.141.90

$ dig +short +dnssec easydnssec.com
72.8.141.90
A 5 2 300 20160227161002 20150218151002 25875 easydnssec.com.
Gv1qQXykeiBvmxk2ASUGuMf/b9uSJv88gy2m
```

# Reverse lookups

To obtain the PTR record for an IP address, the **-x** switch is useful:

```
$ dig +short -x 205.210.42.42
corp.easydns.com.
```

Without the -x switch, you would need to specify the IP in the in-addr.arpa format and specify the PTR RR type:

```
$ dig +short -t ptr 42.42.210.205.in-addr.arpa
corp.easydns.com.
```

# Delegation chains

Whenever I start looking at a zone, I do a **whois** lookup to just quickly validate the delegation of the nameservers and make sure there are no surprises, and then I usually repeat this exercise via **dig +trace**:

```
; <<>> DiG 9.8.3-P1 <<>> +trace packtpub.com
;; global options: +cmd
.                         85241    IN    NS    e.root-servers.net.
.                         85241    IN    NS    l.root-servers.net.
.                         85241    IN    NS    m.root-servers.net.
.                         85241    IN    NS    a.root-servers.net.
.                         85241    IN    NS    h.root-servers.net.
.                         85241    IN    NS    k.root-servers.net.
.                         85241    IN    NS    b.root-servers.net.
```

```
.                          85241    IN    NS    g.root-servers.net.
.                          85241    IN    NS    d.root-servers.net.
.                          85241    IN    NS    i.root-servers.net.
.                          85241    IN    NS    f.root-servers.net.
.                          85241    IN    NS    j.root-servers.net.
.                          85241    IN    NS    c.root-servers.net.
;; Received 241 bytes from 127.0.0.1#53(127.0.0.1) in 8 ms

com.                       172800   IN    NS    a.gtld-servers.net.
com.                       172800   IN    NS    b.gtld-servers.net.
com.                       172800   IN    NS    c.gtld-servers.net.
com.                       172800   IN    NS    d.gtld-servers.net.
com.                       172800   IN    NS    e.gtld-servers.net.
com.                       172800   IN    NS    f.gtld-servers.net.
com.                       172800   IN    NS    g.gtld-servers.net.
com.                       172800   IN    NS    h.gtld-servers.net.
com.                       172800   IN    NS    i.gtld-servers.net.
com.                       172800   IN    NS    j.gtld-servers.net.
com.                       172800   IN    NS    k.gtld-servers.net.
com.                       172800   IN    NS    l.gtld-servers.net.
com.                       172800   IN    NS    m.gtld-servers.net.
;; Received 490 bytes from 199.7.91.13#53(199.7.91.13) in 4308 ms

packtpub.com.              172800   IN    NS    dns3.easydns.org.
packtpub.com.              172800   IN    NS    dns1.easydns.com.
packtpub.com.              172800   IN    NS    dns2.easydns.net.
packtpub.com.              172800   IN    NS    dns4.easydns.info.
;; Received 236 bytes from 192.54.112.30#53(192.54.112.30) in 48 ms

packtpub.com.              86400    IN    A     83.166.169.231
packtpub.com.              86400    IN    NS    dns4.easydns.info.
packtpub.com.              86400    IN    NS    dns1.easydns.com.
packtpub.com.              86400    IN    NS    dns2.easydns.net.
packtpub.com.              86400    IN    NS    dns3.easydns.org.
;; Received 340 bytes from 198.41.222.254#53(198.41.222.254) in 127 ms
```

I find this invaluable and have written my own code classes and scripts that can do this mainly for the sake of finding that last hop, the authoritative nameservers *as they are delegated in the TLD*. Many times, when you use a lookup (such as **host -t ns** or **dig -t ns**), you will get the NS RRSet as they are listed in the domain's zone, but that may not be the same as what is delegated in the domain's TLD.

# host

Some of the tech reviewers yelled at me for this section, wherein I originally wrote, "it's very good at what it does."

What it is good at is getting the A, AAAA, and MX records in one shot, like this:

```
$ host example.net
example.net has address 93.184.216.34
example.net has IPv6 address 2606:2800:220:1:248:1893:25c8:1946
easydns.net mail is handled by 0 mx.easymail.ca.
```

I like it when I'm strictly interested in the end result and not too concerned with where that came from or how it got that way.

The command-line usage is straightforward:

```
host -t <qtype> <hostname> [<nameserver>]
```

By default, it often returns results in a more human-readable format:

```
$ host easydns.com
easydns.com has address 205.210.42.135 easydns.com mail is handled by 0
mx.easymail.ca.
```

But it also comes with an explicit verbose format, which returns results similar to **dig**:

```
Trying "42.42.210.205.in-addr.arpa"
;; ->>HEADER<<- opcode: QUERY, status: NOERROR, id: 46547
;; flags: qr rd ra; QUERY: 1, ANSWER: 1, AUTHORITY: 3, ADDITIONAL: 5

;; QUESTION SECTION:
;42.42.210.205.in-addr.arpa.     IN      PTR

;; ANSWER SECTION:
42.42.210.205.in-addr.arpa. 600 IN      PTR     corp.easydns.com.

;; AUTHORITY SECTION:
42.210.205.in-addr.arpa. 81     IN      NS      dns1.easydns.com.
42.210.205.in-addr.arpa. 81     IN      NS      dns2.easydns.net.
42.210.205.in-addr.arpa. 81     IN      NS      dns3.easydns.ca.

;; ADDITIONAL SECTION:
dns1.easydns.com.        23      IN      A       64.68.192.10
dns1.easydns.com.        388     IN      AAAA    2400:cb00:2049:1::a29f:1835
dns2.easydns.NET.        141     IN      A       198.41.222.254
dns2.easydns.NET.        167     IN      AAAA    2400:cb00:2049:1::c629:defe
```

```
dns3.easydns.ca.          190     IN      A       64.68.196.10

Received 272 bytes from 64.68.199.53#53 in 470 ms
```

It makes assumptions, some of them useful, so it's fairly easy to use without having to specify everything the way **dig** requires. For a simple IP lookup, use this:

```
$ host 205.210.42.42
42.42.210.205.in-addr.arpa domain name pointer corp.easydns.com.
```

Having said all that, if you are actually *debugging* something, such as a CNAME chain that spans multiple zones or multiple nameservers, use **dig**.

# named-checkzone and named-checkconf

These utilities come bundled with the BIND package and are used to check the syntax of an individual zone file or an overall named configuration file, respectively.

There are relatively straightforward to use in their basic cases, as shown here:

```
# ./named-checkzone dom.org ./zones/dom.org.zone zone dom.org/IN: loaded
serial 1433182606
OK
```

Now I've introduced a few errors into the zone (I've removed the preference value from the MX record and entered an illegal RR for "www" because it is already a CNAME):

```
# ./named-checkzone dom.org ./zones/dom.org.zone
dns_rdata_fromtext: /zones/caprica/easydns/primary/dom.org.zone:22: near
'intake.easyrpz.com.': nodns_master_load:
/zones/caprica/easydns/primary/dom.org.zone:25: www.dom.org: CNAME and
other data zone dom.org/IN: loading from master file
/zones/caprica/easydns/primary/dom.org.zone failed: not zone dom.org/IN:
not loaded due to errors.
```

The **named-checkconf** will traverse your entire bind configuration and any included files. When managing many thousand domains this is useful: Any configuration syntax error introduced will usually cause the nameserver to stop processing at that error. In other words, any zones specified after the error will not get loaded into the nameserver:

```
# ./named-checkconf ./named.conf;echo $?
0
```

And now we've left out a "." in an IP address within an **allow-transfer** statement:

```
# ./named-checkconf ./named.conf;echo $?
./named.conf:724: undefined ACL '72167.238.111' 1
```

# dnstop

Most of these tools help us diagnose a single zone. However, it would be nice to have something at our disposal that enables us to look at the aggregate usage of our environment and help us tease out any anomalies, such as abusive clients or zones under attack.

Enter **dnstop**, think of it like your Unix **top** command (which shows you which processes are consuming the most CPU resources) but one that shows you similar usage patterns for DNS queries. Take a look at the following:

**Usage: dnstop <interface> -l <level>**

```
# dnstop eth0:0 -l3 -p
```

The **-l** switch tells dnstop how many levels deep to count the hostnames being queried:

-l 1: com / net / org / biz

-l 2: example.com / example.net / example.org / example.biz

-l 3: example.com.br / example.gov.co / www.example.com

**-p** prevents it from putting the interface into promiscuous mode. Once invoked, you can look at the query activity by source IP, as shown here:

```
Queries: 966 new, 34393 total                    Sat Jun  9 16:16:43
2018

Sources                    Count      %    cum%
--------------------    ---------  ------  ------
45.77.82.193               1432    4.2    4.2
35.184.172.191              284    0.8    5.0
64.68.199.53                207    0.6    5.6
208.80.194.123               77    0.2    5.8
2001:4ca0:108:42::21         71    0.2    6.0
65.55.37.40                  61    0.2    6.2
138.246.253.22               52    0.2    6.4
65.55.37.38                  52    0.2    6.5
138.246.253.21               47    0.1    6.6
2001:4ca0:108:42::22         46    0.1    6.8
```

```
65.55.37.39              45      0.1      6.9
65.55.37.41              45      0.1      7.0
103.243.110.240          44      0.1      7.2
65.55.37.37              42      0.1      7.3
50.19.247.208            38      0.1      7.4
212.1.244.98             37      0.1      7.5
141.207.145.254          34      0.1      7.6
2a04:e4c0:20::71         32      0.1      7.7
65.55.37.36              31      0.1      7.8
```

Hit the numeric key to switch to a view of query targets to that numeric level:

; level "1"

```
Queries: 823 new,  99813 total            Sat Jun  9 16:17:59
2018

Query Name        Count       %    cum%
------------   ----------  ------  ------
com               61580     61.7    61.7
net                7190      7.2    68.9
org                5158      5.2    74.1
uk                 2907      2.9    77.0
au                 2524      2.5    79.5
in-addr.arpa       2418      2.4    81.9
ar                 1682      1.7    83.6
ca                 1454      1.5    85.1
pt                 1184      1.2    86.3
br                 1087      1.1    87.3
top                1032      1.0    88.4
as                  711      0.7    89.1
us                  645      0.6    89.7
ru                  630      0.6    90.4
sk                  515      0.5    90.9
info                472      0.5    91.4
mx                  428      0.4    91.8
edu                 416      0.4    92.2
ch                  412      0.4    92.6
```

## Here are the second-level domains:

```
Queries: 821 new, 168701 total                    Sat Jun  9 16:19:20
2018

Query Name               Count       %     cum%
------------------       ---------- ------ ------
zoneedit.com             21361    12.7    12.7
ultimate-guitar.com      17708    10.5    23.2
fidelity-media.com        7942     4.7    27.9
co.uk                     4338     2.6    30.4
com.au                    3446     2.0    32.5
com.ar                    2412     1.4    33.9
tenaxsoft.com             2259     1.3    35.2
marktest.pt               1958     1.2    36.4
ranincusa.com             1923     1.1    37.5
com.br                    1903     1.1    38.7
123.top                   1746     1.0    39.7
wediacloud.net            1689     1.0    40.7
popo8.com                 1495     0.9    41.6
cbi.net                   1381     0.8    42.4
letzebuerg.net            1208     0.7    43.1
beck-thom.as              1167     0.7    43.8
74.in-addr.arpa           1106     0.7    44.5
qrpune.com                1066     0.6    45.1
dnsbl.org                 1031     0.6    45.7
```

## And here are the third-level domains:

```
Queries: 827 new, 248066 total                    Sat Jun  9 16:20:53
2018

Query Name                  Count       %    cum%
----------------------      ---------- ------ ------
x.fidelity-media.com        11602     4.7    4.7
ns.ultimate-guitar.com       5036     2.0    6.7
api.ultimate-guitar.com      2906     1.2    7.9
w14.ultimate-guitar.com      2853     1.2    9.0
ws.ultimate-guitar.com       2736     1.1   10.1
zoneedit.co.uk               2490     1.0   11.1
123.porn                     2420     1.0   12.1
ns1.ultimate-guitar.com      2408     1.0   13.1
netscope.marktest.pt         2378     1.0   14.0
zoneedit.com                 2189     0.9   14.9
tabs.ultimate-guitar.com     2042     0.8   15.7
www.ultimate-guitar.com      1798     0.7   16.5
umotion.com.br               1689     0.7   17.2
track.ultimate-guitar.com    1657     0.7   17.8
```

```
ns18.zoneedit.com           1587     0.6     18.5
ns3.zoneedit.com            1549     0.6     19.1
ex.dnsbl.org                1512     0.6     19.7
t2.zoneedit.com             1492     0.6     20.3
ns2.zoneedit.com            1479     0.6     20.9
```

With "t" you can see your incoming queries by QType:

```
Queries: 861 new, 342205 total              Sat Jun   9 16:22:42
2018

Query Type      Count        %     cum%
----------   ----------   ------   ------
A?              193047    56.4     56.4
AAAA?            95974    28.0     84.5
SOA?             15841     4.6     89.1
MX?              12806     3.7     92.8
TXT?              6503     1.9     94.7
SRV?              5878     1.7     96.4
PTR?              5608     1.6     98.1
NS?               4212     1.2     99.3
SPF?              1081     0.3     99.6
CNAME?             406     0.1     99.8
#257?              316     0.1     99.8
ANY?               313     0.1     99.9
A6?                 75     0.0    100.0
#52?                56     0.0    100.0
DS?                 23     0.0    100.0
#35?                22     0.0    100.0
DNSKEY?             21     0.0    100.0
#44?                12     0.0    100.0
#13?                 5     0.0    100.0
```

Here are some response codes ("r"):

```
Queries: 842 new, 376289 total              Sat Jun   9 16:23:23
2018

Rcode          Count        %     cum%
-------     ----------   ------   ------
Noerror        376289    100.0    100.0
```

Here are some opcodes ("o"):

```
Queries: 947 new, 415333 total              Sat Jun  9 16:24:09
2018

Opcode      Count       %    cum%
------  ----------  ------  ------
Query      415090   99.9    99.9
Update        132    0.0   100.0
Notify        111    0.0   100.0
```

In the event of a DDoS or other network anomaly, dnstop is very useful for isolating problem domains and clients.

Be aware that dnstop intercepts its data before any firewall rules you enable on your interface. If you enter an iptables rule to drop all packets for a specific domain or source IP, for example, you will still see them show up in dnstop, even though your nameserver will never see those queries.

# Web-based debugging tools

While there are a number of web-based DNS diagnostic tools, the reader is cautioned against taking some of their pronouncements too seriously.

With the odd exception, the majority of web-based tools tend to throw "warnings" and "errors" about issues that aren't actually impacting the operation of a zone's DNS. They tend to be oblivious to the practice of hidden primaries and complain a lot about refresh and retry intervals, which for all practical purposes don't matter.

In other words, a lot of web DNS tools generate a lot of "look busy" output that doesn't actually convey anything useful. From there, people are prone to opening spurious tickets with their vendors.

# DNS stuff

http://www.dnsstuff.com/tools

This is a decent enough high-level diagnostic toolbox; the **DNS Report** will traverse a zone's nameservers and report back on general consistency and configuration issues.

This site also contains a number of useful functions, such as an IP lookup tool that will drill down to the appropriate netblock entity, and an SSL certificate explorer.

# whatismydns

https://www.whatsmydns.net/

This self-described **Global DNS Propagation Checker** comes in very handy for two scenarios in particular:

- **Anycast deployed DNS**: Recall that under anycast deployments, multiple servers worldwide are responding to the same IP address. When things get iffy, this architecture can be difficult to debug. Somebody observing a problem where they are may not be able to reproduce it where you are. This is because different physical POPs may be handling the queries.
- **GeoDNS**: This is similar to anycast, except in this use case, answers are intentionally different based on the location of the originating query.

In either case, this tool has a multitude of lookup probes deployed worldwide that each run your diagnostic query and report the results back. Take a look at this screenshot:

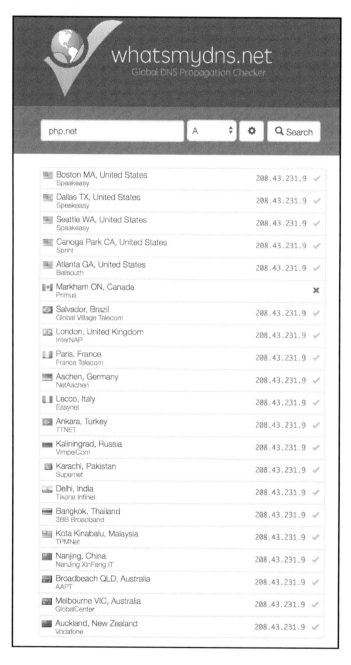

The screenshot shows the results of a lookup on **php.net**, which is using GeoDNS to distribute its responses.

# dnsviz

```
http://www.dnsviz.net
```

This is the rare DNS tool that, in my opinion, is actually suited to a web-based tool, given that it visualizes and diagnoses DNSSEC trust chains for specified domains. This is an open source tool; you can run it on your own web server or `on the command line`, which makes it useful when debugging DNSSEC from within private networks.

Simply enter a DNSSEC-enabled domain name and let 'er rip. Take a look at this diagram:

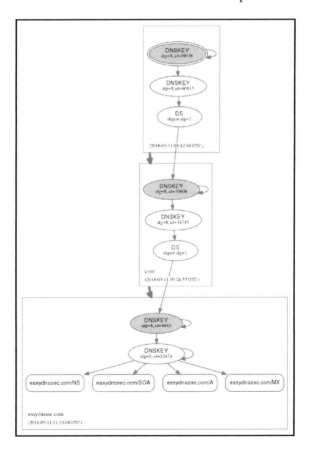

The tool will then output an interactive visual representation of the entire trust chain for the domain.

## easywhois

`http://easywhois.com`

This is one of ours; it is just a simple universal whois lookup tool that will (try to) return the whois record for domains under any TLD.

It will also do simple DNS lookups, IP address lookups, a "what is my resolver" utility, and add new functions, from time to time.

## domaintools

`http://www.domaintools.com`

Originally founded by Jay Westerdahl under the name **whois.sc**, domaintools is, if not the only, then certainly the most comprehensive, historical archive of whois records in the world.

Using this site (premium membership required), you can examine historical iterations of whois records, as well as the changes to a domain's IP address and nameserver delegations over time.

# Summary

Debugging DNS can be tricky and, in this chapter, we examined the tools that can help us figure out exactly where a problem lies so that we can work toward remedying it.

There are numerous command-line utilities that can help us drill down quickly to find a problem and that come with the added bonus of being able to be incorporated into scripts and automated.

Despite the plethora of web-based DNS tools out there, not all of them are terribly useful, and many are prone to spewing verbose "look busy" output that doesn't actually convey any useful information or assist in debugging actual issues.

We did cover the few truly useful web-based tools that stand apart from the crowd, either in their uniqueness (such as domaintools being the only known historical archive of whois records) or their utility (whatsmydns being very handy for debugging anycast or geo-distributed zones).

# References

- `https://thde.io/whois-command-line-new-gtld-guru-watch-zone-link/`

# 11
# DNS Operations and Use Cases

In this chapter, we'll cover the most common DNS use cases. While some may seem straightforward at first glance, there are usually some best practices to be applied that may not be obvious. In some cases, failure to adhere to them can lead to outages.

We'll start with a few domain operations that are typically done on domain names, such as transferring a domain, changing a domain's registrant, or adding secondary nameservers.

From there, we will move to DNS use cases that involve doing something to the zone data *within* a zone, such as global load balancing, implementing GeoDNS, or configuring the DNS component of email deliverability schemes, such as SPF and DKIM.

Some typical use cases we'll cover include the following:

- Transferring domain names
  - Changing a domain registrant
  - Moving nameservers (redelegations)
  - Redelegating DNSSEC-signed domains
  - Registrar transfers
- Adding additional nameservers
- Moving to new nameservers
- Moving entire portfolios of domains to new nameservers
- Round-robin DNS
- Load balancing/global weighted load balancing
- DNS failover
- Dynamic DNS
- Geo DNS

- Zone apex aliasing
- Reverse DNS and Netblock subdelegations
- Implementing SPF, DKIM, and DMARC

# Transferring domain names

It may sound simple, but there are various permutations of a plain "domain transfer." The phrase can have very different implications to different parties, and, to make matters even more complicated, any given transfer can involve one or more of these disparate meanings within the same operation.

In other words, a **domain transfer** could refer to any of the following:

- Changing the **owner** or **registrant** of a domain name from one entity to another (Change of registrant)
- Moving a domain from one registrar to another (Registrar transfer)
- Changing the nameserver delegation of a domain name (nameserver redelegation, Change of Operator or even DNS Transfer–the last of which can easily be confused with AXFR or IXFR zone transfers)
- Moving a domain name between user accounts within a registrar, web provider, managed DNS provider or similar (domain push or account push)

# Change of registrant

This refers to changing the owner of a domain name.

In the olden days (during the Network Solutions monopoly), this was considered a non-trivial undertaking and required sending in a notarized piece of photo ID, and this cost somewhere in the neighborhood of $150 to process.

But there is still more to it, if the reason for the change is because the domain is being sold or transferred from one entity to another.

The way a change of registrant procedure works today came into effect relatively recently with an ICANN policy that took effect December 1, 2016. This applies to all TLDs under the oversight of ICANN (.COM/.NET/.ORG and all new TLDs).

The new process requires that both the current (outgoing) Registrant and the new (incoming) Registrant explicitly approve the change request.

It also adds a new **transfer lock** period of 60 days; this is similar to the way new domain registrations cannot be transferred to a new registrar within 60 days of initial registration. The new change-of-registrant process also imposes the 60-day transfer lock period.

This is typically done as follows:

1. The current registrant navigates to their registrar control panel for the domain and makes the edit (usually in the Whois or Domain Contact or Domain Information sections of their domain).
2. The change assumes a pending state, and a confirmation is sent out-of-band to the current registrant and the proposed new registrant.
3. *Both* the current and the new Registrant explicitly acknowledge and accept the change.

At this point, the Registrant contact set for the domain is updated.

# Nameserver redelegations

A change of nameserver delegation is the act of moving a domain from one set of nameservers to another. There are two permutations to this operation:

- Changing the delegation and changing the primary master for the domain
- Changing the delegation while preserving the primary master for the domain

In the first case, the approach is simply to set up the new environment in stealth, meaning the zone is live on the new nameservers but they are not receiving any queries, and then pick a band-aid moment, when you throw the switch and cut everything over to the new delegation.Look at these steps:

1. Set up new master nameserver, modify the NS RRset to reflect the new/incoming nameserver delegation.
2. Set up the new secondaries as slaving their zone from the new master.
3. Change the delegation for the zone at the Registry of the zone's TLD.
4. Leave the old nameservers up to answer queries for at least as long as the greater of a) the TTL for the NS RRSET or b) the TTL of the zone apex (while optionally setting up the old nameservers to slave from the new master).
5. Decommission the zone on the old nameservers and master.

The second case is a little more streamlined:

1. Set up the zone on the new nameservers.
2. Add your new nameserver NS RRs to your zone's existing NS.
3. Update the nameserver delegation in the parent zone (usually parent TLD)–this includes removing the old nameservers from the delegation.
4. After NS RRSET TTL expires for the old nameservers, remove their NS records from your zone.

The modifications to the NS RRSET are done with *the DNS provider*, or on your *master nameserver* if you are the DNS operator.

The nameserver delegation update is done via the *Registrar* for the zone (domain), which will update the Registry with the new list of nameservers for the domain in its TLD.

Most gTLD registries will modify the delegation without checking whether you've actually done this coherently and the new nameservers become authoritative for the zone.

Many ccTLDs will test the new nameservers first and will not implement the delegation if they are not authoritative for the zone or if the NS RRSET for the zone being reported by the new nameservers do not match the new delegation.

There may be an interval of time in which some resolvers receive data that is not entirely consistent, but still gets the job done from the client's perspective.

For example, the resolver may obtain a referral to the old NS RRSET from the delegating TLD the domain, and upon following the glue to an old authoritative nameserver, end up seeing an NS RRSet with additional data (the new NS RRSet coming into effect). This is normal.

# Redelegating DNSSEC-signed domains

With DNSSEC (see `Chapter 13`, *Securing your Domains and DNS*), you have to execute this nameserver redelegation in a way where the trust chain will not break (RFC6781).

While there is work being done to help facilitate key transfers between DNS operators using the Registry/Registrar EPP protocol, interest in this from registrars and registries is currently lacklustre at best. Until that changes and deployment gets further along, we are stuck working with redelegating zones across (hopefully cooperative) DNS operators.

This is done in a fashion somewhat akin to DNSSEC key rollovers, where you prepublish new keys with the new provider while signing the current zone with both sets of keys: the losing DNS provider's key and a new key with the new DNS provider.

Given the Gaining and Losing DNS providers, where the zone is moving away from Losing nameservers and on to those of the Gaining, consider the following:

- Gaining generates new ZSK, KSK, and DS records
- Losing publishes both new and old ZSKs in the current zone
- Losing signs the zone containing both ZSKs
- Gaining obtains Losing's ZSK and KSK
- Gaining signs the zone containing Losing's ZSK
- Gaining signs both ZSKs with its own KSKs
- New DS record into the parent zone/TLD
- Nameservers redelegated
- Both sets of nameservers operate past length of TTL
- After TTL elapses, Gaining may drop Losing KSK and ZSK and resign zone

The objective of all this is to provide resolvers that have cached data the ability to validate records, regardless of whether they have data from the losing provider or are receiving fresh responses from the gaining provider.

This scenario describes how to redelegate between *cooperating* DNS providers. If the loser is uncooperative, it gets a lot harder. So much harder, in fact, that I will go out on a limb and suggest that if you're in a corner because of an uncooperative losing DNS provider, you should unsign your zone long enough for global caches to expire, then just exit the old provider, generate new keys, and sign in at the new provider.

Whether this type of redelegation occurs within an accompanying Registrar transfer or not only impacts the step at which the new DS key will be inserted into the parent zone/TLD and at what point the Registrar transfer will be executed.

# Registrar transfer (without changing nameservers)

The ability to move your domain between domain registrars is one of the basic rights all domain registrants possess, and all registrars are required under the terms of their registrar accreditation agreements to both allow you to transfer your domain away, and provide you with the mechanisms to do so.

It is not necessary to wait until your domains are close to expiry before transferring them, in fact you may be doing so at your own peril, in case you run into problems or delays. After a registrar transfer completes, the domain expiry is extended by at least one year. Transferring your domain to a new registrar is akin to an early renewal.

This used to be one of the safest operations you could do because very little could go wrong and if it did, the consequence was simply that your change of registrar failed, requiring a do-over which was a simple matter of your gaining registrar resubmitting the request after the necessary issues that caused the initial failure had been remedied. Now, because of what can happen to your domain *after* the transfer, you need to be aware of certain things beforehand.

## IMPORTANT – make sure your new registrar knows what to do with the nameservers

This use case and the next outline registrar transfers, with or without a corresponding nameserver change, respectively. It is critical that your gaining registrar knows whether to change the nameservers when the transfer occurs.

Many gaining registrars automatically change the nameservers when an inbound transfer succeeds.

Conversely, many *losing* Registrars *automatically drop your DNS* when an *outbound* transfer succeeds.

Or, you may be using third-party nameservers unrelated to either registrar and don't want any nameserver changes at all!

It is crucial then, when initiating a registrar transfer, that you and your gaining registrar are on the same page regarding what is supposed to happen with the nameservers post-transfer.

Once the transfer is done it will, under the generic Top-Level Domains and the new gTLDs, trigger an ICANN **Whois Accuracy Process** (**WAP**). If you're unaware of this (which you shouldn't be because you read `Chapter 2`, *Registries, Registrars, and Whois*), it can take your domain offline 15 days after your transfer completes.

## Beware! Transfers may trigger the WAP!

Under the gTLDs and new TLDs, the act of executing a registrar transfer on a domain name triggers an ICANN WAP procedure. (See `Chapter 2`, *Registries, Registrars, and Whois*).

If you do not verify your new contact data when requested by your new Registrar within 15 days of the WAP commencing, then *the registrar* **must suspend** *the domain until it is verified.*

With these caveats out of the way, let's look at a plain Registrar transfer.

## Steps of a registrar transfer

On the Losing Registrar side, perform the following:

- Unlock the domain at the losing registrar. There should be a mechanism within the user control panel to do this.
- Obtain the domain's **auth code.** Usually this is done from the Registrar control panel by triggering an email to the domain's **Admin Contact** email address.

On the Gaining Registrar side, perform the following:

- Initiate the Registrar transfer, pay attention to any options you are presented with about whether to automatically update the nameservers or retain current nameservers upon completion.
- Confirm the transfer request by entering the **auth code** where prompted.

This is generally all there is to it. Once the transfer is requested and confirmed, the Losing Registrar sends the Request to the Registry where, in the case of gTLDs, it can sit for approximately five days.

The Losing Registrar may send a confirm request that the transfer is in progress. If ignored or not actioned, the transfer will complete within five days. The Registrant may also explicitly cancel the request.

In some cases, the Losing Registrar offers the Registrant the opportunity to explicitly *approve* the request, if this happens, the transfer can take place immediately, without the five-day waiting period.

As previously mentioned, you don't need to wait for the domain to approach its expiry date before transferring a domain name away. However, if you wait too long, many registrars will not allow a domain transfer to occur if the domain is past expiry.

Finally, you should be aware that domains that are less than 60 days old typically cannot be transferred between Registrars. This is a fraud-prevention measure.

After the registrar transfer completes, the nameserver delegation remains the same.

# Registrar transfer and nameserver redelegation

If you want to move both your registrar and your nameserver delegation, there is a definite order to go in.

*First,* do your nameserver redelegation. After you have completed this step, *then* execute a registrar transfer (as in the preceding section).

The reason for this is because, usually in a scenario where you are moving both DNS nameservers and the registrar, it's the losing registrar that is the current DNS operator.

When the registrar transfer clears the registry, the losing Registrar may drop the DNS from their nameservers *immediately* (always a pet peeve of mine). Ideally, they keep the DNS past your zone's longest TTL *and* you've presumably already paid them through to the end of your term. They *should* keep your DNS warm until your paid term ends. But many end up not doing that.

In these situations, there can be a window-of-limbo when the registry has cleared the registrar transfer, the losing registrar has dropped DNS for the zone, but the gaining Registrar may not have processed the transfer completion yet (there are different processes at work with different Registrars—it could be a cron job that runs every so often that polls the registry, or a number of other things). This can lead to outages until the new registrar is fully in effect.

# Adding additional nameservers

(Also known as **Secondary DNS** or sometimes **Backup DNS**.)

Note that the terms Primary and Secondary nameservers only have meaning within the authoritative set of nameservers for a given zone itself. In that context, "primary" simply means where all of the other authoritative nameservers (the so-called "secondary" and "tertiaries") obtain their copy of the zone from.

Even this distinction is blurred when using nameservers that do not share their zones via transfer mechanisms such as AXFR/IXFR (BIND, nsd, Knot) or even rsync (tinydns). A fleet of nameservers using PowerDNS or BIND-dlz employing MySQL replication or LDAP to syndicate their zone data would be an example of where "primary" and "secondary" meanings becoming obscured.

It is also worth recalling from our *Anatomy of a DNS Query* that the order of nameservers (which may be confused with being "primary," "secondary," and so on) in no way governs the order in which the query load will be distributed. In other words, a common notion that the secondary nameserver will get the queries if the primary is down is not how it works. *All* of the delegated nameservers will receive queries based on the selection algorithms of the recursors.

Let's just call it "adding more nameservers" with the objective of increasing redundancy and resiliency. Traditionally, the bare minimum was two nameservers on disparate networks. When it comes to DNS, more is better, up to a point.

Ideally, you want multiple nameserver nodes across multiple networks and multiple datacenters (preferably multi-homed).

By node, I mean a logical nameserver hostname (such as ns1.nameserver.dom) that may itself be an anycast constellation of multiple physical nodes.

In fact, this is how the internet root works, which is why it is so resilient. Most of the 13 root servers (a.root-servers.net through m.root-servers.net are themselves an anycast constellation operated by varying entities–take a look at this table).

| Hostname (.root-servers.net) | Operator | Number of sites (as of May 2018) |
|---|---|---|
| a | Verisign | 8 |
| b | Information Sciences Institute | 2 |
| c | Cogent | 10 |
| d | University of Maryland | 136 |
| e | NASA | 192 |
| f | ISC.org | 220 |
| g | U.S. DOD Network Information Center | 6 |
| h | U.S. Army Research Lab | 2 |
| i | Netnod | 60 |
| j | Verisign | 162 |
| k | RIPE NCC | 58 |
| l | ICANN | 160 |
| m | WIDE Project | 9 |
| | Total Sites: | 1,025 |

Table 11-1 The number of sites in each of the internet root server nodes

From career experience and drawing on the wisdom of the root operators, I have found that true redundancy is achieved from using multiple disparate DNS operators. Having a single provider, albeit operating multiple nameserver nodes in a redundant fashion, is not enough. For reasons we don't need to explore here, any single provider is a single entity and thus a **Single-Point-Of-Failure (SPOF)** unto itself.

# External secondaries

When specifically setting out to add DNS redundancy via secondaries or tertiaries, it is best to select a completely separate DNS operating entity for it, and then come up with a coherent methodology to federate your zones across those separate entities.

The easiest way is to simply setup AXFR/IXFR zone-transfer access to another set of nameservers operated by somebody else. This can be an informal *ad-hoc* arrangement with a peer or a commercial DNS provider that offers secondary DNS as a service.

One way to do this is to operate your own (hidden) primary and set up multiple mirrors to publish your zones.

The steps in setting this up, using BIND as an example, would be as follows:

1. Enable transfers of the zone to the external nameservers, or their entity's ingress point (see the *Other Considerations* section):

```
acl "ourdns" {
        192.0.2.183/32;
        192.0.2.48/32;
};

acl "theirdns" {
        203.0.113.3/32;
        203.0.113.22/32;
};

zone "myzone.dom" {

        type master;
        file "zones/myzone.dom.txt";
        allow-transfer { ourdns; theirdns; 198.51.100.165; };
};
```

In our preceding BIND snippet, we've defined two ACLs, which would be within the **options** section of our `named.conf`.

In the configuration block for `myzone.dom`, we've allowed transfers to our nameservers, the other DNS provider's nameservers via the ACL "theirdns," and we've also added another third-party nameserver by simply specifying its IP address.

2. Arrange for NOTIFY packets to be sent to the relevant nodes. Here we are expanding on the preceding snippet:

```
zone "myzone.dom" {

    type master;
    file "zones/myzone.dom.txt";
    allow-transfer { ourdns; theirdns; 10.0.19.165; }; also-notify
    { 192.168.1.1; }
};
```

It's possible the nameservers at "theirdns" will not accept NOTIFY packets directly from our master, instead they may have an "ingress" point created that will receive all notifies that originate external to their own network, which will then distribute them internally as they arrive.

3. Add the additional nameserver NS records to your zones. Remember to add NS records for your external mirrors to your zone:

```
$ORIGIN myzone.dom.

@  IN SOA  dns0.myzone.dom. hostmaster.myzone.dom. 1453313457
3600 600 604800 10800

@  IN NS    ns1.myzone.dom.
@  IN NS    ns2.myzone.dom.
@  IN NS    ns1.theirdns.dom.
@  IN NS    ns2.theirdns.dom.
@  IN NS    dns.thatotherguy.dom.
```

BIND will send notify packets to each listed NS record, with the exception when an NS RR matches the value in the MNAME of the zone's SOA record (in BIND's mind, that would mean sending a NOTIFY to itself. In these cases, you need to set the MNAME value to a NS that *is* in the delegation and work around the aforementioned issue with an **also-notify** directive.).

The stated nameservers may not necessarily accept any NOTIFY coming from your master. (Perhaps the NS RR contains the anycast address of for a multiple-node anycast constellation—see `Chapter 12`, *Nameserver Considerations*, or perhaps an external provider uses a hidden or non-published ingress point for NOTIFY and zone transfers.) If not, then we again use the **also-notify** to alert the node(s) that *will* accept it.

There also exist various APIs and/or webhooks to publish your data into third-party systems.

For example, Amazon Route 53 is a popular DNS provider, a component of the **Amazon Web Services** (**AWS**), yet it does not operate via AXFR/IXFR. Everything is API-driven. Numerous scripts and services exist to assist in integrating Route 53, including easyRoute53 (`http://easyroute53.com/`), an integration layer we developed at easyDNS that automagically pushes DNS settings from our control panel into Amazon Route 53 (it also integrates several other DNS providers, such as Google Cloud DNS, Linode, and Digital Ocean).

# External masters

In these situations, your registrar/DNS host or webhost supplies DNS and allows third-party AXFR access. They operate your zones' primary master, and you add other mirror nameservers, perhaps even operating them within your own infrastructure, and load from the external master.

Most Registrars, DNS Providers, cloud providers (such as Linode, Digital Ocean), and even the popular web hosting dashboard, cPanel, enable you to add third-party nameservers that can conduct AXFR/IXFR zone transfers from their masters.

# Other considerations

When it comes to working across DNS providers, there are always several factors that need to be taken into account for setting up the initial relationship and then maintaining it.

## Structuring secondary DNS arrangements

In the past, structuring secondary DNS arrangements with external nameserver operators were often *ad-hoc* affairs. When configuring the zone transfers between the operators, it would be done from nameserver to nameserver.

For example, the `ns1.isp.dom` master nameserver would **allow-axfer** to the `mirror1.yournet.dom` and `mirror2.yournet.dom` third-party secondaries.

And `mirror1.yournet.dom` and `mirror2.yournet.dom` would, in turn, slave directly from the `ns1.isp.dom` master.

In other words, each secondary nameserver would be set up to transfer their mirrored zones directly from the primary master.

In practice, this can lead to messy and confusing configurations, not to mention if they are not managed correctly, a phenomenon called "notify storms," where, through a combination of misplaced **allow-notify** and overlapping **also-notify** directives, one update can set off a never-ending barrage of notifies among the participating nameservers.

Ideally, each distinct nameserver operator will provide designated ingress/egress points for AXFRs both into and out of its environment, such as these:

```
axfr1.example.dom
axfr2.example.dom
```

Each participant mirroring from or to will then add those parameters to their respective **allow-transfer**, **allow-notify**, and **also-notify** settings.

The axfr points themselves syndicate any inbound zone transfers out to their own nameserver constellations:

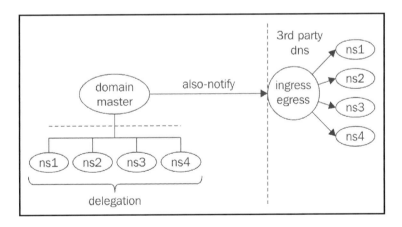

Figure 11-1: Distributing an updated zone within the network of an external secondary DNS provider

With the advent of anycast DNS, this kind of structure becomes even more desirable because it is impractical for a master nameserver to send a NOTIFY or to transfer zones to every node within an anycast constellation.

## Securing zone transfers with TSIG

It is possible to further secure zone transfers between nameservers using **Transaction Signatures (TSIG)**.

This involves the generation of a shared key that will be installed on either side of a master/secondary pair of nameservers:

```
$ dnssec-keygen -a HMAC-SHA512 -b 512 -n HOST -r /dev/urandom mykey
```

This will result in a .key file being created:

```
$ ls Kmykey.+165+34180.key
Kmykey.+165+34180.key

$ cat Kmykey.+165+34180.key
mykey. IN KEY 512 3 165
NiQW6wS0O2OVbmha6/yR0yQa5Ot7Rou7BMz0p3cZQbYeczBl+265YAV+ /eZ/CVNRZRimfPEhM
```

We will be using the following string:

```
NiQW6wS0O2OVbmha6/yR0yQa5Ot7Rou7BMz0p3cZQbYeczBl+265YAV+
/eZ/CVNRZRimfPEhMHQ5t8Wa+VG1nA==
```

The preceding string is the shared key, which must be implemented on each server:

```
key "mykey" {
        algorithm hmac-sha512;
        secret "NiQW6wS0O2OVbmha6/yR0yQa5Ot7Rou7BMz0p3cZQbYeczBl+265YAV+
/eZ/CVNRZRimfPEhMHQ5t8Wa+
};
```

To secure all transfers between a specific server, perform the following:

```
server 192.168.3.26 {
    keys { mykey; };
};
```

This will cause problems in environments where some zones may employ TSIG, while others using the same master may not.

In that case, instead of associating the key to the server, specify it on a per-zone basis:

```
zone "secured.dom" {
        type slave;
        file "secondary/secured.dom.db";
        masters {
                192.168.3.26 key "mykey";
        };
};

zone "unsecured.dom" {
        type slave;
        file "secondary/unsecured.dom.db";
        masters {
                192.168.3.26;
        };
}
```

On its own, using TSIG leaves it to the implementer to distribute the shared keys. GSS-TSIG (RFC3645) defines an extension to TSIG to provide shared key exchange using **kerberos**.

# Syncing zone data across secondaries

Traditionally, zonedata is kept in sync across the master and mirror nameservers via zone transfers (AXFR and IXFR). When a zone is updated, the master sends NOTIFY packets to each NS RR as well as any applicable **also-notify** destinations, and if the SOA serial on the master is higher, the mirrors initiate the zone transfers.

Sometimes, you see arrangements where multiple masters are utilized, especially if separate DNS operators are being employed for redundancy. Unless those disparate masters are themselves synced via some other method, such as SQL replication, this is not recommended. Doing so necessitates making any changes in the zone more than once, at each master location, and this unfailingly leads to oversights and inconsistencies between the masters. Even though, as DNS operators, we seek redundancy at a level that is near obsessive, when it comes to masters, "There can only be one!"

There are alternative methods to syncing data than AXFR/IXFR zone transfers.

In the case of PowerDNS and BIND-DLZ, any number of database backends can be used and with them along with their associated data replication methods. The most common deployment of this being MySQL replication for both server types.

Tinydns recommends using rsync over a secure socket, which again blurs the distinction between primaries and secondaries since each node is running a current copy of the data (although in this context, primary can refer to the origin of the zonedata being copied or replicated to the other nodes).

Git lends itself well to this type of application and is emerging as a viable way to manage the zone data. GitZone (`https://www.dyne.org/software/gitzone/`) provides a way to manage BIND 9 zonefiles via git, while having the nameserver itself reference the repository. Git integration is emerging among managed DNS providers.

# Planning migrations with DNS updates

It is fairly common that various infrastructure upgrades, migrations, and switches will involve making DNS updates, whether those will be temporary or permanent.

When making changes to individual components within a zone, such as migrating webservers or mail hosts, you usually want any changes to your zone to be out across the internet sooner than later. This means changing the effective TTL on either the entire zone or just the records involved in the migration to a low value *before* your maintenance window commences.

How long before? You want any resolvers out there that might have your existing records in their cache to refresh with your new, lower TTL before you start making changes. That means, at a minimum, you lower your TTLs the current value ahead of the window.

Observe this zone snippet:

```
example.dom. IN SOA dns1.example.dom. zone.exampl.dom. 1453310835 7200 3600
1209600 600
$TTL 86400
```

Given the preceding zone snippet, you would lower your TTL at least one day (`86,400` seconds) before the window. You should also allow for broken resolvers that will cache your zone longer than they should, make it two days, and then drop your TTL:

```
example.dom. 300 IN SOA dns1.example.dom. zone.example.dom. 1453310836 7200
3600 1209600 600
$TTL 300
```

The zone now has a TTL of five minutes. Once your maintenance or migration is complete and you're confident you will not need to roll back for any reason, you can restore it to its previous value.

DNS migrations can affect large pools of resources. When dealing with a resource that performs a function across many domains (hundreds or thousands), careful planning of your naming scheme before deployment can make migrations a lot simpler.

Take the `pageeditor.platform.dom` web application, which has an IP address that handles thousands of domains. When each new domain is provisioned, you may be tempted to assign a host record under the new domain:

```
pageeditor.platform.dom. IN A 10.1.0.4

; each of these are within it's own zone
www.customer1.dom. IN A 10.1.0.4
web.customer2.dom. IN A 10.1.0.4
etc.morecustomers.dom. IN A 10.1.0.4
```

When the time comes to move `pageeditor.platform.dom` to a new IP address, it would necessitate also updating the zone for each client hostname referencing it by IP address. It becomes even more difficult when not all of those zones are under your direct control.

Instead, you can create the naming as follows:

```
www.customer1.dom. IN CNAME pageeditor.platform.dom.
```

Then, at migration time, you need to update only a single record, one that's under your direct control.

# Moving to new nameservers

This may seem self-evident, but it's not, because I've seen the following happen countless times: A domain moves on to a new DNS service, they delegate there to the new nameservers, and everything breaks.

What happened?

They forgot to *input their existing zone* into the new nameservers or DNS service before they updated their delegation.

Perhaps this is a throwback to the days when nameserver redelegations took 24 hours or more, and people doing this are trying to get the jump on the new delegation and think they still have a day to put in their zone into the new nameserver system before the new nameservers take effect.

This is not so. Nowadays, almost all TLDs update their zones in real time, or close to it. So, whatever you do, make sure your zone data is in place and loaded on the new nameservers *before* you update your nameserver delegation via your registrar or with the registry.

# Moving single zones

The first order of business is to load your DNS settings into the new nameservers, and there are a few methods.

## Have the new nameservers slave from the current master

This demonstrates the benefit of running a hidden master under your own control from which you allow various remote nameservers to slave the zone, and you update the delegation as required.

The hidden master is more or less static (and stable). In fact, I've always been a proponent of setting up multiplesets of remote secondaries, including hot spares that are not actively delegated. If you run into problems with a given delegation, your spares are already set up and ready to go (this model, with some monitoring and automation is the essence of our "hot swappable nameservers" service).

## Setting up a new master to serve the new nameservers

If you are making a complete move to an entirely new infrastructure, start with setting up the new master nameserver for your zone. If you're using an outsourced DNS provider, it may provide mechanisms for getting your zonedata into their platform. You need to do the following:

- Upload or import a current zonefile
- Open one of your current nameservers to zone transfers to the new system, and import the zone via AXFR
- Use an API method provided by the new vendor

Once you can verify, using your favorite command-line tools, such as **dig**, that the new master and the intended published secondaries are responding authoritatively to queries for your zone, it is now safe to update your nameserver delegation via your registrar or directly with the registry.

# Moving entire portfolios of domains

Sometimes it's the DNS operator itself that needs to migrate nameservers for every domain under management.

The ideal way to do this is to set up the new nameserver constellation and then renumber the host entities for your existing nameservers. This will have the effect of updating all zones under management *whether you have control over the nameserver delegations of each client or not*.

These types of moves are best mapped out over weeks. If you are operating a large multi-variant portfolio, you are almost certainly using a hidden master scheme, Look at this diagram:

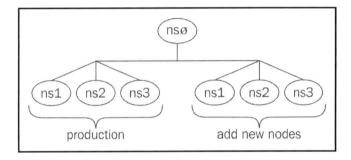

Figure 11-2: Moving all domains to a new set of nameservers

Begin by adding the new nameserver nodes as additional mirrors to your hidden masters for domains for which you are the primary, and your ingress points for domains for which you are providing secondary services.

Populate the new nameserver nodes with new domains as they are being provisioned and keep existing zones in-sync with also-notify.Look at the diagram:

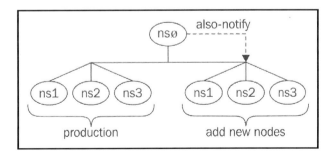

Table 11-3: Keeping both new and old nameservers in sync ahead of cutover

When you are ready to cut over, change the nameservers to the new value, by doing the following:

- Update the host record in the nameserver's zone
- Modify the glue record/host entity for the nameserver in the parent domain. In most cases, this would be the nameserver's parent domain's registry and would be done via the nameserver's domain's registrar. Look at this diagram:

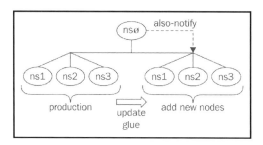

Figure 11-4: Do the cutover by updating the nameserver host and glue records

Note that if you are employing **TLD Redundancy** among your nameservers, it is possible you will be updating your host entities via different registrars or registries, each nameserver having unique procedures for doing so.

Also see `Chapter 12`, *Nameserver Considerations*, as the decisions you make around those topics will directly impact whether your ability to move around huge portfolios of zones, live and on the fly, is a straightforward, routine cakewalk or a harrowing, angst-filled existential crisis.

# Round Robin DNS

Round Robin is a crude way to distributing load across resources and, on its own, is almost never as useful as it might sound. It is *not* a failover mechanism. Without some additional system that monitors and automatically updates your zone, any dead nodes will simply continue to receive traffic and impact your users. Other than that, it's easy to implement and works ok when the resource is relatively stateless. An example would be a pool of URL forwarders.

Most nameservers can implement round-robin without much fanfare; simply add the RRSet for the given hostname, and configure the nameservers to distribute the responses accordingly.

Given `resource.example.com` with multiple servers/IP addresses, it is simply a matter of:

```
resource.example.com.  IN A 10.1.0.1
resource.example.com.  IN A 10.1.0.2
resource.example.com.  IN A 10.1.0.3
resource.example.com.  IN A 10.1.0.4
```

The nameservers then control in what order the records will be returned.

In BIND, it's via the `rrset-order` statement:

```
rrset-order {order cyclic;};
```

Cyclic is the default, and it will cycle through the records returning them in rotating order:

```
rrset-order {order fixed;};
```

It will return them in the order they are listed in the zone:

```
rrset-order {order random;};
```

It will randomize the return order.

With NSD, it's a config option:

```
round-robin: <yes or no>)
```

PowerDNS doesn't support round-robin per se internally, BUT, DnsDist (also from the folks at PowerDNS) *does* support it and has the added benefit of built-in health checks and can be used in front of any nameservers, not just PowerDNS ones. DnsDist a great tool that we take a further look at in `Chapter 14`, *DNS and DDoS Attacks*.

You cannot round-robin CNAME RRs, although some DNS providers facilitate a pseudo-implementation of that. See the *POOL records* section in `Chapter 8`, *Quasi-Record Types*.

It is important to note that round-robin isn't load *balancing* as much as it is load-*distributing*.

# Load-balancing/global weighted load-balancing

Load-balancing is distinct from Round Robin in that one designates desired "weights" or proportions to the various components of the resource being distributed.

In practical terms, this is more often done via hardware implementations (unsurprisingly called load balancers) or open source software packages that run on hardware. Look at this diagram:

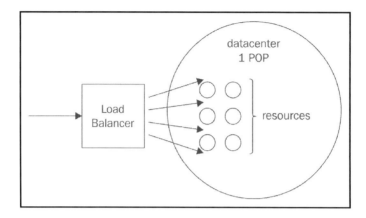

Figure 11-5: Load-balancing within a single POP

However, sometimes the sites you want to load-balance aren't sitting on the same network or even in the same data center. You may be after Global Load Balancing but not necessarily GeoDNS.

When executed via DNS, the load-balancing is implemented by distributing query results along the desired load-balanced weights. Look at this diagram:

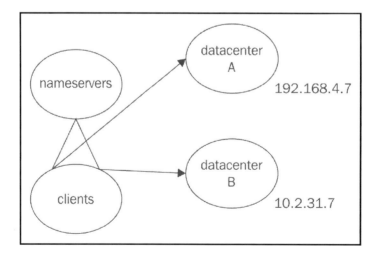

Figure 11-6: Global load-balancing between disparate data centers or POPs

DNS has a couple of built-in mechanisms that can facilitate load-balancing in that SRV and NAPTR records can specify a weight for each RR.

Alas, despite the usefulness of the SRV record in particular, not many applications make use of it. You couldn't load-balance a web server using them, although it would be nice if you could.

Those who insist on using DNS load-balancing are faced with the same implementation choices as those seeking GeoDNS:

- Use a niche server built for the job, such as gdnsd (`http://gdnsd.org`) (I am told Wikipedia uses this)
- Outsource to a DNS provider that has a proprietary implementation
- Build your own implementation, for example, using PowerDNS with a Lua functionality or a custom pipe backend

It is also worth noting that, depending on what it is you want to load-balance, especially globally, this is pretty much what a Content Distribution Network (CDN) does, so another option would be to use a Content Delivery Network (CDN).

# DNS failover

DNS failover is the ability to monitor the health or responsiveness of a given resource and if it is found to be lacking, unresponsive, or severely degraded, the DNS for that resource is automatically modified to direct traffic to another instance of the resource, such as a backup copy or a temporary workaround.

There are several components necessary to make failover effective.

## The target resource must be monitored

The resource being guarded must be continually monitored and care taken that false positives are minimized.

Connectivity and uptime should be polled via some meaningful method. Simply pinging a host isn't reliable since too many routers deny ICMP by default. DNS providers that provide failover enable various mechanisms to fine-tune this, such as minimum thresholds, variable polling intervals, and send/expect dialogs.

Open source packages, such as **nagios** or **sensu**, can be employed and then integrated with various methodologies to dynamically update a subject zone (after all, failover DNS is really a type of an enhanced dynamic DNS use case).

Multiple monitoring points should be used and results cross-referenced. Without using multiple monitoring stations from disparate network locations, it is difficult to know whether an inability to poll a target resource is because the target is down or whether the network between the monitor and the resource is down.

## Its health must be measured and evaluated

Using thresholds, response times, and send/expect dialogs, there needs to be a framework to decide whether a resource's performance necessitates that its DNS records be updated to direct traffic to another resource.

## The standby resource must be ready

This step is spelled out here because I've seen it happen personally (being woken up in the middle of the night by somebody wondering, "Why isn't our failover working?!?"), so apparently this *isn't* so obvious that it doesn't need to be mentioned.

Similar to how merely designating a backup mail spool in your MX settings does not magically convey spooling privileges for your zone on that host, enabling failover at your DNS provider does not magically make it stand-by-ready to your failover device. You have to actually set that up ahead of time, and then *it* also needs to be monitored so that it will only be swapped into production if it's in a ready state.

## There must be a reversion strategy

The final step is to decide what your reversion strategy is once your primary resource is back online and available. You may not want to automatically rollback the DNS to its initial state.

If your secondary environment did any database operations that have not been reflected in your primary environment, you may want to roll back as a delayed or manual process, after any environment alterations that took place during the outage have been reconciled with the primary site.

It may be undesirable to immediately revert back to a previously failed resource if it is "flapping," that is, failing and then intermittently coming back to a working state only to fail again.

# Dynamic DNS

This is perhaps one of the most common DNS use cases, dynamic DNS enables you to map a hostname to a non-static IP address (such as one temporarily assigned to a residential broadband connection and subject to change).

Doing so enables you to do any number of things, such as run a personal mail hub, web server, or PBX on a residential connection.

A process monitors the public-facing IP address of the network demarcation point, such as a router, and when it notices a change, it triggers a process to update the IP address assigned to the hostname in the DNS.

## Standards-based dynamic DNS (RFC 2136)

As defined in RFC 2136, this method of updating a zone sends an update query packet to the authoritative master nameserver and is secured via TSIG.

DHCP servers frequently use this method to update the DNS after assigning an IP address to a remote client.

*Beware of non-secure DDNS updates.*

Even if you are not using RFC 2136-style DDNS updates (and especially if you are), be sure to secure your nameservers against non-secure updates or **zone poisoning.**

A recent paper found that among popular production domains, enough were found to be vulnerable to warrant reporting on (roughly 0.06%). Vulnerable nameservers included those from governments, health care providers, and banks.

This method is typically not supported by DNS providers that offer dynamic DNS as a service. Most often, the way DNS vendors facilitate dynamic DNS is via web requests.

# Dynamic DNS via web requests

Most dynamic DNS clients use http GET method requests to send an update request to a middleware webserver run by the DNS provider. It seems appropriate here to include early tech reviewer Peter Van Dijk's comment on this:

*"It is terrible and dangerous and has forever been forbidden by web standards but what are you going to do?"*

You would hope, given Van Dijk's comment, that any dynamic DNS clients running today would at least use TLS to secure their connections via `https://`. However, my experience from running a couple of the oldest DNS providers in existence and perusing their request logs shows that there are a lot of legacy dynamic DNS clients out there who don't. Look at this diagram:

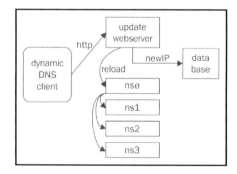

Figure 11-7: Relationship of a web-based DDNS client and the DNS provider

The format can vary from vendor to vendor; however, the parameters created by Tim Wilde back in the early days of dyndns.org, an early dynamic DNS provider (now owned by Oracle), have become a *de facto* standard of sorts. More information about this can be found:

```
http://provider.dom/nic/update?hostname=home.example.com&myip=1.2.3.4
```

The client would authenticate using HTTP basic access authentication. Ideally, today this process should be made more secure by bearing in mind these things:

- Send the requests over TLS.
- Do not use the same end-user authentication credentials in the dynamic update request–instead use another password or token, which, if compromised, would not allow full access to the zone via the customer control panel.

The middleware server then needs to accept the request and perform the following steps:

1. Validate the requestor's credentials and privileges regarding the requested update.
2. Sanity-check the request:
    - Is it a valid domain or zone within the system?
    - Is the requested IP address different from one currently in effect? (Probably 95% of all dynamic update requests are completely superfluous in this respect.)

3. If the update is valid and a change is required, perform the following:
    - Update the backend database with the new IP address for the hostname.
    - Initiate a nameserver reload of the zone.

4. Output a result code back to the client that indicates what happened.

# Geo DNS

GeoDNS is the practice of customizing your responses based on the geographical location of the client making the request.

Before we get into the nuts and bolts of how to do it, there are a couple of aspects you need to be aware of.

## Edns-client-subnet

In the past, when a nameserver received a query, it was only aware of the remote IP of the other nameserver. It had no awareness of the end user client or device making the request, unless they just happened to be on the same host or device.

This can be a problem when trying to do things such as geo-target your DNS responses, especially if end users are employing large public resolver infrastructures that are themselves anycasted (think Google Public DNS, OpenDNS, or Quad9).

edns-client-subnet (`https://trac.tools.ietf.org/html/rfc7871`) addresses this by sending a subnet of the client stub-resolver, usually the first three octets of an IPv4 address or 56 bits of an IPv6 address.

The authoritative nameserver, or any middleware layer, then has the option to factor the edns-subnet-client into its response logic.

Most importantly, when a nameserver "geo responds" to a query, consider the factors that impact what governs the response from the Geo DNS server itself.

As the industry uptake of edns-client-subnet increases, more implementations will key on the client subnet of the requestor in their geo-responses. Most large resolver operations (Google and OpenDNS) already support edns-client-subnet, but be aware that for any for any of your users with resolvers that do not, it will be the location of their *resolvers* that will govern your Geo DNS responses, as opposed to the location of the end users/clients themselves.

# Native support for Geo DNS

Native support for GeoDNS is beginning to appear in some nameserver software.

## PowerDNS and GeoIP backend

PowerDNS has the GeoIP backend (`https://doc.powerdns.com/md/authoritative/backend-geoip/`) that incorporates both Geo DNS and a load balancer. Take a look at this:

```
domains:
  - domain: geo.example.com
    ttl: 30
    records:
      geo.example.com:
        - soa: ns1.example.com hostmaster.example.com 2014090125
          7200 3600 1209600 3600
        - ns:
            content: ns1.example.com
            ttl: 600
        - ns: ns2.example.com
        - mx: 10 mx.example.com
      fin.eu.service.geo.example.com:
        - a: 192.0.2.2
        - txt: hello world
        - aaaa: 2001:DB8::12:34DE:3
# this will result first record being handed out 30% of time
      swe.eu.service.geo.example.com:
        - a:
            content: 192.0.2.3
            weight: 50
        - a: 192.0.2.4
```

```
  services:
# syntax 1
    service.geo.example.com: '%co.%cn.service.geo.example.com'
# syntax 2
    service.geo.example.com: [ '%co.%cn.service.geo.example.com',
    '%cn.service.geo.example.com']
# alternative syntax
  services:
    service.geo.example.com:
       default: [ '%co.%cn.service.geo.example.com',
        '%cn.service.geo.example.com' ]
       10.0.0.0/8: 'internal.service.geo.example.com'
```

This snippet is from the documentation at
`https://doc.powerdns.com/md/authoritative/backend-geoip/`.

In your `pdns.conf`, you need to specify the backend and the location of the geoIP data files, as shown here:

```
; check the geoip backend first, then try the mysql backend
launch=geoip,gmysql
geoip-database-file=/var/lib/GeoIP/GeoIP.dat
```

The **services** define the granularity you can offer, provided you have the requisite data file and the following tokens available:

- **%cn**: Three-letter country code (iso3166-3)
- **%cc**: Two-letter country code (iso3166-2)
- **%cn**: Continent
- **%ci**: City
- **%af**: Address format, either v4 for IPv4 or v6 for IPv6
- **%as**: ASN (**Automonous System Number**)
- **%ip**: Remote IP

## BIND and Geo IP

BIND added GeoIP support in Version 9.10; it involves defining separate BIND views based on each geographical area.Take a look at this code block:

```
options {
        geoip-directory "/path/to/geoip/database";
};

acl "redwoodcity" {
        geoip country US;
        geoip region CA;
        geoip city "Redwood City";
        /* names, etc., must be quoted if they contain spaces */
};

view "redwoodcity" {

        match-clients { redwoodcity; }; zone "isc.org" {
                file "locals/db.isc.org"; type master;
        };

};

view "default" { zone "isc.org" {
        file "nonlocals/db.isc.org"; type master;
};
```

On its own, you might find it unwieldy to try to implement a public-facing GeoDNS implementation using BIND views—it would necessitate creating ACLs for each geographical region. Enter http://phix.me/geodns/ (it used to be a patch for BIND to implement Geo DNS before BIND did it natively); it has a suite of tools and scripts that can be used in automating the import, parsing, and generation of BIND configs to easily use its Geo DNS capability.

## A GeoIP fork for djbdns

geoipdns by Adrian Ilarion Ciobanu, is a fork of djbdns meant to function as a drop-in replacement for it. It also uses the Maxmind GeoIP database (lite version). Take a look at this code block:

```
.example.com:1.2.3.4:a
%boston:71.233.148.0:24
%boston:71.232.0.0:16
%new-york:71.250.0.0:16
%new-york:71.251.10.0:24
```

```
+www.example.com:11.11.11.11:1200::boston
+www.example.com:22.22.22.22:1200::new-york
+www.example.com:99.99.99.99:1200::nomatch
```

## GeoDNS-centric nameservers

A few nameservers have been created specifically for the purpose of facilitating Geo DNS; Here is a list of them:

- `gdnsd` "is an Authoritative-only DNS server which does geographic (or other sorts of) balancing, redirection, weighting, and service-state-conscious failover at the DNS layer."
- `https://github.com/abh/geodns` is a standalone geodDNS nameserver, written in Go and created by Surfeasy VPN co-founder Athir Nuaimi.

## Anycast method

Another way to do GeoDNS is to leverage your existing anycast deployment. Instead of keying down to country-level granularity, or finer, you instead serve a region-based Geo DNS implementation.

Dividing responses into zones can effectively cover off a large chunk of users because, in general, the requirements for GeoDNS are fairly coarse. Splitting responses out into the East and West coasts of North America, Europe, Asia, and South America will cover a lot of ground. Look at this diagram:

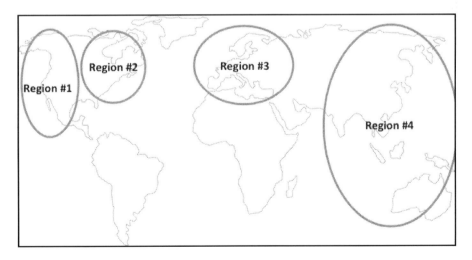

Figure 11-8: Global region-based GeoDNS using anycast deployments

Under this scenario, you create different sets of zone data for each region you are defining, and you deploy that data to the corresponding nodes of your anycast constellations in those regions.

This approach is advantageous in the respect that you don't need to maintain a geoIP database. You're simply letting the routing protocols do all the work, and you're putting plain zone files or zone data tailored for specific regions on each node.

The task is in automating the maintenance and deployment of each region's copy of the zonedata, both within your customer-facing user interface and then under the hood in getting each copy of the zone out to the correct nameserver(s) for each region. Have a look at these examples:

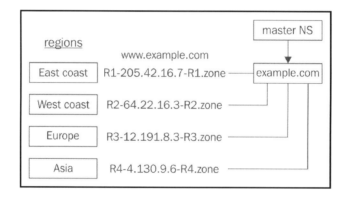

Figure 11-9: Splitting your zone data out into per-region versions

We used this methodology for a while at easyDNS before writing our own PowerDNS backend, which gave us the country-level granularity some clients wanted.

# Custom PowerDNS backend method

This method involves writing and creating a GeoDNS pipe backend for PowerDNS.

We took this route at easyDNS, creating our own PowerDNS pipe backend in Python, which could support round-robin CNAMEs (POOL records).

The backend simply queries a Maxmind GeoIP database with the IP address of the client and, then it looks to see whether any Resource Records specifically match the resulting country-code, returning those if found, or, if they aren't found, a default result.

More recently, as we began the final review on this book, we did end up switching to the PowerDNS GeoDNS backend described earlier.

# Zone apex aliasing

We covered this in depth in `Chapter 8`, *Quasi-Record Types*, (we called it the ANAME). We'll quickly survey some commercial implementations of this:

- Cloudflare offers **CNAME flattening**, which they bill as "RFC Compliant aliases" at the zone apex.
- DNSimple provides a CNAME Round Robin mechanism they call "POOL Records."
- DNSMadeEasy created a mechanism to alias a zone apex to another hostname, called "ANAMEs".

(At easyDNS, we copied DNSMadeEasy's methodology–with their permission–and in our GeoDNS implementation for PHP.net, we inadvertently came up with our own POOL mechanism, which is similar to DNSimple.)

Further more, PowerDNS introduced the **ALIAS** type quasi-record in Version 4.0 (again, see `Chapter 8`, *Quasi-Record Types*, where we dissected this in more detail).

# Reverse DNS and netblock subdelegations

In the case of the address space, that is, the netblocks, you will either be assigned a block of addresses from your regional numbering authority or you will be subdelegated a netblock from your upstream network connectivity provider.

In the case of the former, you will have your own Autonomous System Number (ASN) and be responsible for maintaining your own routing announcements for your netblocks. You will enter your nameserver delegations for your netblocks directly to your regional numbering authority.

Delegating /24 and larger is simply a matter of specifying NS records for the corresponding in-addr.arpa notations as shown here:

```
$ORIGIN 168.192.in-addr.arpa.
        IN NS ns1.telecom.dom.
        IN NS ns2.telecom.dom.
        ; delegates the netblock 192.168.0.0/12 to the ns1.telecom.dom and
ns2.telecom.dom. nameservers

14      IN NS dns1.otherco.dom.
14      IN NS dns2.otherco.dom.
        ; delegates 192.168.14.0/24 range of addresses to otherco.dom
nameservers
```

Then ns1.telecom.dom will contain the relevant PTR records for its delegated netblock:

```
$ORIGIN 13.168.192.in-addr.arpa.

1 IN PTR gateway.example.com.
2 IN PTR somehost.example.com.
```

The PTR records for `14.168.192.in-addr.arpa` (192.168.14.*) will reside on dns1 and dns2.otherco.dom.

But as the internet grew, there increasingly became requirements to carve up and subdelegate address space in chunks smaller than /24. While the terms Class A, B, C, and so on, are still used casually, allocations are now done as **Classless Inter-Domain Routing (CIDR)**.

This is probably one of the more vexing use cases, because there are many ways to subdelegate reverse netblocks among non-dns-ops types, it is one of the least understood aspects of DNS. It requires active cooperation of upstream netblock admistrators (ISPs, connectivity providers), and this process is seldom automated the way a simple forward domain registration is.

But you need reverse DNS, especially for Mail Transport Agents (MTAs), lest it becomes near impossible to send email, as most mail servers will refuse to accept email from any MTA that does not have its reverse DNS configured.

IP addresses are assigned from the geographical numbering authorities known as **Regional Internet Registries (RIRs)** in blocks in 256 address increments (or /24).

Subdelegating a /24 to a downstream entity is relatively simple: You just create NS records for the netblock in the zonefile for the parent zone as follows:

```
42.210.205.in-addr.arpa. 86400 IN NS dns1.easydns.com.
42.210.205.in-addr.arpa. 86400 IN NS dns2.easydns.net.
42.210.205.in-addr.arpa. 86400 IN NS dns3.easydns.org.
42.210.205.in-addr.arpa. 86400 IN NS dns4.easydns.info.
```

You then set up your corresponding PTR records within the delegated netblock's zone on the authoritative nameservers.

# Classless reverse DNS

Many times, you want to be able to directly control reverse mappings for address blocks that are not on a network boundry/smaller than a /24 (Class C) block. This is where **Classless Reverse Mapping** (RFC 2317) comes into play.

When addressing CIDR blocks, there are a two major approaches: RFC 2317 and its variants, which some would argue is an *inferior* method (because they are prone to misunderstandings and breakages), and the more-cumbersome-but- resilient method of delegation at octet boundaries. We'll start with this method, courtesy of tech-reviewer extraordinaire, Peter Van Dijk.

## The proper way to do sub-/24 PTR records

"The only sane way to delegate sub-/24 PTR authority is to delegate per /32.

Assuming the parent holds authority over 192.0.2.0/24, they have this zone:

```
2.0.192.in-addr.arpa. IN SOA .... IN NS ..
```

Now, suppose we want to delegate 192.0.2.0/25 to our example.com customer, we do:

```
0.2.0.192.in-addr.arpa. IN NS ns.example.com.
1.2.0.192.in- addr.arpa. IN NS ns.example.com.
2.2.0.192.in-addr.arpa. IN NS ns.example.com.
...
127.2.0.192.in-addr.arpa. IN NS ns.example.com.
```

Our customer, example.com, then creates 128 zones (yes, really) to receive these 128 delegations. Yes, it looks cumbersome, but if you run mission critical stuff, you have a management panel or decent automation. If you don't have a panel, it's still trivial to generate these 128 files from a single text file.

This is the only sane way to delegate sub-/24 authority, because it does not rely on hacks that confuse people and software. It just uses DNS as it was intended."

## The RFC 2317 method

Many DNS experts, including Peter, view the more common RFC 2317 method as technically inferior, and they may be right. As I mentioned, the following method is prone to misunderstandings and breakages, but it does work and, to be frank, in my entire career, I've never seen a client *not* use it.

In other words, this method of setting up reverse DNS is still prevalent and will probably remain so. Even if you decide to do the delegation-for-each-IP-address way, the odds are you will encounter this method when *others* employ it, so you'll need to understand how it works. If you are going to function as a DNS operator or provider in any capacity, you are almost certainly going to encounter this.

There are variations on the main method defined in RFC 2317; what is important is that the same method must be used by both the upstream and the child nameservers and this is the part that usually breaks.

At the upstream/ISP/netblock admin, the upstream adds a delegation to the zone for the parent netblock:

```
$ORIGIN 38.IN-ADDR.ARPA.

38.in-addr.arpa. 43200 IN SOA auth1.dns.upstream.dom. dns.upstream.dom.
2015071702
        IN NS ns1.upstream.dom.
        IN NS ns2.upstream.dom.

; subdelegation to our client netblock
128/25.251.98.38.in-addr.arpa. 43200 IN NS dns1.managed-dns.dom.
128/25.251.98.38.in-addr.arpa. 43200 IN NS dns2.managed-dns.dom.

; we're still not done, the upstream also needs to add a CNAME
; for *each address* in the sub-delegation....
154.251.98.38.in-addr.arpa. 43200 IN CNAME 154.128/25.251.98.38.in-
addr.arpa.
155.251.98.38.in-addr.arpa. 43200 IN CNAME 155.128/25.251.98.38.in-
addr.arpa.
156.251.98.38.in-addr.arpa. 43200 IN CNAME 156.128/25.251.98.38.in-
addr.arpa.
```

The DNS provider on their end sets up a zone for **128/25.251.98.38.in-addr.arpa.**, again this must exactly match what was used in the zone cut from the parent:

```
$ORIGIN 128/25.251.98.38.in-addr.arpa.
@ IN SOA dns0.managed-dns.com. zone.managed-dns.dom. 1452178728 43200 10800
604800

@ IN NS dns1.managed-dns.dom.
@ IN NS dns2.managed-dns.dom.

154 IN PTR mailgateway.somecustomer.dom.
155 IN PTR mailhub.somecustomer.dom.
156 IN PTR www.somecustomer.dom.
```

The reason this can get tricky is because of the variations.

## RFC2317 modified

The slash (/) character was not always legal to be used so the hyphen (-) was used in its place (**RFC 2317 modified**). In fact, RFC 2317 specifically warns against using slashes and to use some other character in its place. That said, a lot of implementations use the slash.

A dash (–) is commonly used in place of the slash. In this case, everything would be as before, except:

```
; subdelegation to our client netblock

128-25.251.98.38.in-addr.arpa. 43200 IN NS dns1.managed-dns.dom.
128-25.251.98.38.in-addr.arpa. 43200 IN NS dns2.managed-dns.dom.

; we're still not done, the upstream also needs to add a CNAME
; for *each address* in the sub-delegation....
154.251.98.38.in-addr.arpa. 43200 IN CNAME 154.128-25.251.98.38.in-
addr.arpa.
155.251.98.38.in-addr.arpa. 43200 IN CNAME 155.128-25.251.98.38.in-
addr.arpa.
156.251.98.38.in-addr.arpa. 43200 IN CNAME 156.128-25.251.98.38.in-
addr.arpa.
```

In the child zone, you would find the following:

```
$ORIGIN 128-25.251.98.38.in-addr.arpa.
@ IN SOA dns0.managed-dns.com. zone.managed-dns.dom. 1452178728 43200 10800
604800

@ IN NS dns1.managed-dns.dom.
@ IN NS dns2.managed-dns.dom.

154  IN PTR mailgateway.somecustomer.dom.
155  IN PTR mailhub.somecustomer.dom.
156  IN PTR www.somecustomer.dom.
```

For a long time, this used to make my brain seize up. I don't know why, because it's not that hard, but it still got to me for a long time, until one day Steve Job (from DNSMadeEasy) got on a call with me for well over an hour and very patiently stepped me through it. (The problem then was that we had just acquired Zoneedit and I was finding all kinds of client-reverse zones in it that were totally hosed and I was panicking that we had royally screwed up the migration. It turned out that all of the affected zones were already broken long before we ever came along, we just discovered that they were broken.)

What really helped drive this all home for me was to step through the delegation with **dig +trace** (see `Chapter 8`, *Quasi-Record Types*, in section *Debugging Without Tears*):

```
$ dig -t ns +trace -x 38.98.251.154

; <<>> DiG 9.8.3-P1 <<>> -t ns +trace -x 38.98.251.154
;; global options: +cmd
;; ...
;; snip earlier hops

38.in-addr.arpa.    86400  IN NS auth1.dns.cogentco.com.
38.in-addr.arpa.    86400  IN NS auth2.dns.cogentco.com.
38.in-addr.arpa.    86400  IN NS auth4.dns.cogentco.com.
38.in-addr.arpa.    86400  IN NS auth5.dns.cogentco.com.
;; Received 140 bytes from 203.119.86.101#53(203.119.86.101) in 344 ms

154.251.98.38.in-addr.arpa. 43200 IN CNAME 154.128-25.251.98.38.in-
addr.arpa.
128-25.251.98.38.in-addr.arpa. 43200 IN NS dns2.easydns.net.
128-25.251.98.38.in-addr.arpa. 43200 IN NS dns1.easydns.com.
;; Received 129 bytes from 80.91.64.50#53(80.91.64.50) in 129 ms
```

We queried the NS RR one of our final destination IP addresses, the last two hops are instructive. They tell us that our client's address block has been subdelegated from the parent `38.in- addr.arpa`, a /8 block allocated to Cogent.

Next we see that they're using RFC 2317-modified (dashes not slashes) to delegate down to us:

```
128-25.251.98.38.in-addr.arpa. 43200 IN NS dns2.easydns.net.
```

We can also see the CNAME in the parent:

```
154.251.98.38.in-addr.arpa. 43200 IN CNAME 154.128-25.251.98.38.in-
addr.arpa.
128-25.251.98.38.in-addr.arpa. 43200 IN NS dns2.easydns.net.
128-25.251.98.38.in-addr.arpa. 43200 IN NS dns1.easydns.com.
```

Knowing what we know now, this makes perfect sense:

```
$ dig -x 38.98.251.154

; <<>> DiG 9.8.3-P1 <<>> -x 38.98.251.154
;; global options: +cmd
;; Got answer:
;; ->>HEADER<<- opcode: QUERY, status: NOERROR, id: 63236
;; flags: qr rd ra; QUERY: 1, ANSWER: 2, AUTHORITY: 2, ADDITIONAL: 3

;; QUESTION SECTION:
;154.251.98.38.in-addr.arpa.    IN  PTR

;; ANSWER SECTION:
154.251.98.38.in-addr.arpa. 43164 IN CNAME 154.128-25.251.98.38.in-
addr.arpa.
154.128-25.251.98.38.in-addr.arpa. 564 IN PTR mailgateway.somecustomer.dom.

;; AUTHORITY SECTION:
128-25.251.98.38.in-addr.arpa. 43138 IN NS dns1.easydns.com.
128-25.251.98.38.in-addr.arpa. 43138 IN NS dns2.easydns.net.
```

# Implementing SPF, DKIM, and DMARC

As we outlined in the preface and described briefly in `Chapter 5`, *A Tale of Two Nameservers*Sender, **Policy Framework (SPF)** and **DomainKeys Identified Mail (DKIM)** data are examples of DNS going beyond name-to-number translation and conveying metadata over DNS.

In these cases:

- SPF publicly broadcasts which mailserver hosts are allowed to originate or relay email for a specified domain.
- DKIM cryptographically signs an email message or sections of a message to guarantee that it has not been modified or altered in transit.
- Both mechanisms optionally operate in conjunction with a **Domain-based Message Authentication, Reporting and Conformance (DMARC)** policy, also published via a TXT record, which provides further guidance on how remote MTAs should process email based on the results of their SPF and DKIM verification.

## SPF

Implementing SPF is a simple matter of enumerating the complete list of hosts that can send or relay for a domain and publishing that list into a TXT RR within the zone:

```
$ dig +short -t txt example.com
"v=spf1 -all"
```

SPF data fits into the rdata of a TXT RR. It starts with **v=spf1** (the current version of the specification) and is composed of **mechanisms**, where each mechanism is prefixed with a **qualifier** and optionally **modifiers**

The available mechanisms are:

- **ip4**: `<address>` or `<address_range>/<prefix>` example: `"v=spf1 ip4:192.168.0.1/16 -all"`
- **ip6**: `<ip6-network>/<prefix-length>` example: `"v=spf1 ip6:1080::8:800:200C:417A/96 -all"`
- **a**: `<hostname>` or `<hostname>/<prefix>` example: `"v=spf1 a:mail.example.com -all"`

If <hostname> is omitted, then the current domain is used.

The preceding example specifies that email originating from the mail.example.com host is permissible. Add a prefix to the specification:

```
"v=spf1 a:mail.example.com/24 -all"
```

This ensures all hosts within the same /24 that mail.example.com resolves to are sender-permitted.

- **mx**:<domain> or <domain>/<prefix>

The mx handlers for <domain> (or current domain if omitted) are permitted senders.

In this case, if a <prefix> is used, it will permit IPs within the same range as the specified MX:

```
"v=spf1 mx:example.com/24 -all"
```

If example.com's MX handler is mail.mailers.dom, then any IP within the /24 that mail.mailers.dom resolves to will be permitted senders.

- **ptr** [do not use]

As per RFC 7208, even though this is still part of the SPF specification, do not use the ptr mechanism. The other available mechanisms accomplish whatever you would put here more efficiently.

- **exists**: <domain>

A lookup is performed on <domain> and if it resolves *to anything* the sender is permitted. This may not seem useful at first glance, but it can be combined with SPF's macros to create per-user rules or conduct RBL-style lookups:

```
"v=spf1 mx:example.com/24 -exists:%{i}.sbl.spamhaus.example.org -all"
```

In the preceding case, the "-" qualifier in front of the "exists" mechanism, after macro expansion would reject any sender IP that had an entry within the sbl.spamhaus.example.org RBL.

- **include**: <domain>

This mechanism processes the SPF data of an external `<domain>` domain. This is for allowing third-party services that send email on your domain's behalf.

Only the result of the evaluation other domain is used and the processing continues at the next directive (the SPF record from the other domain is not literally included into the current record).

The available modifiers are:

- `redirect=<domain>`

The SPF record for <domain> will replace the current record. Note the difference in syntax between include:<domain> and redirect=<domain>

- `exp=<domain>`

An "explanation" can be defined that the senders will see if their message is rejected. A TXT lookup is performed on <domain> and its contents are used as the message to sender.

These mechanisms, qualifiers, and modifiers combine to specify which senders are permissible for originating email from the subject domain.

For an SPF record to accomplish anything, it has to end with the special **all** mechanism, which matches everything and has the effect of defining what should happen with all other senders that *aren't* matched by the data explicitly asserted in the record:

- **-all** means "fail," the MTA should reject the email with a permanent failure.
- **~all** is a "soft fail," the MTA will still accept the email (usually) and optionally tag the message.
- **?all** is "neutral," don't change processing based on this.
- **+all** is "pass," in this case, adding the + qualifier to the special "all" mechanism allows everything to be a permitted sender and thus, quite ineffectual.

Although you usually see the qualifiers only at the end of the record with the "all" mechanism, they can be used in any mechanism. For example, if there is a known address block (`192.168.44.0/24`) that is emitting forged email for a domain, you could explicitly confront that by putting `-ip4:192.168.44.0/24` into your record.

There are numerous SPF wizards online to enable you to create SPF records:

- `http://www.mailradar.com/spf/`
- `http://www.spfwizard.net/`
- `http://wizard.easyspf.com/`

# SPF – things to know

Before you publish SPF records for your domain, especially any key domains that originate email for your organization or business, there are a couple things you must be aware of.

## SPF breaks email-forwarding

We can see example.com has the following SPF:

```
"v=spf1 a:mail.example.com -all"
```

This means that mail.example.com is the permitted sender for email originating with example.com in the envelope from.

If somebody has a `.forward` file, or is forwarding email through their registrar or ISP to another location, if the final destination MTA is checking SPF data, they won't check mail.example.com where the message originated, they'll check the forwarder, and that check with fail:

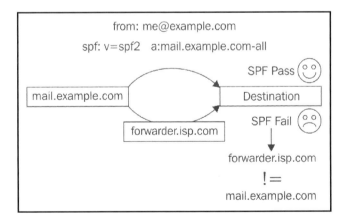

Figure 11-9: If the recipient MTA checks SPF then SPF breaks email-forwarding

The workaround is either that the recipients who are using forwarding need to explicitly whitelist their forwarders on their destination MTAs, or forwarders need to enlist **Sender Rewriting Schemes (SRS)** within their mailers.

SRS was created to solve the forwarding problem for SPF. Instead of forwarding messages to their next hop, the messages are instead *re-emailed* after their envelopes are rewritten with a new address that will:

- Pass an SPF check at any next hops that are checking SPF
- Preserve the original address within the rewritten one to handle replies or bounces

An example of an envelope for an email coming from `mary@foobar.net`, being forwarded by example.org, and rewritten with SRS looks something like this:

```
Return-Path: <SRS0=U1g+=H7=foobar.net=mary@example.org>
```

Oftentimes, a provider implementing SRS will use a specific domain for it, at easyDNS we use easysrs.org, and all SRS rewrites thus happen under that domain.

### Overcomplicated SPF records can lead to bounces

The SPF validation process involves DNS lookups. Given that you can fit a lot of strings into a TXT RR, or that SPF records can refer to external SPF records, which may themselves refer to yet more SPF records, it is possible to construct an SPF record that takes a lot of DNS lookups to evaluate, or even create a circular reference. It is possible to craft a type of Denial-of-Service (DoS) attack.

For these reasons, the SPF specification now caps the maximum number of DNS lookups to evaluate an SPF record at 10. If your record generates more than 10 lookups, the result will be a PermError and your email can be rejected.

You can use this SPF validator (`https://www.kitterman.com/spf/validate.html`) to test an SPF record.

# DKIM

As with SPF, DKIM publishes its data via a TXT RR within the zone, in this case the public key used to verify the signed emails.

However, it doesn't end there; the other side of the equation requires that the originating mail server (MTA) also has the DKIM private key installed and signs each outbound message with it.

The receiving servers will them use the public key from the zone's DKIM TXT RR to authenticate the signature on the inbound email, and optionally refer to a DMARC policy to decide how to handle the message.

The DKIM record uses a **selector** to identify which public key should be used in verifying the signature. Organizations can use multiple selectors for multiple signatures corresponding to any logical distinction of their choosing (office location, departments, servers, or even per-user).

The selectors become part of the `name` field in the DNS TXT RR and are located via the DNS lookup to here:

```
<selector>._domainkey.<domain>
```

We'll use the supportemail selector as we go through this.

The DKIM TXT RR consists of a DKIM DATA formatted within a normal TXT RR:

```
$ORIGIN <domain>.
<selector>._domainkey <ttl> IN TXT "<DKIM-DATA>"
```

For example.com, using our selector:

```
$ORIGIN example.com.
supportemail._domainkey IN TXT "<DKIM-DATA>"
```

or

```
supportemail._domainkey.example.com. IN TXT "<DKIM-DATA>"
```

For the `mail.example.com` host:

```
$ORIGIN example.comsupportemail._domainkey.mail IN TXT "<DKIM-DATA>"
```

or

```
supportemail._domainkey.mail.example.com. IN TXT "<DKIM-DATA>"
```

DKIM information is conveyed via **tag=value** pairs. In the <DKIM-DATA> portion of the TXT RR, they are specified using the following tags:

- `v=<version>`:

```
v=DKIM1;
```

- `p=<public key>` contains the public key of the DKIM key pair. This can be generated using a command-line tool such as **openssl**.

Generate a private key as shown here:

```
$ openssl genrsa -out dkim.private 2048 Generating RSA private key, 2048
bit long modulus
..+++.....................+++ e is 65537 (0x10001)
```

Now generate a public key:

```
$ openssl rsa -in dkim.private -out dkim.public -pubout -outform PEM
writing RSA key
$ cat dkim.public

-----BEGIN PUBLIC KEY-----
MIIBIjANBgkqhkiG9w0BAQEFAAOCAQ8AMIIBCgKCAQEA2+ukWe2SwLDUMpnupnMW

4i2yEHnB8aEzdjK5XpcM3bK0ThekUIy6VVdWbqxMfFEHQ8xXPCmm1yOtvCTuf2Ga
G+UIFBhuAbHkWV6h5SNA3nzsXTD466E3nMnNPDT0XK6/jKVHSurlrnrAIfEeayXl
HUBvPN7kzLwoFR92wog/5OyJ4hIsoF7Oy/6g2kmDibz13Xetb5CuSnzZTeTbQhRw
JJGxZGjoQwXLZB9rRXj6DDOmgUH+cnbjloCJ6wZjKcbqevHpHBa+Rd2L5LFsdkAI
MnX/T0ztrjTXQtdMQOJ0hyQmasJiUeVBNO8W/nIC3GX/tgE5XzM8XDwaq7f5KSME VQIDAQAB

-----END PUBLIC KEY-----
```

A DKIM record for `example.com` created from these two tag/value pairs would be as follows:

```
custemail._domainkey.example.com. IN TXT "v=DKIM1;
p=MIIBIjANBgkqhkiG9w0BAQEFAAOCAQ8AMIIBCgKCAQEA2
4i2yEHnB8aEzdjK5XpcM3bK0ThekUIy6VVdWbqxMfFEHQ8xXPCmm1yOtvCTuf2Ga
G+UIFBhuAbHkWV6h5SNA3nzsXTD466E3nMnNPDT0XK6/jKVHSurlrnrAIfEeayXl
HUBvPN7kzLwoFR92wog/5OyJ4hIsoF7Oy/6g2kmDibz13Xetb5CuSnzZTeTbQhRw
JJGxZGjoQwXLZB9rRXj6DDOmgUH+cnbjloCJ6wZjKcbqevHpHBa+Rd2L5LFsdkAIMnX/T0ztrjT
XQtdMQOJ0hyQmasJiUeVBNO8W/nIC3GX/tgE5XzM8XDwaq7f5KSME VQIDAQAB"
```

The record can be further modified with the following optional tags:

- **g**=<granularity>: **Granularity** refers to everything on the left-hand side of the @ sign in the email address. This field is optional and defaults to "*", meaning a DKIM signature without the granularity specified will apply to all senders take a look at this code:

```
Valid for hostmaster@<domain> g=hostmaster;
Valid for all addresses @<domain> g=*;
```

- t=<flags>: A colon-separated list of flags to the validator, of which there are currently two:
    - y = test mode: This will generate additional diagnostic information for the validator, but it does not imply allowing a failed validation attempt to "pass" because of "test mode." It might be more accurate to think of this flag as a "verbose" mode more than as a "test" mode.
    - s = subdomains: This flag signals that the DKIM record is not valid for any subdomains.

An example TXT RR using these records could look like:

```
custemail._domainkey.example.com. IN TXT "v=DKIM1; g=hostmaster; t=s;
p=MIIBIjANBgkqhkiG9w0BAQEFAA
4i2yEHnB8aEzdjK5XpcM3bK0ThekUIy6VVdWbqxMfFEHQ8xXPCmm1yOtvCTuf2Ga
G+UIFBhuAbHkWV6h5SNA3nzsXTD466E3nMnNPDT0XK6/jKVHSurlrnrAIfEeayXl
HUBvPN7kzLwoFR92wog/5OyJ4hIsoF7Oy/6g2kmDibzl3Xetb5CuSnzZTeTbQhRw
JJGxZGjoQwXLZB9rRXj6DDOmgUH+cnbjloCJ6wZjKcbqevHpHBa+Rd2L5LFsdkAI
MnX/T0ztrjTXQtdMQOJ0hyQmasJiUeVBNO8W/nIC3GX/tgE5XzM8XDwaq7f5KSMEVQIDAQAB"
```

This example specifies a DKIM record for our custemail selector under example.com, valid for *hostmaster@example.com*, and not valid for any subdomains.

There are additional tags in the specification, many of them with a single default value, which is why I omitted them here. They are covered on the DKIM website and in the RFCs.

As is frequently the case when discussing the DNS aspects of email functions (such as when we discussed adding backup MX spoolers), merely adding the DKIM records in your zone's DNS does not make DKIM validation happen.

The private keys of those DKIM records need to be made available to your MTAs, the MTA signs any outbound messages matching your record's specifications with its private key, the receiving mail server locates the public key via DNS and uses it to authenticate the signature.

# DMARC

**Domain-Based Message Authentication Reporting and Conformance** (DMARC) sits on top of your SPF and DKIM implementation.

Once you are publishing SPF data and/or signing your outbound email with DKIM, DMARC provides a way to accomplish two things:

- It provides guidance to email carriers about what they should do with any email purporting to originate from your domains that fail their SPF or DKIM validation.
- Provides reporting back to you about the flow of the mail subject to your published SPF and DKIM policies.

Once again, the policy is published via another TXT RR in the zone's DNS, as shown here:

```
$ORIGIN example.com.
_dmarc IN TXT "<DMARC-DATA>"
```

As in the case with DKIM, the DMARC data is in the form of tag=value pairs. Take a look at this point:

- v=DMARC1: The current version.
- p=[none/quarantine/reject]: What to do with messages that fail their validation. This tag must be the second one present (the first must be the preceding v= version tag).
- sp=[none/quarantine/reject: Optional tag, if present it defines the policy for all sub-domains. If not present, the **p=** policy will apply to all subdomains.
- adkim=[r/s]: Relaxed ("r") or strict ("s") enforcement of sender domain matching the d= parameter of the DKIM record. If "s" (strict), they must match exactly, subdomains will fail. If "**r**" (relaxed), subdomains will pass.
- adspf=[r/s]: In strict ("s") mode, the domain used in the SMTP "MAIL FROM" com- mand must match the domain in the "From:" header (message envelope) exactly. In relaxed mode, any subdomain will pass.

- `pct=[0..100]`: An optional tag specifying the percentage of which DMARC processing will be applied to the domain's mail. 100 means all email is subject to the DMARC policy. Using this tag enables you to begin testing DMARC implementation on a small portion of your mail flow before turning it up for everything.
- `fo=[0/1/d/s]`: Defines under what circumstances a report will be generated to the originating MTA:
  - 0 = reports if ALL underlying (DKIM and SPF) checks fail.
  - 1 = reports if ANY of the underlying checks fail (DKIM or SPF).
  - s = generates a report if the SPF check fails.
  - d = generates a report if the DKIM check fails.
  - Multiple values can be set using colon-separated values.

- `ri=N`: Wait N seconds between reports. The default is 86,400 seconds (one day).
- `rua=<uris>`: Comma-separated list of URIs to which aggregate reports will be sent. Here is an example of one.:

```
rua=mailto:postmaster@example.com,mailto:dmarc-reports@example.com
```

The report address must lie within the domain being reported on. If it does not, the domain for the intended report address must publish yet another TXT record advertising that it will accept reports for another domain. Take a look at this:

```
$ORIGIN example.net. example.com._report._dmarc TXT "v=DMARC1"
```

This allows DMARC reports for example.com to be sent to an address within example.net.

- `ruf=<uris>`: Same mechanism as the preceding, only for detailed failure reports. If not present, these will not be sent:

```
_dmarc.example.com. IN TXT "v=DMARC1;p=none;fo=1;rua=mailto:dmarc-
reports@example.com;"
```

The preceding record asserts a policy in which, the following happens:

- An email will still be accepted even if it fails either test.
- A report will be generated if any test fails.
- Aggregate reports will be sent to *dmarc-reports@example.com.*
- No per-incident failure reports will be sent.

DMARC has been somewhat slower in adoption than DKIM or SPF, but several large providers are using it20 (Google, Yahoo, AOL, and Microsoft), which collectively covers a lot of mailboxes.

It would be somewhat illustrative to use DMARC to gain an understanding on how SPF and DKIM is affecting your mailflow, as well as to get an understanding of the scope (if any) of attempts to spoof your domains.

# Summary

There are two types of operations we perform on our domains: things we do to the domains themselves, and other operations we do within the zones themselves.

An example of the former might be transferring a domain between Registrars or deploying DNS anycast.

The latter includes operations such as deploying DNS-based load-balancing or geoDNS, or implementing mail policies such as SPF or DKIM.

In this chapter, we examined these operations and the reader should have an understanding of what's involved in these cases as well as the options available for implementing them.

# References

1. https://www.icann.org/news/announcement-2016-06-01-en
2. But they can be delegated to new nameservers at any time
3. Key Relay Mapping for the Extensible Provisioning Protocol
4. "Hidden primary" means a nameserver from which all other authoritative nameservers load their data, but it is never published in the nameserver delegation for the zone and thus does not receive actual queries from the internet.

5. One logical master, you can still design for high availability at that master level via clustering and mirroring

6. `http://luadns.com` and `http://dns-api.com` to name a couple

7. Zone Poisoning: The How and Where of Non-Secure DNS Dynamic Updates `http://mkorczynski.com/ IMC16Korczynski.pdf`

8. Because of this, I frequently point out to people that by geo-targeting their URL forward instead, which is comparably trivial to do compared to full-on GeoDNS, you probably get more accuracy (at least for now) in terms of matching remote users to intended resources than you would via GeoDNS (at least for web traffic). Almost everybody I tell this to dismisses it.

9. From documentation at `https://doc.powerdns.com/md/authoritative/ backend-geoip/`

10. From documentation at: `https://kb.isc.org/article/AA-01149/0/Using-the- GeoIP-Features-in-BIND-9.10.html`

11. `https://blog.cloudflare.com/introducing-cname-flattening-rfc-compliant -cnames-at-a-domains-root/`

12. `http://blog.dnsimple.com/2012/03/introducing-pool-record/`

13. `http://www.dnsmadeeasy.com/aname-records/`

14. `https://tools.ietf.org/html/rfc7208`

15. `http://www.openspf.org/SPF_Record_Syntax`

16. SPF/Sender-ID DNS & DDoS Threats(`https://www.dns-oarc.net/files/ workshop-2007/Otis-SPF-ddos-threat.pdf`)

17. `https://tools.ietf.org/html/rfc7208#section-4.6.4` 4.6.4. DNS Lookup Limits

# 12
# Nameserver Considerations

In this chapter, we're going to look at various high-level considerations when deploying nameservers.

Whatever you choose here, you will probably be stuck with it for a long, long time. These decisions can come back to haunt you someday when you are under a DDoS attack (see `Chapter 14`, *DNS and DDOS Attacks*), are experiencing some other type of cascading failure, or have some reason to migrate a really large number of domains.

We'll look at questions such as anycast versus unicast, and you'll gain an understanding of the advantages of each, and whether you even need to go with anycast.

You'll be taken through numbering-scheme considerations and the concept of nameserver homogeneity versus heterogeneity. In my experience, many of the factors we examine here are frequently overlooked or glossed over.

By the time you've finished this chapter, you will have put more thought toward these issues than many professional domain registrar companies or webhosts.

In this chapter, we will look at the following topics:

- Anycast versus Unicast
  - Unicast architectures
  - Setting up anycast
- Nameserver Heterogeneity versus Homogeneity
- Nameserver records
- IP space
- Numbering and delegation schemes
- Vanity Nameservers
- Resolvers

# Anycast versus Unicast

When planning a nameserver deployment, one of the decisions in architecture is whether to go with a unicast or anycast deployment.

In a unicast architecture, each nameserver correlates (logically) to a single-server POP on a single IP address. I say logically because that **Point-of-Presence (POP)** may be a group of servers, behind load balancers or other traffic-shaping devices. Also, it is possible that the POP will be multi-homed and thus answer on multiple IP addresses, including multiple IPv4 addresses and IPv6. Take a look at the diagram:

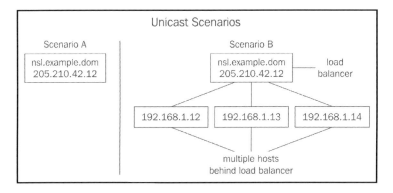

Figure 12-1: unicast nameserver scenarios, each POP has its own IP

Contrast this with an anycast constellation, where nodes in multiple POPs across geographically diverse locations correlate to the same IP address.Take a look at this diagram:

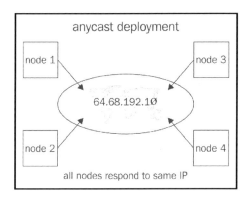

Figure 12-2: Anycast nameserver deployment, multiple POPs respond to the same IP

The address space for the nameservers is advertised from multiple POPs using the BGP routing protocol. Multiple nodes of nameservers are responding from the same IP addresses from different parts of the global internet.

DNS queries originating in resolvers will use network routing to find their way to the closest nameserver listening on the target IP.

An analogy for an anycast nameserver deployment is akin to a Content Delivery Network for your DNS.

# Unicast architectures

Even for large portfolios and many end users, it is possible for unicast deployments to be done well and they can get the job done more than adequately for a majority of domain names. If you are a registrar or a large web host and you have a lot of end user domains under management, most of these can use unicast nameservers. I can tell you from experience, most of your users won't notice or care.

Even single servers that are confined to one network location can be optimized to the point where they are barely distinguishable from an anycast deployment to a majority of users and applications. Multiple CPUs, solid state drives, RAM disks, and proper tuning can make for a unicast deployment that can easily handle hundreds of thousands of domains or more.

Having said that, there is typically a characteristic Achilles' Heel to unicast deployments, and that has to do with the IP address space your nodes are deployed on.

Too often, having decided not to go anycast, a DNS provider will not put a lot of thought into which IP addresses they deploy on or where those addresses come from.

So, they'll take a few IPs assigned to them from their upstream, and maybe some from the data center, or wherever they happen to build out. Then they'll proceed to create their nameserver glue records on those IPs, set up the nameservers, and delegate thousands of domains to them.

This works fine,—perhaps for years,—all the while, more and more domain delegations are being piled on to these nameserver IPs.

Then one day, the DDoS hits.

If you are *Other People's Address Space*, those people have a simple solution to mitigate the DDOS, which in their mind *you* brought to their doorstep: They null-route your nameservers' IP addresses. Once that happens, your nameservers have effectively disappeared from the internet. Different providers have different policies, but once they null-route you, some of them won't even look at you again for at least 24 hours.

Ideally, you are using your own netspace for your nameserver deployments, and, even if you are not deploying via anycast, you have an ASN so that, even if you are not directly announcing your own netspace, you have arrangements with providers whom you've authorized to announce for you (see the next section). That way, when the DDOS hits, you can move your traffic around using BGP and take steps to mitigate the effects.

Anycast or not, you should have a DDoS mitigation plan in place, and have the ability to implement it when the DDoS inevitably hits. It can make the difference between an outage being 35 minutes (which is not great) or a couple of days (catastrophic). Ideally, you have it down to the point where there isn't an outage at all (again, we look at this in `Chapter 14`, *DNS and DDoS Attacks*, in the section *DDoS mitigation services*).

# Anycast DNS

As mentioned earlier, anycast DNS is when you have multiple POPs around the world responding to queries for the same IP addresses. It's like a Content Delivery Network (CDN) for nameservers, where the content being delivered is responses to DNS queries.

To deploy Anycast DNS, you need the following components.

## Your own Autonomous System Number (ASN)

ASNs are required by entities seeking to originate their own routing updates to the global internet. Anycast uses the **Border Gateway Protocol** (BGP) to announce the same IP address (really it's a /24 at minimum) from multiple points around the internet.

To make those announcements, you must have your own routing prefix specified within an ASN.

ASNs are obtained from your regional numbering authority or **Regional Internet Registry (RIR)**.

## Address space to announce

Each logical nameserver (`dns1.example.dom`, `dns2.example.dom`, and so on) will require, at a minimum, its own /24 of address space. If your blocks are smaller than that, your announcements will usually be ignored by the wider internet.

Address space can come from various places:

- Your regional numbering authority (RIR)
- An upstream transit provider who is willing to sub-delegate a portable netblock
- The aftermarket, which is becoming pretty active in recent years given the reality of IPv4 depletion

There are issues with all of these sources, and they can be particularly vexing to DNS providers.

The policy for anycast DNS usually limits such allocations to operators providing DNS to top-level domains or root-server operators. A proposal for ARIN to formally define a policy for micro-allocations (/24s) to non-root or TLD DNS operators has been proposed, but it never went anywhere.

I have to leave it to the reader to come up with a method for obtaining address space for use in anycast DNS from their regional authority. When we did it, we had to apply on the basis of being a web hosting provider, as we were advised we would not receive any allocations strictly for use in DNS anycast.

## Transit providers

Many transit providers have large IP address allocations and may carve out a few /24s for you to use in your anycast deployment. They may want to limit you to their own networks and POPs if they do. If they're willing to let you traverse outside of their own network topology, then the subnets they loan you will have to be "portable."

## The aftermarket

After being a gray area for years, network blocks may now be sold or leased on the aftermarket between entities; however, they are usually still subject to justification within their regional numbering-authority policies.

This means that an acquirer will have to submit a usage plan to their authority as part of the process of taking over the address space.

## Transit providers who will route you

Once you have your ASN and some address space to announce through it, you look for places to colocate or lease your servers that will accept your BGP announcements and aggregate them into their own routing tables.

There are multiple ways to do this. Your provider may simply announce from their routers and put in static routes to your servers within their network. Or, you may control the announcements directly from your own router, gateway or running a routing suite such as quagga, BIRD (brought to you by the same organization that created Knot DNS) or exaBGP on the nameservers themselves.

The advantage of doing the announcements yourself is that you have full control. You can easily drop your announcement when you want, without having to go through your upstream to do it, you can drop your announcement if you want to undertake a maintenance window or are having some issue in a particular POP. The aforementioned exaBGP package was built with these types of operations in mind.

In either case, your transit providers will likely request **Letters of Authority (LOAs)** from you, which codify their authorization to broadcast updates for your routing prefix/ASN.

## Nameserver configurations

After you have your ASN, your address space, and your route peering figured out, you need to tweak a few things on your nameservers to get the final pieces in place.

Most of these issues were enumerated in RFC 3258. Consider the following typical zone:

```
$ORIGIN example.dom.
@  IN SOA dns0.anycast-r-us.dom. zone.anycast-r-us.dom. 1460068247 3600 600
604800 1

@  IN NS dns1.anycast-r-us.dom.
@  IN NS dns2.anycast-r-us.dom.
@  IN NS dns3.anycast-r-us.dom.
```

Normally, when the zone is updated, the master nameserver will send a NOTIFY packet to each NS RR. But if each NS RR is in fact a multiple-node anycast constellation, that won't work, because the NOTIFY will just use internet routing to transmit to the nearest member of each nameserver group.

Either you explicitly send NOTIFY to a non-anycasted IP on each individual node in the anycast constellation (that is, with an **also-notify** declaration), or this may be the impetus you use to switch to an alternate method, such as PowerDNS with a MySQL backend-using data replication.

Each node within the anycast constellation must have the IP address or block of addresses for the anycast configured, and it must also have at least one more routable IP address that will be used in zone transfers, maintenance, and so on Take a look at this diagram:

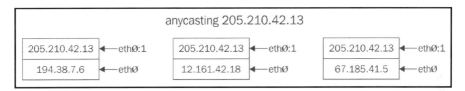

Figure 12-3: Each anycast nameserver node needs at least one other public IP

The nameserver should listen on both IPs so that it can receive NOTIFY packets and zone transfers on the non-anycasted interface. However, the responses to the queries MUST set its source to match the anycasted IP:

```
options {
        listen-on { 205.210.42.13; 194.38.7.6; };
        query-source address 205.210.42.13;
};
```

It is critical that you limit queries to the non-anycasted IP within your own network, so that the wider internet cannot use the non-anycast interface for queries, or DDoS it.

# Debugging under anycast

Debugging under anycast can be tricky ,since there are multiple nodes that could potentially reply to given queries. If what you are debugging is an out-of-sync node, you have to find it.

You can use the existing convention of querying for `bind.hostname`, which can be configured explicitly to any arbitrary string (it defaults to the result of a call to `gethostname()` otherwise):

```
(toronto shell)$ dig @f.root-servers.net CH TXT hostname.bind +short
"YYZ.cf.f.root-servers.org"
(tokyo shell)$ dig @f.root-servers.net CH TXT hostname.bind +short
"ICN.cf.f.root-servers.org"
```

The non-BIND specific ID.SERVER label was later specified, which accomplishes the same thing:

```
(toronto)$ dig @f.root-servers.net CH TXT id.server +short "YYZ.cf.f.root-
servers.org"
(tokyo)$ dig @f.root-servers.net CH TXT id.server +short "ICN.cf.f.root-
servers.org"
```

This enables you to figure out which specific member of an anycast constellation you are talking to.

# Anycast DNS and DDoS mitigation

Anycast is often touted as a DDoS mitigation strategy. Having anycast can help in a DDoS because it diffuses the attack across your different POPs, and if your POPs have more aggregate bandwidth than the attack can muster, it can work, to a degree.

Depending on the amount of capacity at specific locations and where the attack traffic is originating from in relation to those POPs, some of them may fall over even if overall you have more bandwidth than the DDoS can generate.

But, even when that happens, it can be somewhat beneficial overall. If the majority of an attack is originating close to one or a few of your POPs, and those POPs go down as a result but you manage to keep your routing announcements up (it may not be up to you, and your upstream may yank your routes), this can act as a kind of heat sink for the DDoS. Users in those regions will be impacted, but the rest of the world may retain continuity of services.

So, while anycast can help diffuse or sinkhole a DDoS attack, it should not be considered as a main line of defence. Expect attacks to increase geometrically in size over time. Without additional mitigation measures, it's not pessimistic to expect that attacks simply eat up all available bandwidth to all available POPs for the duration of the attack.

We found this out fairly quickly back in the day. Take a look at this diagram:

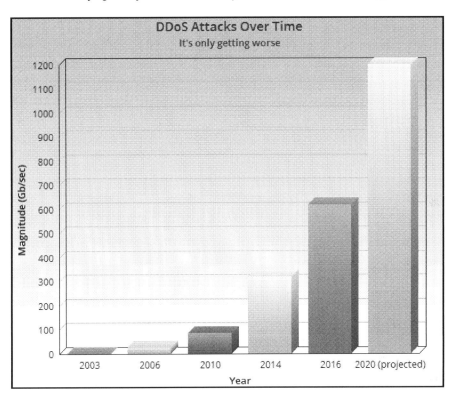

Figure 12-4: DDoS attacks over time

This chart was compiled for one of our white papers using internal attack data and public DDoS incidents. The 2003 and 2006 points were DDoS attacks against easyDNS. The 2010 attack was against DNSMadeEasy, at the time speculated to be a possible record-setting attack. The 2014 data point was composed of NTP reflection attacks. The 2016 point was the attack against security researcher Brian Krebs, while the projected 1.2 TB attack for 2020 came from a Prolexic Technologies white paper. Prolexic's prediction came a couple years early, when memcache reflection attacks hit the 1.2TB/sec to 1.5TB/sec levels in early 2018.

We'll take a closer look at this in the *DNS and DDoS mitigation* section of `Chapter 14`, *DNS and DDoS Attacks*.

# Heterogeneity vs homogeneity in nameserver deployments

There is one kind of mixed architecture that some think should be cultivated and practiced. It is **nameserver heterogeneity**, which means we are running more than one different *type* of nameserver daemon.

Said another way, it means not running the same nameserver daemon in production across all of your namserver nodes. Doing so makes your entire nameserver fleet vulnerable should some kind of bug, exploit, or attack vector come to light that affects your particular choice in nameserver.

Should something arise that could actually neutralize one of your nameservers and you are running in essence, a DNS monoculture, then a vulnerability or attack vector that can take one out can just as easily take them all out.

This is why it is a best practice that whenever possible, you should run a mixed architecture of nameserver daemons.

`Chapter 9`, *Common Nameserver Software*, is written with this in mind; it examines how you would operate various non-BIND nameserver daemons in conjunction with the commonly installed BIND nameserver.

# Nameserver records

Nameserver glue records are those host (A and AAAA) records present in the *parent* zone of a given nameservers' domain. (The phrase "glue" is often misapplied to nameserver hostname records present within the same zone of a given domain.)

In other words, given the `ns1.example.com` nameserver, you would find a host record in the `example.com` zone at example.com's authoritative nameservers, and you would also find copies of those A records in the zone for `.com`, the parent domain of example.com. These latter copies are the actual "glue records":

```
$ORIGIN com.

...

; this $ORIGIN for example.com resides within the .COM TLD zone...

$ORIGIN example.com.
; true glue
```

```
        IN NS ns1.example.com.
  ns1   IN A 192.168.1.13
```

These are required to find the authoritative nameservers for zones these nameservers are authoritative for.

In some TLDs, namely .COM/.NET, glue records are maintained as **nameserver host entities** and are managed via the registrar for their parent domain.

`dns1.example.com` would be updated and modified via the registrar for `example.com`. Most ccTLDs manage glue automatically when you create the delegations.

I mention all this because it comes back into play when you want to update your nameservers, including renumbering, or renaming your nameservers. You will affect all nameserver delegations to your nameserver, even for domains whose registrar is out of your control.

This matters during large migrations or DDoS-renumbering situations.

# IP space

As discussed in the *Unicast vs Anycast DNS* section, which IP space to use for your nameservers deserves consideration.

If you simply use IP addresses assigned to you by your upstream provider, be it a VPS, a data center, and so on, then those IPs ultimately get decided by them. Any initiative to move nameservers to another location (say into a scrubbing center during a DDoS) will necessitate renumbering. Renumbering takes time to propagate as it involves making changes to your DNS. Depending on whether you're the registrar of record for the nameserver's TLD, or the domains delegated to it, it may be out of your control.

On the other hand, if you are using your own IP address allocation, even if you don't use that for an anycast deployment, you have additional flexibility because you can instantly move entire nameserver architectures around via routing updates.

This can be handy, even a lifesaver, in cases such as data-center failover or a DDoS attack.

# Numbering and delegation schemes

Here's where we cover the single worst executive decision I ever made, close to the beginning of my career in the managed-DNS provider business. One that I'm still paying for today.

The year was 1999-ish. The NASDAQ was on fire, Bill Clinton was a lame_duck president, and everybody was bracing for Y2K... One day, Colin Viebrock, one of my co-founders at easyDNS, looked up from his coding and said, "Are we going to just stack domain after domain on to the same nameserver delegation? After a while, that's going to be tens or hundreds or thousands of domains! (Provided we don't go bankrupt!)"

I thought about it. If we *didn't* do exactly that, what were the alternatives? "What are you suggesting?" I asked.

He suggested that we create a large number of nameserver records and multiple nameserver sets, and then we start rotating our delegations on to those nameserver sets. It would mean, he added, that we'd have to keep track of each nameserver delegation for each domain, and where each nameserver set was in terms of numbers of domains delegated.

"That sounds like a lot of extra work," I said. "Just keep stacking them on to ns1, n2, remote1, and remote2."

And, thus, a blunder of cosmic proportions was born. We had another four years to go until, in 2003, our first-ever DDoS attack would knock us offline. When it did, all of ns1, ns2, remote1, and remote2 were squashed as if they were insects, and every single domain under management went dark. Hilarity ensued.

Meanwhile, over in New York City, at around the same time, Erik Aronesty and his partner were working on *their* DNS startup, called `Zoneedit.com`, and when their turn came to have the exact same conversation, they went the opposite way with it.

They created 20 different nameserver records, and began assigning two or three of them, at random, to each domain onboarding into their system.

Every once in a while, one of their domains would get DDoSed too. Except when that happened, it would only take out two or three of their nameserver IPs, and it would *only* affect a small slice of domains that had the exact same delegation.

Now lets fast forward to 2015, when easyDNS acquired Zoneedit. You could still find *many* users who swore up and down that they had never experienced a single instance of downtime with Zoneedit in 15 years. You *cannot* find an easyDNS member who can say the same thing (unless their memories are impaired), alas, because of this one bad decision, we had a few outages and had to spend a lot more money on DDoS mitigation to defend that risk.

Lets go back to IP address considerations: Let's say you had three nameservers and 3/24 net blocks, and the ability to null-route any single IP addresses at the edge of your network.

You could do the following:

- Configure your nameservers to listen to all addresses within the /24 (minus a couple IPs for behind-the-scenes maintenance)
- Create unique nameserver hostnames for each one (253 X 3), that is, ns-a1.example.com through `ns-a253.example.com`, `ns-b1.example.com` through `ns- b253.example.com`, and so on
- Assign a unique combination from three nameserver pools to each domain being served

You would have 253^3 combinations before you had to start recycling combos, giving you the ability to serve 16,194,277 domains without repeating.

Then, when one of those names does get DDoS-ed. Consider the following:

- You can hopefully tell which domain is the target from the IP combination it's hitting, even if you can't from an analysis of the attack traffic.
- Once you null-route those three IPs at your network edge, you have one domain down versus all domains down.

What may seem an innocuous decision on how to number your nameservers, and how to delegate domains to them at scale, will have ramifications long into the future.

When you're not the registrar of a given set of domains, getting existing nameserver delegations updated, especially en masse, is akin to herding cats. It's very slow and cumbersome, and without some band-aid moment, where you arbitrarily shut off nameservice on an obsolete nameserver record, a seemingly never-ending one.

# Vanity nameservers

This is the practice of setting up nameservers under a specific domain being served, such as in the case where BigDNSCo is providing DNS service to example.com, the people running example.com want it to have all of their nameserver records within example.com. They may do this either to appear to be running their own nameserver infrastructure; perhaps they are reselling BigDNSCo's DNS, or, less frequently, because they are ideologically committed to in-bailiwick nameservers.

To do this, they will set up vanity glue records for `ns1.example.com`, `ns2.example.com`, and `ns3.example.com`, and point them at the same IP addresses as `ns1.bigdnsco.com`, `ns2.bigdnsco.net`, and `ns3.bigdnsco.org` (notice that BigDNSCo employs TLD Redundancy, and hence at least two of their nameservers are out-bailiwick).

Some companies will charge for the privilege of doing this, but, in reality, there is nothing preventing your downstream users from doing it on their own, with or without your blessing. You manage nameserver glue records at the registrar of the parent domain of said nameserver records, and if that isn't the DNS provider, it's out of their hands.

Vanity nameservers run the risk that, at some point, those vanity nameserver records will break.

Especially if they are doing it without the explicit consent or blessing of what I'll call the true or underlying nameserver operators. The consequences are further exacerbated when the vanity nameserver records are used across multiple domain names, such as with a reseller of a DNS provider. There are multiple reasons why the underlying nameserver operators may renumber their nameserver records, sometimes with no notice, such as in an extreme DDOS attack. When the old IP addresses stop responding to DNS queries, any vanity nameservers still set to them will cease functioning, and without any out-of-band redundancy, all zones served by them will go dark.

# TLD redundancy

Failure of an entire Top-Level Domain (TLD)is considered a low-risk probability, but it is not unheard of, and if it were to occur in a TLD, which happens to be the super-domain for all of your nameserver records, then all client domains will go dark.

No TLD redundancy:

```
ns1.example.com
ns2.example.com
ns3.example.com
ns4.example.com
```

I consider it a best practice to split your nameserver delegation across multiple TLDs.

TLD redundancy:

```
ns1.example.com
ns2.example.net
ns3.example.org
ns4.example.xyz
```

The author's is not a consensus position. In DNS parlance, there is sometimes a debate over whether a given zone's nameservers should be **in-bailiwick** or **out-bailiwick**. The former means all NS RRs are within the same zone being served. An out-bailiwick nameserver would be a nameserver that is external to the zone being served.

If you are employing TLD redundancy at any level, then, by definition, some of your NS RRs will be out-bailiwick.

For root and top-level nameservers, the bias favors in-bailiwick nameservers, and I can see the logic in that. You will minimize additional out-of-zone lookups, and for top-level domain nameservers that are presumed to have rock-solid infrastructure and not usually prone to outages, the optimization is worth it.

Once we get past the top level, however, my philosophy is to reach for redundancy anywhere we can get it. So, having nameservers under multiple TLDs, ideally, those multiple TLDs being operated by different TLD operators, gives you some downside protection against the unlikely instance of a TLD outage. Conversely, with each new TLD operator and each new registry adds one more attack surface, a compromise in any one of which can cause *Very Bad Things* to happen within your domain.

# Resolvers

While we're concerned primarily with running authoritative DNS for domains under management, every infrastructure requires `resolvers`, and the days of just slapping up a couple of boxes and firing up BIND open to queries are, or should be, over.

Think carefully; who would you want knowing, or having access to, data about every website and internet host your organization interacts with?

I ask because whoever operates the resolvers you use has exactly that.

Looked at in this light, concerns around privacy, data mining, and security may then preclude using one of the big public resolver services. The tradeoff is that the big public resolver services usually add other values, such as security add-ons of their own: protection against phishing sites, malware distributors, and so on.

These are the big public resolver services:

- **Google**: `8.8.8.8` & `8.8.4.4`
- **OpenDNS**: `208.67.222.222` and `208.67.220.220`
- **Quad9**: `9.9.9.9`
- **Cloudflare**: `1.1.1.1`

But if you come to the conclusion that you must run your own resolvers, you should follow these guidelines:

- **Don't make it public**: Public resolver lists get passed around like bottles of booze, usually among the computer underworld with an eye to recruiting them into DNS-amplification attacks.
- **Implement Response-Rate-Limiting** (**RRL**): When your resolver *does* get roped into a reflection attack, which it will if it's public, at least it will detect it and start sinkholing the queries.
- **Enable DNSSEC**: Yes, that will make you more attractive to being used in reflection attacks, but you can mitigate that with RRL. Enable DNSSEC because it's just going to be used more as time goes on. Yes, this is a hotly contested topic, but hating DNSSEC doesn't mean it won't happen. See `Chapter 13`, *Securing Your Domains and DNS*. Turn it on so your resolver fully supports domains that are signed. It won't make any difference to those that aren't.

# Summary

You should now have a decent basis in laying the groundwork for your DNS deployment or rethinking an existing one.

Aside from whether you decide to go anycast versus unicast, what was covered here are often meta-issues that, all too often, are afterthoughts or decided on the fly.

After reading this chapter, you should be better prepared when it comes time you start standing up actual nameservers or developing DDoS mitigation strategies.

# References

1.  One day, a couple of years ago, I put together a list of some of the most illustrious clients easyDNS has, it included names such as Rasmus Lerdorf (PHP creator), Paul Graham (YCombinator), and Larry Wall (inventor of perl). I asked them why they used easyDNS as a vendor and how much of their decision had to do with our using Anycast DNS. Not one of them said, "It's because we need the anycast." More than half of them said, "What's Anycast?"
2. If you are going to be a DNS provider in any capacity, you will be DDOS-ed some day. Not if—when. Plan for it.
3. https://www.arin.net/policy/proposals/2006_5.html
4. https://www.ietf.org/rfc/rfc4892.txt

# 13
# Securing Your Domains and DNS

Over the next two chapters, we'll take a look at a wider scope of domain security:

- Protecting your domains from unauthorized manipulation via a required vendor, such as a registrar or managed DNS provider platform
- Ensuring the validity of your zone data (DNSSEC)
- Mitigating brute-force attacks, such as **Denial-of-Service** (**DDoS**)

We'll also briefly touch on approaches to secure the transport between authoritative servers and resolvers, such as **DNSCurve**.

By the end of this chapter, you should have a set of basic principles that will enhance the security of your domains. You will also understand DNSSEC, what it is, why you may want to use it, and what is involved in doing so.

Then, in the following chapter, we'll continue the discussion with a look at DDoS mitigation strategies.

# Protecting your domains from unauthorized manipulation

DNS security extensions, such as *DNSSEC*, are used to authenticate your query responses and prevent cache poisoning. But it may be easier for an attacker to simply hack into your registrar account or other platform that has the ability to manipulate your domains, and hijack them.

# Cybercriminals hack DNS provider to take over Brazilian bank

Shortly before this manuscript went to final review, news emerged via the 2017 Kaspersky Security Summit in St. Maarten of a sophisticated attack on a major Brazilian bank ,in which the attackers successfully hacked into the bank's DNS provider and then modified its DNS settings to take complete control over its traffic.

For a period of approximately five hours, they substituted a fake online-banking platform operated on servers they controlled, and they duped users into logging into them. The bank reportedly had $25,000,000,000 in assets and 5,000,000 customers worldwide.

You can find the article here: (*Cybercriminals Seized Control of Brazilian Bank for 5 Hours*) `http://www.darkreading.com/attacks-breaches/cybercriminals-seized-control-of-brazilian-bank-for-5-hours/d/d-id/1328549`.

Even if you run your entire DNS infrastructure in-house, the architecture of the DNS system still requires an external registrar or registry component. Those external systems run the gamut in terms of security options and practices and through which control over your domains can be effected.

The following are basic best practices we'd prefer to see for any third-party platform that can exert any control over our names.

## Account ACLs

The ability to limit logins by netmasks, IP addresses, or geographic regions is a start. If your company is based in Toronto, and suddenly somebody is logging into your registrar account from Romania, that's probably not a good sign.

Ideally, you require those logins to originate from within your organization's secured network. Remote workers can be controlled by having them use an organizational VPN and then proceed to the vendor platforms from within the company's intranet.

## Multi-factor authentication

**Multi-factor authentication** can avert disaster in the face of a compromised password or other breach. Take a look at this screenshot:

If your vendor doesn't support two-factor authentication, you can still use a password management system, such as LastPass or 1password, using extremely strong passwords, and then enable 2-factor authentication there.

These password management systems also make shared access credentials within an organization easier to manage.

Factor authentication can happen in various forms, from an SMS message to your mobile device, a specific app, such as Authy or Google authenticator, or even an email to an out-of-band address. Anything is a lot better than not having it.

# Event notifications

Whenever something happens in your external vendor account, you want to know about it, right from logins all the way to making changes such as the following:

- Account updates (email change, password change)
- Whois record edits
- Xone updates
- nNameserver redelegations

# Transfer locks

The domain transfer lock, when enabled, causes any domain transfer/change-of-registrar requests to summarily fail.

All gTLDs and new TLDs support the transfer-lock, which can be observed in a Whois lookup:

```
$ whois example.com
...
Status: clientTransferProhibited
https://www.icann.org/epp#clientTransferProhibited
```

If the lock were turned off, we would see this instead:

```
$ whois example.com
[snipped]
Status: ok https://www.icann.org/epp#ok
```

Which is actually *not* OK, because we never want to see our domains in this status, unless we are preparing to transfer them to another registrar.

Transfer locks are not implemented by all **Country-Code TLDs (ccTLDs)**.

# Registry locks

Registry locks are not the same as a transfer. The transfer locks are usually directly accessible to the end user via the web-control panel and can be enabled or disabled there (preferably triggering an event notification when they do).

Registry locks are an additional level of security provided by the registry itself, which raises the bar on what has to happen before a given domain is unlocked or its nameserver delegation changed. These measures can include telephone voice confirmation between set business hours with a designated list of approved contacts that can grant authorization to proceed,Take a look at this table:

| Registry Operator | TLDs |
|---|---|
| Verisign | .COM, .NET, .TV |
| CIRA | .CA |
| SIDN | .NL |

There is, however, a tradeoff with the registry-level lock: You lose the ability to rapidly change your nameserver delegation at will.

In my own experience, I see more DNS outages occur from nameserver unavailability, such as network failures or DDoS attacks, than from unauthorized nameserver delegations (hijackings). It is more important to me to have the ability to change the nameserver delegation on a domain, or a large portfolio of domains, than it is to lock in the nameserver delegation.

# DNS Security Extensions (DNSSEC)

DNS, for the most part, happens over UDP. That means it is not subject to IP address validation. On its own, it is possible to for an attacker to create a DNS query response packet with whatever payload they want to put in there. Without authentication, to a resolver the bar is fairly low as to what it will accept in a response. If certain elements are present, a resolver will accept a response as authentic. On their own, DNS responses are spoofable. Source-port randomization was added to make it harder to do this, but that is still defeatable. There have been notable instances over the years of this inherent weakness in DNS being used to hijack domains or otherwise superimpose false DNS responses over legitimate ones.

As such, it was deemed necessary to create extensions to the DNS protocol to provide mechanisms for authenticating a DNS response.

**DNS Security Extensions (DNSSEC)** provide a methodology to authenticate that the responses received for a DNS query contains the true response data for the query and have not been altered by an intermediary.

## What DNSSEC does

DNSSEC provides a method where resolvers can reliably affirm that the responses they've received to their lookup queries are unaltered, and that the DNS lookup chain used to arrive at the authoritative name server for a given query can be trusted (trust chain).

Without this mechanism, it is possible that a response received to a query has been altered in transit, and that can have big implications.

For example, when you enter the URL for your online banking, or your cryptocurrency wallet in your web browser, it is highly desirable to know that the IP address you are connecting to after the DNS lookup is the actual IP address for your bank's web portal or the actual cryptocurrency exchange.

A more common example of an everyday situation where your DNS queries are routinely altered would be in some hotel chains. When using their Wi-Fi or broadband networks, they are known to alter certain DNS responses for their own inscrutable purposes.

The premise of DNSSEC is that each RRSet will be able to be authenticated by a DNSSEC-aware recursor because of the following (we will cover the various terms introduced here as we work our way through this section):

- Each RRSet will have an accompanying RRSig record, which is a signature generated by signing the RRSet with a **Zone Signing Key** (**ZSK**), which is itself a **Resource Record** (**RR**) of the type DNSKEY.
- The DNSKEYs used to sign the RRSets (resulting in RRSigs) will themselves by signed by a separate key called the **Key Signing Key** (**KSK**).
- The zone's parent TLD will have a **Delegation Signer** (**DS**) record that authenticates the delegation to the child zone.
- The DS in the parent zone will contain a hash of the child zone's KSK, and it is signed with the parent zone's ZSK key.
- All of which combines to create a Chain of Trust, which is what DNSSEC is all about. Take a look at the following diagram:

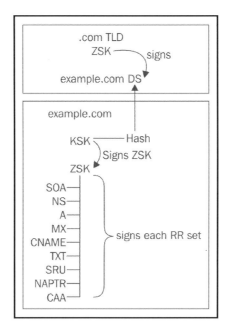

Figure 13-1: The link between a domain and its parent TLD

# Is DNSSEC really a magic bullet for DNS security?

While individual zones have certainly been successfully spoofed or poisoned without DNSSEC or some comparable mechanism, the lower-hanging fruit in these times may be to exploit weaknesses in the DNS operator or the registrar's management platform, or wherever the zone data is being originated to simply hack in and alter the desired responses directly from what would then be an ostensibly trusted origin.

Having said this, as this book was in its final draft, a relatively new attack vector came into being, where the attackers used BGP to hijack the address space of a DNS provider, insert their own face nameservers, and direct victims to a fake cryptocurrency wallet. Had the target domain been DNSSEC-signed, the number of victims would have been greatly reduced.

This event was a bellwether and adds a new urgency to the need for a mechanism that can be used to authenticate responses in the DNS (not to mention BGP announcements). Thus, my view on DNSSEC has shifted significantly since setting out to write this book, where I now think it is a requirement that mission-critical domains be DNSSEC-signed.

# Drawbacks of using DNSSEC

In practical terms, implementing DNSSEC can appear daunting. Best practices suggest periodic key rollovers, although they are not strictly necessary, and rollovers are known to be done incorrectly. Entire TLDs have screwed up their DNSSEC configurations, and thus gone dark to DNSSEC-aware resolvers, and this happens more often than you may suspect. It happens so often, in fact, that there is a website that tracks TLD outages due to errors in the DNSSEC configuration, and you might be surprised to see that these incidents include numerous government, military, and internet infrastructure domains.

Further, because a relatively small query can generate a much larger response, DNSSEC is also another favorite tool for creating DNS amplification attacks. I've had too many sleepless nights because of exactly that, and it didn't succeed in endearing DNSSEC to me.

These factors sometimes lead to a perception that DNSSEC creates more problems than it solves, or that it doesn't fully mitigate the vulnerabilities inherent in the naming system.

However, having said all that, I do agree that there is a real requirement for being able to create reliable trust chains in the DNS tree. The DNSSEC implementation was designed by people far smarter than I when it comes to this protocol. I may be writing a book on managing DNS, but DNSSEC was created by the likes of people who wrote the RFCs that define the DNS protocol itself and those who coded the nameservers we all use to run our domains.

I don't second-guess DNSSEC or criticize it, because frankly, "I'm not worthy." I just try to understand it and not screw up implementing it. Fortunately, the latter is much easier to accomplish today than it was in the past. Read on.

# When to use DNSSEC

In a lot of cases, DNSSEC may be unnecessary. The point where it may be deemed necessary is with zones that provide a high-value target and where the consequences of successful and malicious tampering would be catastrophic, such as the following:

- Financial institutions and payment gateways
- Cryptocurrency exchanges and wallets
- Public infrastructure, including health and safety
- Government organizations and units
- Military

Any website that accepts online payments or any site that, for any reason, might find itself the target of a phishing attack, should consider enabling DNSSEC.

Following this list would be scenarios where it could be highly advisable to use DNSSEC because compromising the zones would greatly amplify the ability to attack high-value targets, and assist in widespread malware infection or botnet construction. Take a look at these points:

- Internet infrastructure domains
- High-traffic sites
- Domains that are referenced by many other domains, such as ad networks, embedded widgets, and API services

Having said this, there are still many domains within the preceding categories that are still not DNSSEC-signed. Why? I think it's for the simple suspicion that DNSSEC-signed zones are at a higher risk of operator error. Some may argue that by signing a zone, you elevate the odds of an outage from DNSSEC-related operator error to being higher than those from a successful DNS spoofing attack. Further more, as in the aforementioned case of intentional DNS alterations, such as what happens on some hotel networks, you run the risk of unpredictable results for users in those situations who access resources dependent on your internet infrastructure zones.

There are other methods of providing DNS authentication (we touch on DNSCurve and DNS over TLS later), but even if they succeed in attaining widespread adoption, DNSSEC will be the frontrunner for the foreseeable future. In 2008, the US government mandated that all federally-owned DNS zones had to be DNSSEC-signed by December 2009. While this doesn't guarantee DNSSEC entrenchment, it certainly goes a long way toward attaining the status of a *de facto* standard.

# Signing your zones

Implementing DNSSEC is a three-stage process, and we'll go over the various components and terminologies. Take a look at these points:

- **Stage 1**: We need to generate our keys.
- **Stage 2**: We use them to sign the elements of the zone.
- **Stage 3**: We generate our DS records and insert them into the parent zone. This is the go-live moment for your DNSSEC deployment and what completes the Chain of Trust from the " . " internet root to your zone.

# Preparing a DNSSEC deployment

Before enabling DNSSEC for any of your zones, you have to work out what your approach will be for implementation. We'll step through them.

As we cover these issues, you'll see references to RRSIGs (a digital signature for an RR Set), various keys (ZSKs, KSKs, CSKs, and DNSKEYs, used to sign data), and Delegation Signers (DS records). If you're unfamiliar with them, they are described in the *DNSSEC Resource Record Types* section.

## Key structure

There are a couple of approaches to setting up the digital keys. The most prevalent approach is to generate two keys: a **Zone-Signing Key** (**ZSK**) and a **Key-Signing Key** (**KSK**).

Both of these keys are **Resource Records** of the DNSKEY type:

```
example.com. 551 IN DNSKEY 256 3 8 (
AwEAAZu77tLm4/O9ZDVp9O9zzV/wsDCunJSWx65+0e8l
i0Hh/5Wbl9kyrhgDs4q2zCD1q4cP8jQUBnnWPn3ZQRhW
Ipa8emWpWPiTVxsqohBC1Cfm5FGA2qL86S5MW29i3Np7
BXHIrtv4er7Y45xgSwZ8XCEUdmJ11Vc3CnyuH1pLi0YH ss41) ; key id = 21214
```

The various DNS records within the zone, such as SOA, NS, MX, A, CNAME, and TXT, are generated using the zone's ZSK, generating an RRSIG for each RRSet:

```
example.com. 569 IN SOA sns.dns.icann.org. noc.dns.icann.org. (
                                    2016110791 ; serial
                                    7200 ; refresh (2 hours)
                                    3600 ; retry (1 hour)
                                    1209600 ; expire (2 weeks)
                                    3600 ; minimum (1 hour)
                                    )

example.com. 569 IN RRSIG SOA 8 2 3600 20170430062944 (

20170409082358 21214 example.com.
IAmTLnX5VglPdIxslSQFZ8SinjbiJEBxoLBOfZizcvSx
E160P/B0NQwvt/9dV41vLGrAh1YSPbULuR8Yq3KqY0bB
b1j2M6nS8u1apkhCuVO+UooASOcZEGWGBWD+Zbhbnvja
03g06+iX28iA9I0mWEQVTOXXt6j3+nGeHGzQETDwyk0= )

example.com. 337 IN NS a.iana-servers.net.

example.com. 337 IN NS b.iana-servers.net.

example.com. 569 IN RRSIG NS 8 2 86400 20170427121451 (

20170406002358 21214 example.com.
B56AKtsmSb50Ey7lb6CvjyhAA85IbPiiPWpF/by5VAuO
1VTxQlvS1+bnkdZpjTHk8+NDEAUmbE84cnPqLxC2pM5N

33EQB+PnqZLLr2k/Jr3MrIoRI6a69VI/zm9fLVysFnmp
2zvS75MQWhwOqhn4ABj4/HDaNT5o5c30Izw9hqQ5N7E= )
```

The KSK is used to sign the zone's DNSKEY RRSet, which will generate a corresponding RRSIG:

```
example.com. 69 IN DNSKEY 257 3 8 (
AwEAAbOFAxl+Lkt0UMglZizKEC1AxUu8zlj65KYatR5w
BWMrh18TYzK/ig6Y1t5YTWCO68bynorpNu9fqNFALX7b
Vl9/gybA0v0EhF+dgXmoUfRX7ksMGgBvtfa2/Y9a3klX
NLqkTszIQ4PEMVCjtryl19Be9/PkFeC9ITjgMRQsQhmB
39eyMYnal+f3bUxKk4fq7cuEU0dbRpue4H/N6jPucXWO
wiMAkTJhghqgy+o9FfIp+tR/emKao94/wpVXDcPf5B18
j7xz2SvTTxiuqCzCMtsxnikZHcoh1j4g+Y1B8zIMIvrE
M+pZGhh/Yuf4RwCBgaYCi9hpiMWVvS4WBzx0/lU=
) ; key id = 31406

example.com. 69 IN RRSIG DNSKEY 8 2 3600 20170428223343 (
20170407202358 31406 example.com.
g0PvvYFHanfd5UTQxdAF+cJhJsH8aV98aRa3rQaC4Rih
WKEjoiDE65a8Hz0vXQXCLpqqJp7RXkIcCvKsgYqwJgS+
GsqfT1WaG3ZSanb8H5NZy+6ooBmCuciXwRiAtGWPQ+oY
sZ74UqD4rZvbVJ8bDNrZleXNGvKIEPzsXkKM3mXGLspW
tixE9mPBAk0N/1+QGuUraFxnPOehTXV5bdYOmks0wV1l
+80YaabH6h/LsGLyUXzT5AHLIFceHVUB8gSdeaK6m2Le
f9TdYW2FgEs2tauoqTsD7gF8d2nCrSC/uSt7g6wZCrib
KSCFlpWrsyPTh60vEh8jiG+4dOtLAnJWEg== )
```

In other words, the ZSK is used to sign the zone's authoritative data, while the KSK is used specifically to sign the DNSKEY RRs themselves.

A hash of the KSK is used in the DS, which gets sent up to the parent domain.

There is another approach for key generation, which is to combine the keys into a **Combined Signing Key (CSK)**. Using a CSK is said to reduce complexity and query response sizes. When using a combined key, the key assumes the role described by the "ZSK" or "KSK" terms, depending on the context it is being used (PowerDNS defaults to the CSK method).

The downside of the CSK method is that you have to update your DS in the parent any time you rollover your key. If you use a separate ZSK/KSK method, you can rollover your ZSK without having to update your DS at the parent.

## Key rollover policy

While it is not mandatory to rollover your keys (as one tech reviewer put it, "How often do you roll over your ssh keys?"). Keys that last for ever were specifically prohibited in earlier operational definitions of DNSSEC, and many tutorials and literature around it still specify a rollover interval. But the operational practices have since evolved and it is now permissible to create keys that do not expire. Consider this:

> *"In general, the available key length sets an upper limit on the key effectivity period. For all practical purposes, it is sufficient to define the key effectivity period based on purely operational requirements and match the key length to that value. Ignoring the operational perspective, a reasonable effectivity period for KSKs that have corresponding DS records in the parent zone is on the order of two decades or longer. That is, if one does not plan to test the rollover procedure, the key should be effective essentially forever and only rolled over in case of emergency."*

> *- Section 3.3 Key Effectivity Period https://tools.ietf.org/html/rfc*

Would periodic rollovers be considered a best practice? Consider that a majority of the high-profile DNSSEC outages I mentioned earlier arose from botched rollovers; I guess it would come down to what you define as a "best outcome." Personally, I have a pathological aversion to DNS outages, so I consider things that actually increase the odds of an outage not to be a "best practice." That said, the major name servers (including BIND and PowerDNS, which we'll look at later in this section) now provide rollover tools that can minimize these dangers. If you elect to implement regular rollovers, use these tools (we'll cover this in the *Rolling your keys* section).

Further more, as another tech reviewer points out, employing the practice of periodically rolling over, and knowing how to do it properly, gives you an advantage when a key is lost or compromised and you find yourself compelled to do a rollover.

## Trust chains

If you simply generated a key pair for its own zone and signed it, you havn't really accomplished much to make the zone secure. An attacker could still spoof responses by generating their own keypair and simply signing their spoofed responses with it.

Think of they way websites are secured via TLS. The TLS certificate authenticates the hostname component of the URL being visited, however it doesn't prevent an attacker from simply obtaining a TLS certificate for a counterfeit version of the target domain.

To truly authenticate a DNS response, there needs to be a mechanism by which the resolver can prove that the signed response it is receiving is actually signed by the correct key.

It does this by verifying the delegation to the authoritative nameservers from the domain's parent zone.

In turn, the delegation from the zone's parent must also be authenticated from its parent domain, and this process must be repeated all the way up to the "." DNS root, as shown in the following diagram:

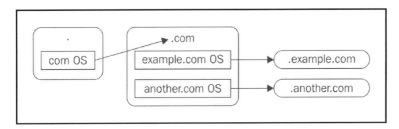

Figure 13-2: This chain is constructed using Delegation Signers (DS Records), which connect each child zone to its parent in a verifiable manner.

## How is the internet root authenticated?

There is no parent zone to the "." internet root.

The "." root then needs to be signed and authenticated by a KSK in a secure way, as it terminates (or originates) all trust chains for the entire DNS tree.

This is accomplished by splitting the KSK into pieces. First, there are two redundant datacenter locations where the root keys are kept, currently on the east coast and west coast of the US; and then there are seven trusted individuals, called **Trusted Community Representatives** or **TCRs**, within the naming community assigned to each location.

A minimum of three is required to undertake a key signing. Look at this diagram:

Figure 13-3: Permission of Cloudflare license: CC BY-ND

At designated intervals, when the root KSK is to be rolled over, the requisite numbers of crypto-officers along with various other Administrators and Controllers convene at an elaborate Key-Signing Ceremony, which is tightly controlled, videotaped, and web casted.

Alas, as mainstream media often does, it tends to get dumbed-down to a lowest-common denominator narrative that is disappointing, but hardly surprising. Look at this screenshot;

The "Internet is Controlled by Secret Keys" meme seems to be persistent, this cited writer even doubled-down with "The internet is still actually controlled by 14 people who hold seven secret keys" in late 2016. It prompted ICANN to issue a blog rebuttal on its website. The TL;DR is, "No, it isn't."

# Operational ramifications of DNSSEC

While most operational TLDs today are DNSSEC-signed, enough of them still aren't to have to make it a point to ensure that your zone's parent domain (TLD) is itself DNSSEC-signed. The following table lists all the TLDs, which at the time of writing are not DNSSEC-enabled. If you want to sign a domain under one of these TLDs, you cannot successfully create a chain-of-trust:

| | | | | | | | | | |
|---|---|---|---|---|---|---|---|---|---|
| ae | aero | ai | al | ao | aq | as | ba | bb | bd |
| bf | bh | bi | bj | bn | bo | bs | bv | cd | cf |
| cg | ch | chart | ci | ck | cm | cu | cv | cw | cy |
| dj | dm | do | dz | ec | eg | er | et | fj | fk |
| ga | gb | ge | gf | gg | gh | gm | gp | gq | gt |
| gu | gy | hm | ht | im | iq | ir | je | jm | jo |
| kh | km | kn | kp | kw | kz | ls | ly | mc | mh |
| mk | ml | mo | mp | mq | ms | mt | mu | mv | mw |
| mz | ne | ng | ni | | np | nr | pa | pf | pg |
| ph | pk | pn | ps | py | qa | rs | rw | sd | sk |
| sm | so | sr | st | sv | sz | tc | td | tg | tj |
| tk | to | tr | uz | va | ve | vg | vi | xn‑‑54b7fta0cc | xn‑‑80ao21a |
| xn‑‑90a3ac | xn‑‑d1alf | xn‑‑j1amh | xn‑‑lgbbat1ad8j | xn‑‑mgba3a4f16a | xn‑‑mgbaam7a8h | xn‑‑mgbayh7gpa | xn‑‑mgbc0a9azcg | xn‑‑mgbpl2fh | xn‑‑mgbtx2b |
| xn‑‑mix891f | xn‑‑node | xn‑‑qxam | xn‑‑wgbl6a | xn‑‑ygbi2ammx | ye | zw | | | |

*Table 11-2: TLDs which are not DNSSEC signed as at June 2018*

## Zone updates

In the past, DNSSEC was not a set-and-forget affair, the zone had to be re-signed any time one of its resource records was updated. This could lead to mistakes and glitches, but servers, such as BIND's inline signing or PowerDNS' live signing, can fully automate the process. As we'll emphasize in the section on signing your zones, don't do it by hand–use the tools.

## Using multiple providers with DNSSEC

If I haven't belabored the point too much already, I'm a huge fan of achieving 100% DNS availability via multiple DNS solutions. How does signing one's zones affect this approach?

Once you publish your DS record into the parent zone, all validating resolvers will expect authenticated data from all nameservers.

If your additional DNS providers are simply slaving your zones via IXFR/AXFR, then their nameservers should respond accordingly. Even if that DNS provider doesn't support DNSSEC natively in that they don't provide mechanisms to sign zones, they'll typically mirror signed zones just fine.

Some other DNS platforms, such as Amazon Route 53, don't use IXFR/AXFR and are utilized via API calls. At the time of writing, Route 53 does not support DNSSEC. If you signed your zone and published the DS record into the parent zone, your queries from validating resolvers would fail querying the Route 53 nameservers.

# DNSSEC Resource Record Types

DNSSEC introduces several new RR types that are used to build trust-chains and provide the authentication mechanisms for DNSSEC.

## RRSIG

The RRSIG is a DNS RR that contains the digital signature that will authenticate its corresponding RRSet.

Every RRSet set within a DNSSEC-enabled zone will be accompanied by an RRSIG record of the same owner, hence each RR Set has its "RR SIGnature."

This is the exception to the "CNAME and other data" rule mentioned earlier. CNAME RRs normally cannot coexist with another record with the same owner-name; however, they can be DNSSEC-signed and thus have a corresponding RRSIG.

Because the RRSIGs contain large cryptographic hashes (compared to the size of the rdata they serve to validate), and that their presence can increase the number of RRs in a zone, enabling DNSSEC vastly increases the size of the zone. The size of the DNS responses can consequently trigger a response over TCP:

```
$ dig -t dnskey tap.ca @pdns0.zoneedit.com
```

The format of the RRSIG is as follows this:

```
<HOSTNAME> IN RRSIG <TYPE_COVERED> <ALGORITHM> <NUM_LABELS> <ORIG_TTL>
<EXPIRY> <INCEPTION> <KEY_TAG> <SIGNER_NAME> <SIGNATURE>
```

It's quite a mouthful. Let's step through it with an example for a CNAME query:

```
; <<>> DiG 9.8.3-P1 <<>> -t a +dnssec +multiline www.easydnssec.com
;; global options: +cmd
;; Got answer:
;; ->>HEADER<<- opcode: QUERY, status: NOERROR, id: 22517
;; flags: qr rd ra; QUERY: 1, ANSWER: 4, AUTHORITY: 0, ADDITIONAL: 1

;; OPT PSEUDOSECTION:
; EDNS: version: 0, flags: do; udp: 4096
;; QUESTION SECTION:
;www.easydnssec.com.     IN A

;; ANSWER SECTION:
www.easydnssec.com.      297 IN CNAME easydnssec.com.
easydnssec.com.          297 IN A 64.68.200.46
www.easydnssec.com.      297 IN RRSIG CNAME 8 3 300 20180704161556 (
                             20180604154213 9054 easydnssec.com.
HgP+P+MJZ4iXUNOcefkJxjekdMscfvlTbyWay8UlxbIC
Np7GUybxbms1jehxsWT6JllotCmnmvyGHr+mSsv6Gg5k
k+4GPecATtOPRNlLyFHrPvVr9R41txgdPKAHXxTFDZWw
QY1MVSKj7Ae7gYUmmrPtp1d9MGJEf3xQFRj/n0JHGbT/
QV3x0iPV6Uy9vJUf4UDq6QW2Rm2joEJt2qVwdUGK1SIw
7Oqqr+k1S5xGWhfZ8PGIFnIpkAKk1Qjj+v7V8G40TPpD
uXfSl4FPSx/2BV1X81dSwzLBzTPNAqQHeGevwXbGfs7c
HgP+P+MJZ4iXUNOcefkJxjekdMscfvlTbyWay8UlxbIC
Np7GUybxbms1jehxsWT6JllotCmnmvyGHr+mSsv6Gg5k
k+4GPecATtOPRNlLyFHrPvVr9R41txgdPKAHXxTFDZWw
QY1MVSKj7Ae7gYUmmrPtp1d9MGJEf3xQFRj/n0JHGbT/
QV3x0iPV6Uy9vJUf4UDq6QW2Rm2joEJt2qVwdUGK1SIw
7Oqqr+k1S5xGWhfZ8PGIFnIpkAKk1Qjj+v7V8G40TPpD
uXfSl4FPSx/2BV1X81dSwzLBzTPNAqQHeGevwXbGfs7c
 L/Vz4BaMqibofhQ+LFIgCxEuSgLr7Wxe3w== )easydnssec.com.
 297 IN RRSIG A 8 2 300 20180705002151 (20180604232151 9054 easydnssec.com.
                             VMbQluuFRj4Q1Yb+GksBYNVwup3OcpZECEV93vyAK2nB
j0M8B9ya5El3ExVLBaOhq7GLnnmoJT8TQuAXnMk0qenS
P65waDPs44SjBIBg4tLauKfu/kGGaDDZZpjoqGzTaGsB
tXylyY2fvaJk1ZkOnxqOwFCy1XC+ojWgtQrRRUpYVz1/
yS4pYmOoYjaqIM1UQelG/je0Zrj84+hEYj1RoubDAOHU
sv9uXN95O4+Xhp18WZkt9vgb9rKhTnlaHunvTV3/eQxx
AETrEZWmZM8kqgTDJt3ipmaknhbmgPC1emXEbpoIK4UC
 +B3WE2IYbjCQbWlOwF0cbWakh2jb4Ths7A== )

;; Query time: 0 msec
;; SERVER: 127.0.0.1#53(127.0.0.1)
;; WHEN: Mon Jun 11 13:19:41 2018
;; MSG SIZE  rcvd: 681
```

- **OWNER_NAME** : The owner name of the RRSet. Here it is `www.easydnssec.com`, and because that is a CNAME, we are also receiving back the A record and its corresponding RRSIG for `easydnssec.com`.
- **TTL**: The TTL of the current response.
- **TYPE_COVERED**: The CNAME for the original query and the A of the CNAME target.
- **ALGORITHM**: The type of signature used, in this case RSA/SHA-256.
- **NUM_LABELS**: Tells you the number of labels in the owner-name of the RRSet being queried (for www.easydnssec.com it's three, for easydnssec.com it's two). If this value is less than the number of labels in your actual query, this response is part of a wildcard.
- **ORIG_TTL**: The stated TTL of the original underlying record being validated. Validating resolvers need this in order to validate records returned from a cache.
- **EXPIRY**: When the current signature expires.
- **INCEPTION**: A date from which point *onward* the signature is valid.
- **KEY_TAG**: Keys are assigned a "key id" or "key tag", which are labels with which they themselves can be identified.
- **SIGNER_NAME**: The value of the entity that owns the **DNSKEY** that was used to sign this record.
- **THE_SIGNATURE**: The actual signature that a DNSSEC enabled resolver will use to compute the validity of the answer it just received.

# DNSKEY

When you generate your ZSK or your KSK, you end up with DNSKEY RRs.

The DNSKEY RR type contains the public half of the key used for signing and the associated metadata.

The format is:

```
<OWNER NAME> <TTL> IN DNSKEY <FLAGS> <PROTOCOL> <ALGORITHM> <PUBLIC KEY>
```

The wire format is this:

```
                            1 1 1 1 1 1 1 1 1 1 2 2 2 2 2 2 2 2 2 2 3 3
       0 1 2 3 4 5 6 7 8 9 0 1 2 3 4 5 6 7 8 9 0 1 2 3 4 5 6 7 8 9 0 1
      +-+-+-+-+-+-+-+-+-+-+-+-+-+-+-+-+-+-+-+-+-+-+-+-+-+-+-+-+-+-+-+-+
      |                  flags          |S|   protocol   |   algorithm   |
      |                                 |E|              |               |
      |                                 |P|              |               |
      +-+-+-+-+-+-+-+-+-+-+-+-+-+-+-+-+-+-+-+-+-+-+-+-+-+-+-+-+-+-+-+-+
      |                                                               /
      /                      public key                               /
      /                                                               /
      +-+-+-+-+-+-+-+-+-+-+-+-+-+-+-+-+-+-+-+-+-+-+-+-+-+-+-+-+-+-+-+-+
```

Source: `http://www.ietf.org/rfc/rfc3757.txt`

Bit 15 of the flags section is the **Secure Entry Point** (**SEP**) bit, which differentiates between a KSK (1) and a ZSK (0). SEP being set to 1 indicates to a validating resolver that there should be a matching DS record in the parent zone.

Bit 7 will be 1 for any DNSKEY that is to be used for DNSSEC.

The flag being 256 means this a ZSK; if it were 257, it would be a KSK.

The Protocol field will always be 3, and the next field is the algorithm; here, 8 means RSASHA256:

```
$ dig @dns1.easydns.com DNSKEY easydnssec.com +multiline
; <<>> DiG 9.8.3-P1 <<>> @dns1.easydns.com DNSKEY easydnssec.com +multiline
; (2 servers found)
;; global options: +cmd
;; Got answer:
;; ->>HEADER<<- opcode: QUERY, status: NOERROR, id: 40758
;; flags: qr aa rd; QUERY: 1, ANSWER: 2, AUTHORITY: 0, ADDITIONAL: 0
;; WARNING: recursion requested but not available

;; QUESTION SECTION:
;easydnssec.com.              IN DNSKEY

;; ANSWER SECTION:
easydnssec.com.         300 IN DNSKEY 256 3 8 (
AwEAAauzv+3RAS7/6UHZKBOZyoovIe292XUDRiDgwK1a
sb6KZ22iT+sA5Janhko1Wtage5eT0ie3litJGQV015L0
r8PIGPaSX1seG9zmH/OBPYbA/eOwIgqh7KdQZ4enp7uf
0IqBi8UnNFNBTSOMvrDZm7GSapeWi1b7xIeaYmbyLHo2
R+ljKqlJHJNKJIc80OgDjyQ0+kA6tHtF7KlmjSFT6vNu
HEYSFs9rgGl8cDip2Y3eEQ8P584wDW4DM7ps3NxJOIHJ
```

```
G+oC9SaUqmY8KkiZyhOfphRAuTEhDKcuPH5fODYReRuJ
                                A8iwyJU3LjNllM3bJJaLHgFjAd8EN//2Ree2vp8=
    ) ; key id = 9054
easydnssec.com. 300 IN DNSKEY 257 3 8 (
AwEAAdfOoWYa6Ce3voZHZbDQuAP/SEqP9Q5JrDGD+AZO
1N+pqqJpybH2H0s4MndsfWs66nLdyXJiZlcgSCMRHEbc
+X0QyUhK+cqEG6DMS4rZm6odjmjA4mRfkDklpuv71LbM
EZw/L0mdxpeoW0nyGCB0ZYLSaZyDBx9MtG12EOfFsRks
bAKRqZETtL59h5cWAOKLAT1Av8NY2v/fnVdV2fpWd9PT
C5SOgJfj8SB+ILnh87nz5/Yd9+z8CJ1JmztQ0Ait1C7v
jGOf1glnyBg47B6myhW1rqzc+TUeHNd6CI/E1MWRmlts
CS1CL/DCwKJ0TMz9KW2VcmyIqohqFVbEUN+Hr6c=
    ) ; key id = 754
```

In this example, the first DNSKEY returned is the ZSK ,the second the KSK. The ZSK key ID is `12474`, and the KSK key ID is `8665`.

## DS (Delegation Signer)

DS RRs are used to establish the chain-of-trust from the "." internet root all the way down to an eventual DNSSEC-signed hostname being queried.

Each DNSSEC-enabled zone has a **Delegation Signing (DS)** RR (RFC 3658) in its parent zone. The DS RR from the child contains a hash of the child's public KSK. It is placed into the parent zone where it is signed by the parent's ZSK. It is up to the child zone administrator to facilitate secure transfer of the DS into the parent zone. Some registries allow this via their own platforms (see sidebar), typically this operation is done via the child zone's registrar:

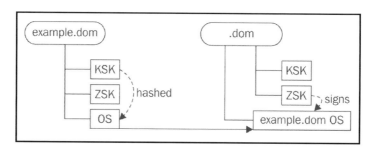

Figure 12-4 The DS record establishes the link between parent and child zone

```
easydnssec.com. 86400 IN DS 28744 5 1
86BBF031318BC809502DD4118C9FB326B8B2B89
```

The format of the DS is as follows:

```
<OWNER-NAME> TTL IN DS <KEY-TAG> <ALGORITHM> <DIGEST-TYPE> <DIGEST>
```

- **OWNER-NAME**: The name of the domain being anchored to the parent.
- **TTL**: The Time To Live for the DS record
- **KEY-TAG**: Specifies the key ID of the DNSKEY used to generate the hash
- **DIGEST-TYPE**: Describes which algorithm was used in the hash
- **DIGEST**: The generated hash that will be signed by the parent zone's ZSK

## Effect of key rollovers on the DS

It is not a requirement that you periodically roll over your keys. It is often suggested. In most discussions of DNSSEC, they almost invariably assume that you will be rolling their keys.

When rolling over your ZSK, you don't need to regenerate your DS record, and, thus, no reinsertion into the parent domain is required.

You will need to regenerate your DS when you rollover your KSK, because the associated hash of your KSK in the DS will change.

## How do I get my DS records into the parent zone?

If you are signing the subzone of a registry-level domain (`example.com` or `example.on.ca`), where your parent is an actual registry (.com and .on.ca, in these cases), you typically have your registrar perform the DS-key insertion for you.

Not all registrars provide this functionality ,and those that do do so at varying levels of automation. Also be aware that your DS keys may originate elsewhere from your registrar, such as cases where you are operating your own nameserver master or using a third-party provider.

Some Registries allow end user Registrants to insert their DS keys directly, those include the following:

- `.AT`
- `.BG`
- `.CA`
- `.DK`
- `.IO`
- `.IS`
- `.UK`

If you are maintaining a subdomain whose parent is not a TLD operated by a registry, then treat the maintainer of the parent zone as "the registry," and coordinate with them to get the DS keys inserted into that parent zone. For example, subzone.example.com DS RRs will be delivered to the administrator of example.com for insertion.

A joint proposal from Cloudflare, Red Hat, and Rightside has tabled a model where third-party DNS operators could, among other things, do DS key insertions and many other functions currently done exclusively via the registrar or registry. It's an interesting proposal, time will tell whether it gains traction.

# Maintaining DS keys after initial setup (CDS/CDNSKEY)

One problem with DNSSEC can occur when you're rolling their KSK: They need to update their DS record in the parent zone. There is no standardized way to do this yet. Worse, it can involve multiple parties who may not even be known to one another.

With CDS/CDNSKEY, the DNS operator can control what they want to see in the parent zone for their DS records via CDS or the CDNSKEY RRs they publish within their own zone.

At the time of writing, no Registries or TLDs actively support CDNSKEY, but there are a few test beds in progress so I expect to see this being deployed someday. Once this happens, one of the last big caveats of DNSSEC will become a lot more managaeable.

Also see: `https://tools.ietf.org/id/draft-ietf-dnsop-maintain-ds-05.html`

# NSEC/NSEC3

While RRSIG records prove the authenticity of a DNS record that exists, there also needs to be a method to authenticate the non-existence of a given record. In other words, we need to be able to sign NXDOMAIN responses.

The initial implementation of this used the NSEC record (Next SECure):

The records in the zone are sorted into canonical order and an NSEC record is computed for each one.

The format of the NSEC RR is:

```
<OWNER-NAME> TTL IN NSEC <NEXT-LABEL> <RR-TYPES>
```

Given a `bar.example.dom` record with the SRV, TXT, MX and NS RRs, and the next record in the zone being `foo.example.dom`, the resultant accompanying NSEC record would be:

```
bar.example.dom. 3600 IN NSEC foo.example.dom. NS SRV TXT MX RRSIG NSEC
```

A bar.example.dom query for on an RR type that doesn't exist would return the NSEC. Any queries for labels that fall between bar.example.dom and foo.example.dom would also return this NSEC.

From looking at the NSEC results, we can determine the next canonically ordered labels within the zone that do exist, thus the NSEC method makes it possible to host walk an entire zone and enumerate every hostname within it.

To fix this, NSEC3 was created. Instead of spelling out the literal label that comes next in the zone, it returns a base-32 string that was derived from multiple iterations through a hashing function:

```
$ dig +dnssec idonotexist.beer
; <<>> DiG 9.8.3-P1 <<>> +dnssec +multiline idonotexist.beer
;; global options: +cmd
;; Got answer:
;; ->>HEADER<<- opcode: QUERY, status: NXDOMAIN, id: 41983
;; flags: qr rd ra; QUERY: 1, ANSWER: 0, AUTHORITY: 8, ADDITIONAL: 1

;; OPT PSEUDOSECTION:
; EDNS: version: 0, flags: do; udp: 4096
;; QUESTION SECTION:
;idonotexist.beer.        IN A

;; AUTHORITY SECTION:
beer.                     3563 IN SOA dns1.nic.beer.
```

```
hostmaster.nominet.org.uk. (
                                2100019916 ; serial
                                900        ; refresh (15 minutes)
                                300        ; retry (5 minutes)
                                2419200    ; expire (4 weeks)
                                3600       ; minimum (1 hour)
                                )
N0DBO49BN7VJGNOJ2EK7PD0P08552BHC.beer. 3563 IN NSEC3 1 1 10 497E730B
N2M0VGKJLS3UIBCUAIGLIAO0MFJJF8SF NS SOA RRSIG DNSKEY NSEC3PARAM
V87TOT23DS3IOKC7PM37NISJDE9HKN1O.beer. 3563 IN NSEC3 1 1 10 497E730B
VI4OALJ7N49FKH833523LBB0U6HI4UL7 NS DS RRSIG
beer. 3563 IN RRSIG SOA 8 1 172800 20180716165302 (
 20180611155302 9250 beer.
te15Dcm0jKAVMtLDtG7W7Y6rkfvrqmAEv2IhcnqGTQ78
odrFD5Afk78+uQOgQZD2F3cfNDzDg4qvRr9VJxgNPXQh
LFKWb88J5vXWfQN639qkIcz39my7jC1gTQSw7qni5bBv
1SZXIzPO2uSuUdir09HqAmlpRNmxPHzPkbcgmFOt86dc
p5u7qa7A+ClXCXiwgttYrMeubMZY17H5Q4W005mr+rYm
Ol/oOfQqpSA5vK7TKK1KXPJY1skE7Yj9B4o8Mb6RGAST
7Ij4H+qpZhRuW65LkYfYGf8bpKiOHac+TpiO7+4JrtUs
k4Ni0G92axgkjlHibWRVHFoZLfcZYjvo9w== )
N0DBO49BN7VJGNOJ2EK7PD0P08552BHC.beer.
3563 IN RRSIG NSEC3 8 2 3600 20180711150601 (
20180606141322 9250 beer.
g8Ed+AjMIt9TmyVdulnFaT1YfgEDqsS0mbCu3gveEd2J
h4zv2Qr4zqaDdFhG/jcqZD/iQrxemg9rq6xE4ei71NFq
Ef3Z+aFWxwCJkt4GxIMdKIYUZVGuFHq08Tik133A4cGD
9grL9M8qvmMI/i9sfSoZevhNr9GEpEzigBnummNWwLe4
qT5drnjYT1+4fhTtbTMWN/YAaKC6GdcYaVaYZdWKxRLH
7HE3gvBPhV1YTyZ4UtFJzx1h/pGbaPfeTZdeU2ZkTZD9
HRv4c+pAoC28JHOFGOF5M9Nz/Wi8NhPPRwecuTzRBOUF
uJKVihd8q9U948cIfjjxiXspsD4M+0S5pw== )
V87TOT23DS3IOKC7PM37NISJDE9HKN1O.beer.
3563 IN RRSIG NSEC3 8 2 3600 20180711103409
(20180606095309 9250 beer.
xzYk6OwmUghYnWqgmp7qXWvj/YYO06lt2ooIB5/Nqr/H
iJBjqT13fb5cZdm+a6CHkNK+wGiatQmzEMcCjEtuYJet
A1D8kCREXyy6k+NLlEN8MK/JqS+oKBi7BJgzCk3LZhz8
V/96g+OqkEd4m/1T/XJCP7c6oXABP7qbULYxNbI/rLds
REUNVbhOaOCXZ0mfV7vvBW0qemjX4TrIkOkXhUmDJNbS
WYCPWX41BkiSFbEZQ1W1XxYTj19e35iXNZtA13fcc8A3
/BWzLQCJHrBSHonehrIghRy9QxlNkYc+pobNK0vTIC5D
 FozhhMy5qvUoako8jnNGyU3jQiq0YQaaTg== )
GK4D2M1CMB9OIUF0GMQ8KE3FSCMH96V8.beer.
3563 IN RRSIG NSEC3 8 2 3600 20180715041037
(20180610035349 9250 beer.
lsdYn5mSon/fOCwtIrS+qbUla96WlrLRPLEwCXTXuaAj
8kAns+a5usKUJmKdz6B4N8qmCbo9FKMTTUg9aZw97rAd
```

```
hN56Ooun03VZ1YynZUiqnS4DnNCUgngiqc09Nt9vGIgT
1T5Cb3Z2lqzWtdAjJsFsMvxMuuTD9rWrLmzZmhOfVAdp
7N2qGz5QTKqLfCxvaelLhQ3jRVN/3MEyniLTA9Zv2pTg
SjfPxLByq1tQ5Jh+DCLtHfdGkOyjmRYxv1EK3bJ1a7SY
rwJNdrK3Coqw3xuoqOta0i0AgBJRFwXJDCsfC2Z/7VaF
 T3dyPBmcUTBGPk9NxtHbhz5lbogXhverQQ== )
```

The format of the NSEC3 RR returned is:

```
<HASHED-LABEL> TTL IN NSEC3 <ALGORITHM> <FLAGS> <ITERATIONS> <SALT> <NEXT-
HASHED-LABEL> <RR-TYPE>
```

The algorithm at present is always 1: SHA1. Iterations means the number of times the process was repeated, and SALT contains the salt used.

# Implementing DNSSEC on your nameservers

If you've decided to sign your zones with DNSSEC, the next question may be, "What nameserver do I use?"

You probably don't want to switch name servers daemons in order to implement DNSSEC. Fortunately, most of the major ones support it.

The other good news is that the major nameservers have all come a long way in DNSSEC deployment, making the signing, maintenance, and rollovers close to fully automated. There are also numerous third-party tools to assist in automating these tasks.

If you are starting a deployment from scratch, I recommend against using manual methods of signing and re-signing after changes and rollovers. Use the tools.

In this section, we'll cover deploying DNSSEC on both the BIND and PowerDNS nameservers.

## What if your main DNS solution doesn't support DNSSEC?

If you've decided you want to DNSSEC-sign one or more of your key domains but for whatever reason you are saddled with either an in-house nameserver that doesn't support it (whether it's not enabled or getting it set up would be non-trivial), or an external DNS provider who doesn't offer it (not all do, even among managed-DNS providers), you could still do a workaround, provided your existing solution supports IXFR/AXFR zone transfers.

The workaround is to set up or acquire services of a master name server that does support DNSSEC, and use it to sign the zones you want to deploy with DNSSEC. Then simply set up your current name servers (or vendor) as a secondary DNS to this master. DNSSEC-related elements will transfer to your mirrors via AXFR/IXFR zone transfers and you're all set.

# PowerDNS

PowerDNS offers a flexible and easy DNSSEC implementation using the `pdnsutil` utility and can operate in a number of modes:

- **live signing**: This is the default. PowerDNS stores the zone records separately from any keys, it then calculates signatures on the fly as queries are received and the RRSIGs are heavily cached:

```
$ pdnsutil secure-zone example.com Securing zone with default key size
Adding CSK (257) with algorithm ecdsa256 Zone example.com secured
Adding NSEC ordering information
```

Notice that the setup defaulted to using a CSK.

We can also switch to using NSEC3 instead of NSEC fairly easily (contrast with BIND where we have to decide that we're going to use NSEC3 at the time we generate our keys):

```
$ pdnsutil set-nsec3 x9.to
```

NSEC3 set, please rectify your zone if your backend needs it:

```
$ pdnsutil rectify-zone x9.to
```

Add the NSEC3 hashed ordering information for `x9.to`:

```
$ dig +multiline +dnssec nxdomain.x9.to @192.168.2.17 [snip]
sn6tnosij76fo8j179mkpdpfguskpblj.x9.to. 3600 IN NSEC3 1 0 1 AB
EJ63G8F72KJQ1HVFL4LEDT3O8F485M9K A

sn6tnosij76fo8j179mkpdpfguskpblj.x9.to. 3600 IN RRSIG NSEC3 13 3 3600
20170504000000 (
20170413000000 46608 x9.to.
AdTTkknyGoEk+V0KUNy3QARzNK2FwDY5BaIFWNAc6nli
ytcM2RqAEAzN1EREr6xPEoaJnjQX+ymCvHutwhzDTw== )
```

## pre-signed

In this mode, PowerDNS serves zone records with previously generated RRSIGs, such as slaving from a remote master or having the records signed using external tools such as OpenDNSSEC, ldns-signzone, or dnssec-signzone.

## front-signing

This is pretty neat. If PowerDNS has suitable keys available, it can slave an unsigned zone from an external master and then sign the records as they are served.

Once you've enabled the zone for DNSSEC, you obtain your DS records using pdnsutil show-zone:

```
$ pdnsutil show-zone x9.to

Apr 20 02:08:45 [bindbackend] Done parsing domains, 0 rejected, 0 new, 0
removed This is a Native zone

Metadata items: None

Zone has hashed NSEC3 semantics, configuration: 1 0 1 ab keys:

ID = 1 (CSK), flags = 257, tag = 46608, algo = 13, bits = 256 Active (
ECDSAP256SHA256 )

CSK DNSKEY = x9.to. IN DNSKEY 257 3 13
plllM0pzeY+HhmpFQ0YfOUjjXEgtAJmw50vdQeDd9oJZI+CaEcErbwFeOl/ DS = x9.to. IN
DS 46608 13 1 ba74f38822d7bff5f230a4b45568c4534b599e24 ; ( SHA1 digest )

DS = x9.to. IN DS 46608 13 2
185a3ce2b69265ac2130448c5afcf2966a8823778d9b72fbdc4a44e7921ce29f ; ( DS =
x9.to. IN DS 46608 13 3
159746c3dd2111c1429d36542813761221ba71a8fb5e341b92404c034be5e642 ; ( DS =
x9.to. IN DS 46608 13 4
ae845787a83ec67b8b9b611874288b137a1996f83df9d47110f1ea34218a5a8a7d228
```

For further reading, start with: https://doc.powerdns.com/md/authoritative/dnssec/

# BIND

BIND, as of Version 9.9, implements rollovers and automatic re-signing via the new auto-dnssec and inline-signing options:

```
zone "x9.to" {

        type master;
        file "/etc/bind/x9.to.zone"; key-directory "/etc/bind/keys"; auto-
dnssec maintain;
        inline-signing yes;
};
```

On BIND, we still need to generate our keys ourselves:

```
root:/etc/bind/keys# dnssec-keygen -a RSASHA256 -b 2048 -3 x9.to Generating
key pair..+++ ................++++Kx9.to.+008+55719

root@:/etc/bind/keys# dnssec-keygen -a RSASHA256 -b 2048 -3 -fk
x9.toGenerating key
pair..........................................................................
........ Kx9.to.+008+31246
```

In the first command, we generated a KSK using the -fk flag, and used an NSEC3-capable algorithm via -3.

Now it's pretty simple to sign the zone (remember to chown these keys to the uid of the nameserver first):

```
$ /usr/sbin/rndc loadkeys x9.to
```

You have to look at the logs after running rndc loadkeys to see that something actually happened:

```
Apr 20 01:20:26 mark-sandbox2 named[469]: received control channel command
'loadkeys x9.to' Apr 20 01:20:26 mark-sandbox2 named[469]: zone x9.to/IN
(signed): reconfiguring zone key
Apr 20 01:20:26 mark-sandbox2 named[469]: zone x9.to/IN (signed): next key
event: 20-Apr-2017 02:2
```

Now we sign the zone and since we generated keys for NSEC3, we pass the - nsec3param argument, along with a random hash of 8 hexadecimal digits:

```
# rndc signing -nsec3param 1 0 10 A67EB653 x9.to.
```

And now we're signed. Take a look at this code block:

```
# dig -t soa +dnssec +multiline x9.to @0.0.0.0 [snip]

;; ANSWER SECTION:
x9.to. 300 IN SOA dns1.easydns.com. zone.easydns.com. (
                        1487112285 ; serial
                        3600 ; refresh (1 hour)
                        600 ; retry (10 minutes)
                        1209600 ; expire (2 weeks)
                        300 ; minimum (5 minutes)
                )

x9.to. 300 IN RRSIG SOA 8 2 300 (
20170520012027 20170420002027 55719 x9.to.
FSm9KD1miE7REj+LQPuZichuwBc54O4px9mDZwfLRjWe
kzZXWMzDpGGoL8rLkNNEzJI7wP4TsrWA+tKPXhNNZ5MI
1gw9A3V99vNAkPnhTLmrG0pbP38BIK5XTWxwweTeMXv8
DrdCmqmaifcsMIywniAa0CdT6ADCAf/3P1Q865/csKKU
vEk348gLDnrWmy8loNDhjX4F3FvxOzpxI95S2kQoAF1J
tvPWx5MwFLeYRz79HDHyrmWHgluXFwRm3TotMyAAE4iN
KCseMTijqAaJWmgw7ctqcST67GVTDDnhRM8jXu62S1ac
w6EO56xmxtVKtrlsRX+6sbbn8NUYqG3jRw== )
```

What's nice about inline signing and auto-maintain is now you can make any modifications to your zone normally, and BIND will detect those changes and re-sign accordingly. It keeps the signed version of the zone in a separate file, leaving your original zonefile alone. This means you can continue to manipulate them via whatever internal processes you use to maintain your zones.

To obtain our DS records16, you use the `dnssec-dsfromkey` utility, either by querying the live zone itself, as shown here:

```
# dig @0.0.0.0 -t dnskey x9.to | dnssec-dsfromkey -f - x9.to x9.to. IN DS
31246 8 1 F5DB9FE64B8B43EE199F256D9400AFCE37215962

x9.to. IN DS 31246 8 2
DF611193C998C00881EBF8C949640CD01D061B6F6B09EBF1C86A790D05EFFBF0
```

You can also pull them from the keyfiles (make sure you use the KSK file, which you can verify via manual inspection), as shown here:

```
# cat Kx9.to.+008+31246.key
; This is a key-signing key, keyid 31246, for x9.to.
; Created: 20170420011342 (Thu Apr 20 01:13:42 2017)
; Publish: 20170420011342 (Thu Apr 20 01:13:42 2017)
; Activate: 20170420011342 (Thu Apr 20 01:13:42 2017)
x9.to. IN DNSKEY 257 3 8
AwEAAb/ayJAf/ojJp9aX4r+nv8qVjMRXo+XUOb/hNjqgi+w0ak87MI95 w5A5HGTbnXYcen6K


# dnssec-dsfromkey -a SHA-1 Kx9.to.+008+31246.key x9.to. IN DS 31246 8 1
F5DB9FE64B8B43EE199F256D9400AFCE37215962


# dnssec-dsfromkey -a SHA-256 Kx9.to.+008+31246.keyx9.to. IN DS 31246 8 2
DF611193C998C00881EBF8C949640CD01D061B6F6B09EBF1C86A790D05EFFBF0
```

Also see `https://deepthought.isc.org/article/AA-00711/0/In-line-Signing-With-NSEC3-in-BIND-9.9-A-Walk-through.html`

# NSD

NSD also supports DNSSEC, the following tutorial via DigitalOcean steps you through how to set it up: `https://www.digitalocean.com/community/tutorials/how-to-set-up-dnssec-on-an-nsd-nameserver-on-ubuntu-14-04`

# Tinydns

Tinydns does not support DNSSEC natively. The `http://www.tinydnssec.org/` project adds this support via a series of patches. D.J. Bernstein has stated he believes DNSSEC doesn't actually solve the DNS security issue cannot be proven to have prevented any attacks. He takes a different approach to securing DNS in "DNSCurve," which we touch upon a little later in this chapter.

# Key rollovers

A key rollover (see `http://tools.ietf.org/html/rfc6781`) is the process of obsoleting an old or compromised DNSKEY within a zone and then re-signing the zone and all of its component RRs with a new signature.

When we sign our keys, the signatures have a TTL that governs how long resolvers will cache any keys and optionally an expiry date, which is a hard cutoff after which RRSIGs should be refreshed even if they are still within the TTL interval in the cache.

When it comes to rollovers, what needs to be understood is that when you transition from one key to the subsequent key, there will be an interval of time during which some resolvers will have old values of various RRs cached. Consider the following:

- They may have the old DNSKEYs cached but will need to validate RRSIGs signed with a new key.
- They may have RRSIGs signed by the outgoing key in cache, but the outgoing DNSKEY may not be in the cache. How then will the cached RRSIGs be validated?

## Double-signing method

When rolling over to a new key using the double-signing method, you add the new key to the zone but then also retain the outgoing key in the zone for an amount of time greater than the TTL of the outgoing key and the longest TTL of any RRs (RRSIGs) signed with the outgoing keys. The zone is then signed using both the incoming and outgoing keys.

The drawback with this method is that for the cutover period when both keys are active, the size of the zone nearly doubles, because there will be two RRSIGs for each RRSet, one using the outgoing key and one using the incoming key.

Given that one criticism of DNSSEC is that signed zones lend themselves well to use in DNS amplification attacks (see `Chapter 14`, *DNS and DDoS Attacks*), this doesn't help.

Double-signing is the recommended method of rolling ZSKs. To roll KSKs, you should use the `Prepublish` method.

## Prepublish method

**Key prepublishing** is when you put the new incoming key into your zone before you re-sign your RRs with it.

This is done at a time interval greater than TTL of the outgoing DNSKEY and any RRs signed with it.

By prepublishing the incoming key in your zone, you will ensure that once the rollover occurs, resolvers will have already obtained the new key and be able to pair that up with any new RRSIGs they receive that have been signed with the new key.

In either case, the outgoing DNSKEY is discarded from the zone after the maximum TTL for any RRSIGs that referenced it has elapsed.

## Key-rolling utilities

Given the high frequency of outages that occur owing to flubbed key rollovers, it is no surprise that a number of utilities have sprung up to ease the process (if you are turning up a fresh deployment, the best thing would be to use the tools within the nameservers themselves):

- BIND auto-dnssec `https://users.isc.org/~jreed/dnssec-guide/dnssec-guide.html`
- rollerd `https://www.dnssec-tools.org/wiki/index.php/Rollerd` (BIND)
- pdnsutil `https://doc.powerdns.com/md/authoritative/dnssec/` (PowerDNS)
- zkt `http://amo-probos.org/post/9` (nsd)
- OpenDNSSEC `https://www.opendnssec.org/`

## Further resources

- `http://www.opendnssec.org`
- `https://www.dnsviz.org`
- `https://www.dnssec-tools.org/`

## Securing DNS lookups

DNSSEC authenticates that responses to DNS queries are valid. But it doesn't do anything to secure your DNS lookups against snooping. There are a couple of mechanisms emerging to protect the DNS lookups against this.

# DNSCurve

DNSCurve is an alternative method of providing DNS security created by Daniel J. Bernstein (the creator of DJBDns/Tinydns and qmail).

I have seen DNSSEC versus DNSCurve become the subject of vigorous debate. As is with most theological schisms, I find these discussions are usually misplaced and a waste of time and energy. In this case, each mechanism helps to secure different aspects of the DNS system, and in my mind these are not either/or decisions.

While DNSSEC authenticates the records being returned from nameservers and validates that there is an unbroken chain-of-trust from the root through to the responding nameserver, DNSCurve secures the communications channel between the client resolver and the responding authoritative nameserver.

The analogy would be that DNSSEC is like GPG-signing an email message to guarantee that it is unaltered and from its true author, while DNSCurve is more like a TLS connection between your computer and the server that it's exchanging sensitive information with.

OpenDNS, whose business is to provide DNS resolution, adopted DNSCurve in 2010.

They then went one further and created DNSCrypt. Where DNSCurve provides security between an authoritative nameserver and the resolver, DNSCrypt uses the same principle, right down to the same encryption algorithms, to encrypt queries between the client resolver and the client.

# DNS over TLS

Another way to secure security between a resolver and authoritative nameserver is **DNS over TLS**, which is now an RFC.

DNS over TLS is an emerging method for protecting the queries between the end user stub resolver and their full resolvers. It fills the same space as DNSCrypt. The more applicable debate in this context would be one of DNSCurve/DNSCrypt versus DNS over TLS.

DNSCurve/DNSCrypt was first in attaining adoption by a major DNS resolvers in OpenDNS.

DNS over TLS has made it along the standards track to have an RFC, and in July 2016, Google's Public DNS launched a beta program to support it.

In the absence of some mechanism, such as DNSCurve/DNSCrypt or DNS over TLS, to encrypt the queries from our applications to our resolvers, a lot of our online activities can be monitored and analyzed, and this is especially true when you use any third-party resolver or resolver service.

# Summary

In this chapter, we worked our way through various aspects of securing your naming infrastructure. There are numerous attack vectors to defend against and a blind spot to any one of them can have catastrophic consequences even if everything else is bulletproof.

We now know that there are some cases where we must use third-party vendors, and the issue then is how we can tighten things up on their platforms to protect ourselves.

From there, we looked at DNSSEC, which enables us to securely authenticate DNS responses to queries. We also took a brief glance at DNSCurve, DNSCrypt, and DNS over TLS, to at least show that they are not competitors to DNSSEC *per se*, but address a different attack surface than DNSSEC does.

In Chapter 14, *DNS and DDoS Attacks*, we'll look at mitigating DDOS attacks.

# References

1. We generally advise that email addresses associated with our domain names, such as in Whois records and logins to vendor consoles, be at domain names under our direct control, even if they ultimately forward to another destination.
2. This preference remains intact even in the aftermath of the very visible, professionally embarrassing Government of Ontario nameserver hijacking that happened on my watch in 2014, the one I described in the "It could have been worse" sidebar in the preface to this book. That said, the Government of Ontario now employs registry locks on their key domains.
3. DNS Security: In-depth vulnerability analysis and mitigation solutions by Anestis Karasaridis.

4. Like when Eugene Kashpureff hijacked the Network Solutions internic website in 1997: `http://www.theatlantic.com/technology/archive/2011/02/when-the-internet-nearly-fractured-and-how-it-could-happen-again/71662/`

5. `https://www.theregister.co.uk/2018/04/24/myetherwallet_dns_hijack/`

6. `https://ianix.com/pub/dnssec-outages.html`

7. That said, pretty well everybody complains about it. See `https://dnsreactions.tumblr.com/post/157393449539/do-you-know-what-sucks`

8. This article by one of the TSRs is an `excellent account` of the process.

9. There was a workaround mechanism to provide chain-of-trust for unsigned TLDs called "Domain Lookaside Validation" (DLV); however, that system is being sunsetted and no longer accepts new entries.

10. Defined in RFC 4034 `http://tools.ietf.org/html/rfc4034`

11. `http://www.iana.org/assignments/dns-sec-alg-numbers/dns-sec-alg-numbers.xhtml`

12. `https://tools.ietf.org/html/draft-ietf-regext-dnsoperator-to-rrr-protocol-03`

13. CIRA and APNIC are currently running CDNSKEY test beds.

14. It has been asserted that this may not be as big of a deal as it was in the past, given the availability of computing power today. You can enumerate entire zones via brute force anyway: "You are running bare naked through the internet, covered in honey, whether you allow AXFR or not. So, disallowing AXFR is at best a professionalism matter, and not really a security matter" - Paul Vixie, `https://lists.dns-oarc.net/pipermail/dns-operations/2015-April/013140.html`. He was referring to whether one allows AXFR access to the world but the same principle applies to using NSEC vs NSEC3.

# 14
# DNS and DDoS Attacks

Because of the pivotal role DNS plays in all things internet, remember absolutely nothing happens without it, the DNS system provides a tempting attack vector to those bad actors who want to knock targets inoperable or offline.

If you take out somebody's authoritative nameservers, you take that somebody right off the internet.

Alas, DNS attacks against nameservers aren't exactly surgical strikes. As a rule, there is a lot of collateral damage.

Given a target domain `example.dom` using nameservers: `dns1.someisp.com` and `dns2.someisp.com`, and someisp happens to have thousands, or even millions of other downstream domains on those same nameservers (and *only* those same nameservers). If the attackers are successful in knocking over those nameservers, not only will `example.dom` go offline, so will every other domain using the same nameserver set.

Statistically, your odds are very low that one of *your* domains will be the direct target of a DDoS attack.

However, the odds are comparatively highthat you *will* be affected as collateral damage in an attack against somebody else using the same ISP, Registrar, web-hosting provider or managed DNS provider.

DDoS attacks against DNS take a couple of broad approaches:

- To directly attack a target domain on your nameservers (Direct attack)
- To leverage your infrastructure to attack a target someplace else, called a DNS Reflection or DNS Amplification attack

In this chapter, we'll go through the options for dealing with this scourge upon the internet. We'll look at some quick fix tactical things you can do in a hair-on-fire situation, and we'll look at the differences between implementing mitigation gear within your own POPs versus using external scrubbing centers.

We'll look at this from the perspective of a DNS operator, managing many downstream customer domains, as well as from an end-user looking after your own domain.

# What DNS operators can do to mitigate attacks

As stated earlier in `Chapter 12`, *Nameserver Considerations*, if you're going to be offering DNS services, you're going to get hit. It's a matter of when, not if. The first time it happened to easyDNS, we were completely oblivious to the spectre of DDoS attacks and our infrastructure absolutely pancaked under the hit. It knocked all of our nameservers completely off the internet and and most of our customers went offline with them.

Since that day, devising ways as a DNS operator to withstand and parry DDoS attacks has become somewhat of an obsession. Again, some of the decisions I made pursuant to `Chapter 12`, *Nameserver Considerations*, came back to haunt me. Some of them still do today. That's why I said that whatever you decide in that section, think about it carefully. You'll be living with some of those decisions longer than you might with your own spouse.

## Separating the target

The first order of business if you're hosting the direct target of a DDoS attack is to identify who that target is. Utilities, such as **dnstop**, can show the inbound queries broken down by domain, RRtype, and originating resolver, among other criteria.

Packet analyzers, such as **Wireshark**, can help you discern patterns in the attack traffic that can be used to create firewall rules or filters to discard hostile traffic.

Identifying the target helps you decide your course of action. As I've remarked elsewhere, there are two types of DDoS targets you will find on your system: the first, and the minority of instances, are legitimate customers, and you have to figure out how to separate them from your other clients and help them out if you can.

The second are the type of customers you didn't know were on your system and now that you do, you probably want to take a shower. In my experience, these are the most common DDoS targets. As much as blaming the victim is universally frowned upon, these types of users generally have it coming. Kick them from the system and wait for the DDoS to follow them.

There are pariah domains traipsing around the internet... bringing one long perpetual DDoS attack close on their heals... endlessly looking for hapless DNS providers to allow them to dock for a few hours, before the attack hits and they get kicked loose again. Lather, rinse, repeat.

The most effective way to deal with pariah domains is to have and enforce policies on what kind of domains you will allow on your system.

You can automate checks of domain names before you allow them to open an account. The mechanics of doing so is outside the scope of this chapter.

# Response-Rate Limiting (RRL)

RRL is standard issue in BIND and NSD now. The team behind PowerDNS also recently released dnsdist, which is a "DDoS-aware" DNS proxy layer with built-in RRL and packet filtering:

```
options {
        rate-limit {
        responses-per-second 5;
        };
};
```

RRL will prevent your nameservers from being used in an amplification or reflection attack by limiting how many responses it will send to each client.

When thresholds are exceeded by a client sending too many identical queries per second, the nameserver can be configured a variety of ways. It can send back a TC response, forcing the client to retry over TCP, it can not respond at all, or provide an occasional response known as a leaked response, governed by the leak rate parameters.

Also see *A Quick Introduction to Response Rate Limiting*.

# Dnsdist – the Swiss Army knife of DNS middleware

I frequently call *PowerDNS* "The Swiss Army knife" of DNS servers. It is appropriate to fit the same analogy to Dnsdist as a middleware component for a robust DNS infrastructure.

Dnsdist is not confined to use with PowerDNS. It can sit as an intermediary layer in front of any nameserver, and can even be configured to proxy queries to external third party nameservers on multiple criteria and at a level of per-domain granularity.

Given my personal opinion that multiple provider/multiple DNS solutions are the emergent best practice I think there will be a huge role for middleware DNS traffic directors such as Dnsdist. It's an open source product, available via `https://dnsdist.org/`.

Also, see the *DnsDist* project homepage.

# Kernel filtering of queries

Sometimes you find yourself in a situation where you need to get tactical and resort to some low-rent workarounds, if only to buy yourself some breathing room and time to think.

This can mean using kernel rules on your actual DNS server, such as iptables, to calm down a nameserver in the midst of a bad episode.

For example, our nameservers were once used in a pretty bad DNS amplification attack before the days we had RRL.

The attackers had compiled a list of domains delegated to our nameservers and were flooding us with ANY queries for our own domains and forging the source IP in the packets so that we would respond back to their intended target. Not only would that attack the target, it did a severe number on us as well.

We ended up inserting rules to drop all ANY queries:

```
# iptables -A INPUT -p udp --dport 53 -m string --from 40 --algo bm --hex-
string '|0000ff0001|' -j
```

So, we put the fire out, but dropping all ANY queries is a controversial measure to take.

Similarly sometimes you just want to drop all queries for a specific domain:

```
# iptables -I INPUT -p udp --dport 53 -m string --hex-string
"|07|example|03|com" --algo bm -j DROP
```

In this case, you need to prefix each label in the domain with its byte-count; that's what the 07 and the 03 before "example" and "com" respectively are.

Typically, what happens in a DDoS attack is that the queries are auto-generated within a botnet, and frequently the queries have some kind of telltale marker that you can key on and filter.

Perhaps all queries are coming in from the same source port:

```
# iptables -I INPUT -p udp --dport 53 --sport 6666 -j DROP
```

Again, if you're operating at this level, it points to a deficiency in or an absence of an overall DDoS mitigation strategy. Ideally, you don't have to resort to this because you have some other method in place to mitigate DDoS attacks.

# Mitigation devices

The market abounds with hardware and virtual appliance DDoS mitigation devices and they are nice to have. The issue I have with these is no matter how good they are, if the attack fills up the pipes going into the POP where these devices reside, it doesn't matter if they can rinse out all that attack traffic. The attack is still going to crowd out your legitimate traffic.

These devices are effective when the volume of attack traffic is below the threshold of the POP they are protecting. These can be invaluable for protecting TCP/web-based assets, where the attack may be more about the number of packets than it is the bandwidth volume of the attack.

But when it comes to UDP and DNS in particular, I find mitigation appliances are often limited in their effectiveness by the aggregate bandwidth available where it is deployed.

The following are some DDoS mitigation device vendors:

- Top Layer (now corero.com)
- Arbor
- Fortinet
- Checkpoint

# Mitigation services

Even if you have onsite DDoS mitigation gear, they all work well; but if an attack can still be so large that it consumes all the transit into your POP, you'll still be down.

The next line of defence would be to utilize companies that specialize in DDoS mitigation as a service. Such companies operate scrubbing centers and make it their business to have more transit than the largest DDoS attacks. Granted, this is an arms race, but such companies are better suited to fight them than the rest of us.

There are a few variations on this theme of using a DDoS mitigation service. Consider the following:

# Colocated gear

Some mitigation providers will allow you to physically colocate your hardware inside their datacenters or lease servers from them.

Once you have this set up, there are a couple of operational permutations. You can simply run these nameservers as regular active nameservers all the time, even when there is no DDoS. When the DDoS starts, there is nothing to do, the mitigation simply kicks in and does its thing.

# Via BGP

You can run these nameservers as hot spares. They are always receiving NOTIFY updates and are in-sync with your production nameservers, but you are not announcing these nodes via BGP. When a DDoS hits, it's simply a matter of turning up these announcements and making these nodes active.

At easyDNS, we use a combination of this on our DNS1 and DNS3 anycast constellations where we have hardware located with two separate DDoS mitigation providers. For DNS3, those nodes are always active. For DNS1 they aren't, but when a DDoS hits, we start announcing DNS1 from within the scrubbing datacenters. This has the effect of decreasing our global footprint during a DDoS but you are able to maintain DNS availability.

# Via glue records

This alternative method is sub-optimal, for one reason because the TLD glue records will typically hold longer TTLs, but it works better than total outages. If you are perhaps running unicast nameservers, or not announcing nameservers from within your own address space (see `Chapter 12`, *Nameserver Considerations*), you can obtain similar results by doing the following:

- Keeping the TTL on your NS hostname RRs very low, such as 300 seconds or even less
- When DDoS-ed, change the glue records for your nameservers to the IPs of the nameservers colocated within the scrubbing centers

We use this approach on Zoneedit, which has 20+ unicast nameservers scattered around, and we have four nodes within scrubbing centers. When any of the nameservers get hit, we update their glue records and redirect their traffic to the DDoS-protected nodes.

# Reverse proxy

A reverse proxy is a layer-7 application, which talks directly to the client resolvers.

We use this method on our DNS2 anycast. In this scenario, we have an arrangement with a completely separate DDoS mitigation provider who operates their own DDoS-protected CDN.

Then we have a private constellation sitting behind that CDN, and our DNS2 nameserver IP is published as the public-facing CDN.

Queries come in to the mitigation layer, which is always active, and that passes clean traffic back to our layer, which responds back to the CDN, which responds back to the client. Excessive round-trips are minimized by the mitigation layer, optimizing RTTs to the nearest private nodes and by maintaining a query cache, it will answer back from within it directly when it can.

# GRE Tunnels

GRE Tunnels are similar in principle to reverse proxies in that when used in a mitigation context, they filter out hostile traffic and send the rest on to the destination nameservers. This operates at level-3, filtering and forwarding individual packets.

Where the reverse-proxy is akin to a nameserver in front of a nameserver, the GRE tunnel approach is like a firewall in front of a nameserver.

# DDoS mitigation services

- Cloudflare
- Defense.net (acquired by F5)
- Koddos
- Prolexic (acquired by Akamai)
- Staminus (now StackPath)
- Voxility

(EasyDNS currently uses Cloudflare and Voxility. In the past, we've used Prolexic and Staminus–now Stackpath.)

# What individual domain owners can do

The preceding solutions may be out-of-reach for individuals or small organizations, or even big ones whose core competency lies elsewhere.

Thus, when seeking to maximize uptime on your own domains, it's all about *redundancy*.

When the DNS specification and associated RFCs were first published, redundancy was cultivated by simply virtue of having "multiple" (that is, two) nameservers, on disparate networks. To wit, nameservers should be as quoted.

> *"both topologically and geographically dispersed locations on the Internet, to minimise the likelihood of a single failure disabling all of them."*

—*RFC* `https://tools.ietf.org/html/rfc2182.`

This is no longer enough. In the modern, commercialized internet of today, each DNS provider or DNS operator must be treated as a logical **Single-Point-of-Failure** unto itself.

The complexity of deployments today offers a myriad of failure modes beyond the simple "failure of a link to a given Point-of-Presence."

In the case of DDoS attacks, a botnet often targets *all* nameservers within an organization's deployed fleet. Further, because of the complexity of deployments such as anycast, there are additional failure modes within an organization that can cascade across all deployed nameservers, other forms of redundancy notwithstanding.

# Using multiple DNS solutions

The magic bullet to achieving 100% DNS availability is to use multiple disparate DNS providers, not just individual nameserver deployments.

At easyDNS, we've had more than our fair share of DDoS attacks, some causing severe DNS impact, and for the most part, we've been able to sustain end user availability to our control panel throughout them. This at least gave the customers the ability to update their delegations and sidestep the outages.

We do this by using three separate DNS providers for our own domain's DNS, and then our own Nameservers failover system to automatically switch our delegation if one set of nameservers fails. This is different than hostname failover in that it happens at the nameserver level, modifying a domain delegation at the domain TLD registry instead of the at hostname level within a zone.

You don't need to get this fancy. What you need is to have multiple DNS solutions deployed *in advance* and then have a coherent methodology for managing the meta dns structure.

# Keeping your data in sync across those deployments

This can be as simple as using a hidden master that acts as primary for multiple separate providers. Those providers may be commercially-managed DNS companies or privately-run independent nameservers operated by colleagues or peer entities. Look at this diagram:

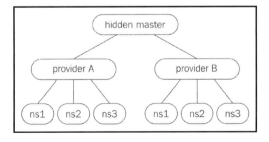

Figure 13-1: Simple layout for mirroring DNS across multiple providers

Data can be synced via traditional AXFR/IXFR zone transfers, which provides the greatest interoperability. Most platforms and providers will have an ingress point designated for third-party zone transfers.

Additionally, many providers have APIs to access their DNS functionality and numerous scripts, code objects and even nice web services exist to facilitate accessing them. At easyDNS, we try to provide as many hooks into external services as possible. Refer to this screenshot:

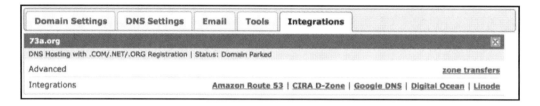

## Monitoring the health of your nameserver delegation

Once your zones are syndicated across multiple providers, you also need to monitor the status of your nameserver delegation.

Options range from third-party monitoring services to open source packages.

Ideally monitoring should be distributed, especially if your nameserver deployment is anycasted.

## Open source monitoring tools

- Cacti
- Nagios
- Sensu

## Monitoring services

- Catchpoint
- Constellix
- Domainsure
- Pingdom
- Site24x7
- ThousandEyes

### The ability to change delegations when required

The usefulness of your monitoring solution decreases drastically if you're precluded from being able to act on what it reports to you.

You need to have the ability to take action when your monitoring reports an outage. One of the reasons provider-wide outages are so bad is because when the provider, such as a Registrar or a web host, is down and their control panel is unusable, nobody can update their nameserver delegations during the outage.

Similarly, when a DNS provider who is *not* a Registrar is down, it simply doesn't occur to many end users that they could, they *should* in fact, head over to their Registrar, and switch their nameserver delegations to their backup DNS provider ...which they setup in advance ...which is up to date with current zonedata and ready to go.

Some DNS providers (such as `https://ns1.com/`) have integrations between third-party monitoring solutions and DNS control. This is great, as are most conventional implementations of DNS failover (see `Chapter 11`, *DNS Operations and Use Cases*) for handling outages within your current zone. What isn't as common, but much needed, are tools to detect and automate failover at the nameserver level. In fact, at the time of writing, there is only one, and we invented it.

# For DNS providers

All of this applies to DNS providers as well: registrars, web hosts, ISPs, managed DNS operators, and so on. What changes is the scale one is operating at and the mechanics of effecting step 3, that of adjusting your DNS setup in response to outages or degraded conditions.

Here, we refer back to our `Chapter 12`, *Nameserver Considerations*, when it comes to selecting address space for numbering your nameservers. Ideally, you control its address space so that you can easily move traffic around, using routing announcements if you have to.

This is what I was alluding to `Chapter 12`, *Nameserver Considerations*, about moving traffic into DDoS scrubbing centers during an attack using BGP.

One model we used for awhile with great success was a combined anycast/unicast architecture, where under normal course operations, a particular nameserver entity was an anycast-deployed constellation.

We would concurrently operate several unicast hot-spares collocated within the data centers of a DDoS scrubbing service.

Whenever an attack hit, we would drop the announcements of the anycast constellations, and bring them back up on the unicast nodes within the scrubbing centers.

This had the effect of collapsing our anycast nameserver constellations into unicast nodes, but the unicast nodes could withstand far more attack traffic than the entire combined aggregate of the anycast deployments. Have a look at this diagram:

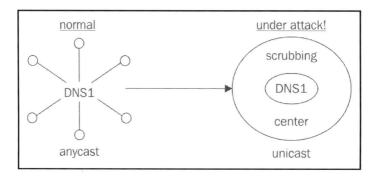

Figure 13-2: During normal operations, DNS is dispersed via anycast, when attacked, it retreats into a unicast node within a scrubbing center.

If you don't have control over your address space or can't update your routing, you can approximate this behavior by updating your nameserver host records, both within your zone and, if applicable, the glue records in their TLD registries.

This should have the effect of updating the IP address for your nameservers across all domains delegated to them, whether you have any control over those domains' delegations or not.

This method isn't as efficient as updating via routing. It won't be instantaneous and normal DNS propagation issues will apply. As such, if you employ this method, it implies keeping the TTLs on these nameserver A and AAAA RRs very low, all the time.

# Summary

In this chapter, we looked at the exigencies of handling Distributed Denial-of-Service (DDoS) attacks against your DNS infrastructure. We examined several aspects of what you can do when they happen, at both the individual domain holder and aggregate provider level.

I can never say it too often, so I'll say it again here: DDoS mitigation is an arms race, and you are usually fighting the last war. The next attack will be bigger, and the next attack will be harder to mitigate, so if you absolutely, positively *must* have 100% DNS availability all the time, the way to achieve that is to use multiple DNS providers or systems and have a coherent methodology for deploying your zone data across them and have the ability to switch between them as the need arises.

# References

1. It was April 14, 2003, bringing to and end five years of 100% DNS uptime.
2. The infamous Godaddy DNS outage of 2012 , which knocked millions of domains offline, was caused by a router misconfiguration (even though responsibility for it was initially claimed by hackers), see: `http://arstechnica.com/security/ 2012/09/godaddy-outage-caused-by-router-snafu-not-ddos-attack/`.
3. Domainsure is an easyDNS subsidiary.
4. It was difficult to write this section because I was always cognizant of the risk of veering into infomercial territory. I'll say it frankly: easyDNS was the first major managed DNS provider to come out and say that you need to use multiple solutions that go beyond any single provider. easyDNS was the only managed provider to build hooks and integrations into other DNS providers, and easyDNS is still the only company that provides automatic nameserver delegation updates in response to outages. But the sentiment that you must use multi-provider redundancy at the DNS level finally became conventionally accepted best practice over the intervening years since I started this book, because of a few spectacular DNS outages.

# 15
# IPv6 Considerations

IPv4 addresses are 32-bit, traditionally represented as four period-separated "octets" of decimal numbers, each octet having a maximum value of 255 (that is, 192.32.45.4). This provides for a possible 4.3 billion ($4.3 \times 10^9$) addresses.

Depending on who you ask, IPv4 depletion is somewhere between "rapidly approaching" and "already here" (the RIRs are already out of IPv4 space). Mechanisms exist to extend the usability of IPv4, from virtual hosting, which can stack thousands of websites on a single IP, to vast privately addressed intranets behind a single public IP, but the fact remains that the number of internet-connected devices will at some point outstrip the number of IPv4 addresses available.

This will become exacerbated by the trend known as the **Internet of Things** (**IoT**). While it could be argued that the jury is still out regarding whether IPv6 will become the *de facto* addressing scheme for IoT, even a reduced role capacity will, in my mind, be more than enough to push the requirement for IPv6 deployment over the top.

Enter IPv6, 128-bit addresses usually represented as 8 colon-separated groups of hexadecimal digits, amounting to 340 undecillion, or *$3.4 \times 10^{36}$* possible addresses. To try to get a mental grasp of this number, consider that the number of grains of sand on the planet is said to be *$7.5 \times 10^{18}$*, or the much smaller number of the 100 billion stars estimated to reside within our galaxy.

In this chapter, we'll look at how to enable your nameservers to respond over IPv6 transit as well as how to add IPv6 records to your zones, followed by a brief look at how to set up reverse DNS for IPv6 addresses.

## IPv6-enabled nameservers

If you have IPv6 transport to your nameservers, said nameservers would ideally be listening on an IPv6 address configured into the nameserver and be dual-stack, responding to queries via both IPv4 and IPv6 transport.

Getting the IPv6 transit is the hard part, but much easier than it used to be. While outside the scope of this chapter, you would discuss this with your upstream connectivity provider. Once that's in place, it's a simple configuration update to get most nameservers responsive over IPv6:

```
listen-on-v6 { 2001:678:5::13; };
###################################
# local-ipv6 Local IP address to which we bind
#
local-ipv6=2001:678:5::13
do-ipv6: yes
```

# Adding IPv6 to your zones

Adding IPv6-enabled hostnames to your zones is simply a matter of adding AAAA (also known as quad-A) RRs, which we looked at in Chapter 6, *DNS Queries in Action*, in the *Types and uses of common resource records* section.

As we observed, A6 records were also defined as another method of specifying IPv6 hosts that have since been deprecated.

# Reverse DNS for IPv6

Setting up reverse DNS for IPv6 blocks works in the same fashion as under IPv4. The reverse mappings under IPv6 occur under the special ip6.arpa namespace (in contrast with IPv4's in-addr.arpa):

```
$ host dns4.example.info dns4.example.info has address 194.0.2.19
dns4.example.info has IPv6 address 2001:678:5::13

$ host 2001:678:5::13
3.1.0.0.0.0.0.0.0.0.0.0.0.0.0.0.0.0.0.0.5.0.0.0.8.7.6.0.1.0.0.2.ip6.arpa
domain name pointer dns4.example.info
```

In our example zonefile, we'll specify our $ORIGIN at the /60 boundary:

```
$ORIGIN 0.0.0.5.0.0.0.8.7.6.0.1.0.0.2.ip6.arpa.
                     IN NS ns1.example.com.
                     IN NS ns2.example.com.

3.1.0.0.0.0.0.0.0.0.0.0.0.0.0.0 IN PTR dns4.example.info.
```

We use PTR RRs for IPv6 addresses, same as we do for IPv4.

# Queries for IPv6

You can use your favorite diagnostic tool to query specifically for IPv6 addresses:

```
$ dig +short -t aaaa dns1.easydns.com
2001:1838:f001::10

$ host -t aaaa dns1.easydns.com
dns1.easydns.com has IPv6 address 2001:1838:f001::10
```

You may also want to run queries specifically over IPv6 transport:

```
$ host -6 dns1.easydns.com dns1.easydns.com has address 64.68.192.10
dns1.easydns.com has IPv6 address 2001:1838:f001::10

$ dig +short -6
dns1.easydns.com 64.68.192.10
```

The transport a query traverses should not affect the resulting response (excepting GeoDNS deployments).

# Operational considerations

*RFC 4472* specifies a number of operational considerations for DNS when dealing with IPv6.

## Transport-independent

Nameservers should return results based on what the query was, not which transport the query arrived over.

If a hostname has both A and AAAA records defined, the nameserver should not assume to return AAAA just because the query arrived over IPv6 transport or vice versa.

## Avoiding IPv4/IPv6 fragmentation

There should be *at least one* nameserver for any given zone's NS RR that is reachable over IPv4, even if that zone only contains IPv6 addresses.

# TTL considerations

When you have a hostname with both A and AAAA records, the TTLs for those records can introduce additional factors in processing, such as when we are dealing with nameserver hostnames that may exist as glue records in the parent zone (See `Chapter 10`, *Debugging Without Tears – DNS Diagnostic Tools*).

Consider the following:

```
ns1.example.com. 500 IN A 192.168.1.13
ns1.example.com. 300 IN AAAA 2001:1838:f001::13
```

A resolver making a fresh NS query for example.com to one of the .COM root servers would receive the A and AAAA records back in the ADDITIONAL SECTION ("courtesy" additional data).

What the resolver should do with the A record after the AAAA record expires is unspecified.

In some situations, it can lead to a window where the one record has expired from a cache, and subsequent queries (without one from the parent that would refresh the cache) return only the remaining record, leading to the other record being unreachable.

# Resolver considerations

Resolvers should either be IPv4 *only* or dual-stack, so that they will be able to reach any other nameserver.

# Summary

In this chapter, we took the bare-minimum look at things to keep in mind regarding IPv6 and DNS. The reader should now be aware that issues arising from the application environment and the network architecture (transport) as they interact with the naming infrastructure (DNS) affect overall performance.

Further reading on this topic would do well to include DNS and BIND on IPv6 (Cricket Liu, O'Reilly).

# References

1. Francis daCosta's Rethinking The Internet of Things, Apress
2. http://www.npr.org/sections/krulwich/2012/09/17/161096233/which-is-greater-the-number-of-sand-grains-on-earth-or-stars-in-the-sky

# Other Books You May Enjoy

If you enjoyed this book, you may be interested in these other books by Packt:

**Practical Network Automation**
Abhishek Ratan

ISBN: 978-1-78829-946-6

- Get the detailed analysis of Network automation
- Trigger automation's through available data factors
- Improve data center robustness and security through specific access and data digging
- Get an Access to APIs from Excel for dynamic reporting
- Set up a communication with SSH-based devices using netmiko
- Make full use of practical use cases and best practices to get accustomed with the various aspects of network automation

## Implementing Cisco Networking Solutions
Harpreet Singh

ISBN: 978-1-78712-178-2

- Understand the network lifecycle approach
- Get to know what makes a good network design
- Design components and technology choices at various places in the network (PINS)
- Work on sample configurations for network devices in the LAN/ WAN/ DC, and the wireless domain
- Get familiar with the configurations and best practices for securing the network
- Explore best practices for network operations

# Leave a review - let other readers know what you think

Please share your thoughts on this book with others by leaving a review on the site that you bought it from. If you purchased the book from Amazon, please leave us an honest review on this book's Amazon page. This is vital so that other potential readers can see and use your unbiased opinion to make purchasing decisions, we can understand what our customers think about our products, and our authors can see your feedback on the title that they have worked with Packt to create. It will only take a few minutes of your time, but is valuable to other potential customers, our authors, and Packt. Thank you!

# Index

Printed in Great Britain
by Amazon